The Minimum Wage and Labor Market Outcomes

The Minimum Wage and Labor Market Outcomes

Christopher J. Flinn

The MIT Press
Cambridge, Massachusetts
London, England

MIT Press books may be purchased at special quantity discounts for business or sales promotion use. For information, please email special_sales@mitpress.mit.edu or write to Special Sales Department, The MIT Press, 55 Hayward Street, Cambridge, MA 02142.

This book was set in Palatino by Westchester Book Composition and was printed and bound in the United States of America.

Library of Congress Cataloging-in-Publication Data

Flinn, Christopher J.
The minimum wage and labor market outcomes / Christopher J. Flinn.
    p.   cm.
Includes bibliographical references and index.
ISBN 978-0-262-01323-9 (hardcover : alk. paper) 1. Minimum wage
2. Labor market. I. Title.
HD4917.F58   2011
331.2'3—dc22   2010014418

10 9 8 7 6 5 4 3 2 1

In memoriam

Arthur S. Goldberger
(1930–2009)

and

Irving M. Piliavin
(1928–2009)

They made quantitative social science important and interesting.

Contents

Appendix: Proofs of Selected Propositions from Chapter 7   269

Preface

This book is based on a collection of papers—Flinn (2002b), Flinn (2006), and Flinn and Mabli (2009)—that develop a model based on search and bargaining to use in investigating the impact of a minimum wage on labor market outcomes. I have often found that when I present this material, which involves equal proportions of simple cooperative bargaining theory, econometric modeling, and empirical analysis, audiences have some difficulty in putting all of the pieces together (as do I). My hope is that this book, which presents this material in a more user-friendly form than is possible in the confines of a professional journal, will allow the interested reader to understand this type of policy-focused research program better, and to become familiar with both its promise and its pitfalls. The reader desiring further details about the models, estimators, or empirical results obtained should refer to the source papers.

The premise of the book is that behavioral models are typically required at some stage of research on policy-relevant questions. While careful statistical and econometric analysis is useful in assessing whether a question is quantitatively interesting, models are required in order to be able to interpret empirical relationships. Models are absolutely essential when the social scientist has the ambition to conduct counterfactual policy experiments. That said, how are we to choose a modeling framework? That fundamental question will not be addressed here. Instead, we use the typical search with bargaining approach to model labor market dynamics and worker–firm interactions. This approach will allow us to make some progress in at least being able to think systematically about how minimum wages can affect labor market careers. There may be better frameworks to use to address this question, and my hope is that some of the results and techniques presented here will spur others to take other, possibly more fruitful, approaches to addressing these and related questions.

I am very much indebted to James Mabli for allowing me to describe some of our unpublished joint work in chapter 10. I am grateful to many students at NYU and in other venues who have helped me refine my thinking on this material, as well as colleagues with whom I have discussed much of this material at length, including Joop Abbring, Pierre Cahuc, Matt Dey, Zvi Eckstein, Fabien Postel-Vinay, Jean-Marc Robin, and Ken Wolpin. I have had the benefit of a careful reading of the manuscript by three extremely conscientious anonymous reviewers, whose comments, not all of which I was able to incorporate, vastly improved the final product.

I am indebted to the Upjohn Institute for Employment Research for their support in the early phases of this project, and for allowing me to publish the monograph with the MIT Press. The C.V. Starr Center for Applied Economics at New York University also provided support throughout the (long) life of the project.

The Minimum Wage and Labor Market Outcomes

1 Introduction

In this book my plan is to look at the minimum wage from a number of different perspectives. I will discuss the role it has played in the various theoretical models of the labor market in which it has been introduced. I will also attempt to assess its impact on unemployment and employment rates and the wage distribution, both using descriptive and model-based estimators. My argument will be that in assessing minimum wage impacts in the US context (or anywhere else, for that matter), in some point in the analysis it is important to have a behavioral framework in hand so as to guide empirical work and facilitate the interpretation of results. The model doesn't have to be explicitly derived from first principles, as it largely is in this monograph, but enough information regarding the proposed mechanism producing the estimated relationships should be provided so that the reader can assess the plausibility of the estimated parameters and what these parameters might imply about the advisability of minimum wage changes. The main contribution of this book is the development of a search and bargaining-based model that is capable of generating empirical implications consistent with observed wage and unemployment spell distributions. This model will serve as the basis for accounting for observed changes in employment rates and wages after a minimum wage change (a type of event study approach). Implications derived from the model will be used to assess whether changes in the shape of the accepted wage distribution following a minimum wage change indicate a positive welfare effect or not. More ambitiously, and perhaps controversially, it will be used to guide in the construction and formal estimation of a search and bargaining model that enables the researcher to directly determine the welfare impacts of observed minimum wage changes. The estimated model is capable of being used to conduct counterfactual policy experiments and can even be employed to determine an "optimal" minimum wage under a variety of welfare metrics. Readers are encouraged to cast a wary eye on the model and all of the assumptions made in its development prior to empirical implementation and the derived policy implications. An aim of the monograph is the propagation of new and improved models of the labor market in which other impacts of minimum wages not explicitly considered here can be fruitfully empirically investigated.

1.1   Plan of the Book

After describing the data to be used in the empirical analyses performed and providing some descriptive evidence regarding minimum wage impacts in chapter 2, I proceed to lay out the model and its implications in chapters 3 and 4. In chapter 5, I provide a very selective, broad-brush review of the minimum wage literature. After giving an overview of the empirical focuses and findings in the literature, I examine five papers that were selected because they analyze "large" minimum wage impacts or employ a methodology worthy of note in regard to the arguments advanced in the book. I provide an interpretation of the findings from each of these papers that is based on my model, and find that it is able to generate coherent and consistent explanations in all cases (this does not imply that other modeling frameworks are not capable of doing the same). The chapter concludes with a consideration of other theoretical models of equilibrium search within which minimum wages have been introduced and a comparison of the implications for minimum wage effects on labor market outcomes drawn from those models with the model I develop here.

In chapter 6, I use the model to derive implications regarding the relationship between observed wage distributions before and after a minimum wage change. As I note, the change in the value of search, which occurs when the minimum wage is binding, is an important component of all welfare measures discussed in chapter 4. In particular, changes in the value of search result in "before and after" steady state wage distributions that may be ordered using first-order stochastic dominance criteria. With these results I attempt to infer whether the value of search has improved on the basis of pre- and post-minimum wage change wage distributions. This analysis, although model based, does not require any estimates of underlying model parameters nor functional form assumptions. It resembles, at least superficially, a quasi-experimental approach to the study of minimum wage impacts on welfare.

I use the basic model, armed with some necessary assumptions regarding the form of functions that play a role in the model, to consider estimation issues in chapter 7. These estimators are implemented in chapter 8, where I discuss and interpret the estimates and look directly at the nature of equilibrium responses to the minimum wage changes of 1996 and 1997. In chapter 9, I use model estimates to answer the question: What would have been the optimal minimum wage in 1996 given a reasonably conventional social welfare function formulation.

All of the analysis in the book through chapter 9 considers only the case of unemployed job search. This situation is remedied in chapter 10, where I allow individuals to search both on and off of the job. This chapter is relatively self-contained (it largely draws on material from Flinn and Mabli 2009), and contains a discussion of partial and general equilibrium versions of the model, estimates of primitive parameters, and a separate policy analysis comparable to that performed in chapter 9. Interestingly, though the models are quite different, the qualitative aspects of the policy analysis are roughly the same in the two model specifications that are estimated using different data sources and estimation techniques.

Throughout the book, attention is devoted to the case of a homogeneous labor market, one in which individuals differ only in the value of the match they happen to have located at a given point in time. Chapter 11 contains a discussion of the manner in which heterogeneity, both of the observed and unobserved variety, can be introduced into the search, matching, and bargaining framework. Chapter 12 concludes with a summary of what I think we have and have not learned at this stage of the research program, and what I view as promising avenues for future analyses of the minimum wage question.

The remainder of this chapter is composed of three sections. In the first, I provide a brief overview of theoretical arguments for and against the imposition of a minimum wage.[1] In the second part, I provide a short history of the federal minimum wage in the United States. The final section contains a motivation for my focus on the federal minimum wages and my omission of explicit considerations of state minimum wages.

1.2 Theoretical Perspectives on the Minimum Wage

The impacts of minimum wage laws, and their desirability, have been debated in textbooks and in policy circles for decades, in the United

States and elsewhere. The standard elementary treatment of minimum wage policy views its impact as unambiguously negative. In a competitive market where unrestricted supply and demand forces combine to determine a unique equilibrium employment and wage level, the imposition of a minimum wage greater than the market-clearing wage creates true unemployment—defined as individuals who are willing to supply labor at the going wage rate and who are unable to find jobs. It creates ex post inequality as well—those individuals fortunate enough to find jobs have a higher welfare level than they would have had in the competitive equilibrium, while those who do not have lower welfare levels. If individuals are risk-averse, this increased "uncertainty" may be welfare decreasing in an ex ante sense as well.

It has long been appreciated that for minimum wages to have beneficial effects (at least for the supply side of the market), there must exist labor market frictions and/or multiple equilibria.[2] The multiple equilibria case (see van den Berg 2003) is perhaps the strongest one for the beneficial effects of government-imposed wage policies. There are a large number of labor market models that are capable of producing multiple equilibria, in the sense that a given set of primitive values of characteristics defining labor market structure can generate two or more labor market equilibria.[3] Each equilibrium is proper in the sense that any agent in the equilibrium has no incentive to change its behavior (Nash). Wage policy, as one possible instrument among many, offers the possibility for the policy maker to select among equilibria, something that is not available to the economist or econometrician. Consider the simple case where two possible equilibria exist, and where both are associated with a unique equilibrium wage rate. Now imagine that the two equilibria can be Pareto-ranked, meaning that in one equilibrium every agent is at least as well-off as in the other, with some being strictly better-off, and that the preferred equilibrium is associated with the higher equilibrium wage rate. Then a minimum wage set less than or equal to the "good equilibrium" wage rate and higher than the "bad equilibrium" wage rate yields nonnegative payoffs for all agents in the labor market.[4]

In terms of rationales for minimum wages that depend on labor market imperfections, perhaps the most extreme case favorable to the imposition of a minimum wage is that of monopsony, where it is supposed that only one firm hires labor in some particular market. Here the friction is that of restricted entry. That is, since a monopsonistic firm is able to earn noncompetitive rents, there would be an incentive for other firms to enter the market and compete over those rents. It is assumed that this does not happen because of large fixed costs of entry.

As pointed out in Stigler (1946), in a monopsonistic market the firm will optimally set employment below competitive equilibrium levels in order to pay a lower wage than the competitive one. A minimum wage has a positive impact in such an environment because it takes the ability to set wages out of the hands of the firm. By removing its incentive to keep employment "artificially" low, the firm will both pay the higher (mandated) wage and increase its employment level—thus amounting to a win–win situation for the supply side of the market. The firm is worse off, of course, but it is still possible for it to earn positive profits depending on the level at which the minimum wage is set.

The equilibrium search models of Albrecht and Axell (1984) and Burdett and Mortensen (1998) offer another avenue for positive minimum wage effects on welfare, once again, at least for the supply side of the market. In the Albrecht and Axell model, potential firm entrants into the market are heterogeneous in terms of quality. A high minimum wage prevents low-quality firms from making nonnegative profits, and hence improves the labor market through a selection effect on the demand side. Having higher quality firms competing for their services improves the wage distributions individuals face while searching. As the model is written, there is no adverse impact on employment rates.

The Burdett and Mortensen (1998) equilibrium framework requires on-the-job search in addition to unemployed search. As in Albrecht and Axell (1984) they assume a wage-posting equilibrium in which firms offer a fixed firm to all potential and actual employees. The Burdett and Mortensen model, however, does not require heterogeneity in the populations of (potential) firms and workers—in fact the basic specification of the model assumes no heterogeneity. They prove the existence of an equilibrium in which the probability that any two firms offer the same wage is zero, namely accepted wages are continuously distributed. Adding a (binding) minimum wage to their model simply shifts the equilibrium wage offer distribution to the right and has no adverse employment effects. As a result binding minimum wages are beneficial to the supply side of the market.

The framework I use posits search frictions, as do the two I have just discussed. Differently from the those two models, an important component of my search and bargaining model is heterogeneous productivity. In particular, when a potential employment opportunity is found after some period of search, the productivity of the match, θ, is determined by taking a draw from some fixed distribution $G(\theta)$. It is typically assumed that the value of the match for a given possible worker–firm pairing is observed immediately by both sides, an admittedly strong assumption.[5] Once the draw is made, the pair can determine if there exists positive surplus to the potential match. "Positive surplus" is said to exist if there exists any wage rate at which both sides would prefer creating the match to their next best options of continued search. If there exists positive surplus to the match, the worker and firm bargain over its division. In general, both sides have some degree of bargaining power, since the other side cannot find a perfect replacement for them without spending additional effort and/or resources. The ultimate source of bargaining power to both is search frictions.

In such an environment a minimum wage might have beneficial effects for the supply side of the market by increasing their "effective" bargaining power in a particular fashion. When two sides bargain, the result is typically strictly beneficial for both of them, in that both are better-off in the sense that the employment contract yields both a welfare level greater than their next best option. For example, a seller wishing to dispose of some good typically ends up selling at a price that is higher than the object's intrinsic value to him, while the buyer typically realizes a surplus as well, in the sense that he values the object purchased more than the price he paid. In these types of "cooperative" problems, economic theory in and of itself does not usually uniquely determine the outcome. Instead, some convention is required to determine the final result of the bargaining process. The most commonly used axiomatic "solution" to the indeterminacy problem is the one first proposed by Nash (1953). By his axioms, the cooperative outcome to the bargaining problem uniquely determines the wage paid to the worker. Formally, the solution is

$$w^* = \arg\max_{w} (V_E(w) - D_S)^\alpha (V_F(\theta, w) - D_F)^{1-\alpha}, \tag{1.1}$$

where $V_E(w)$ is the value to the worker of being employed at a wage w, D_S is her value from not accepting the current employment contract, $V_F(\theta, w)$ is the value to the firm of employing a worker whose productivity is θ and whose wage rate is w, and D_F is the value to the firm from not entering into this particular employment contract. The differences $V_E(w) - D_S$ and $V_F(\theta, w) - D_F$ are the surpluses gained by the worker and firm, respectively, from entering into the employment contract.[6]

The parameter α, which takes values between 0 and 1, determines the share of their surplus that each party receives at the final bargained outcome. For example, when $\alpha = 1$, the worker has all of the "bargaining power" and as a result receives all of their potential surplus from the match. In such a world, when the worker's utility is strictly increasing in her wage rate, the wage would be set so that $V_F(\theta, w^*(\theta)) - D_F = 0$, that is, so that the firm received no surplus from the match. Conversely, when $\alpha = 0$, the wage would be set at a level such that the worker's surplus was 0, or $V_E(w^*(\theta)) - D_S = 0$.

When $0 < \alpha < 1$, both parties receive some positive amount of surplus from entering into the employment contract, with the amount of the surplus going to the worker a strictly increasing function of α. The parameter α is a key determinant of the wage in this setting, and deserves a significant amount of attention. Unfortunately, in most practical situations no particular motivation for a choice of α is readily apparent. There are some exceptions, however. In the most celebrated case, Rubinstein (1982) showed that in an alternating offers game in which a seller announced a price and the (potential) buyer had to take it or leave it, the division of the surplus from the sale of the good was a function of the intertemporal discount rates of the two parties. The individual with the lower rate of discount (i.e., who was less impatient to end the bargaining period), ended up with the larger share of the surplus. Thus bargaining power in this case was related to the relative impatience of the two agents.

In the worker–firm bargaining case, such a simple rationalization of α is not likely to be very useful. The reader may find it more beneficial to think of α as a type of summary statistic, a scalar parameter that is meant to summarize the totality of the labor market environment that the worker and firm inhabit. For example, we may think that α varies with the degree of specialized training a class of workers have. If workers have little training, then the firm may credibly threaten them with replacement by other low-skilled workers or machines. In this case, α may reflect the degree of substitutability between this specific type of labor and other inputs.

Even more simply, α may reflect bargaining prowess. A firm's raison d'être is to make money, and to do so requires that it minimize cost, which may largely consist of wage payments. In the bargaining setup this implies that the firm must be a "good" bargainer in that it secures most of the match surplus for itself.[7] Because searchers generally engage in only a few employment contracts over their labor market careers, they may not have the experience nor the information to be good bargainers. This is especially true for young searchers, who form the core of the minimum wage population, and they are the main subject of attention in this book.

By either one of the arguments above, and a large number of others, those workers whose welfare is likely to be affected by the minimum wage can be expected to have relatively low levels of bargaining power. The more credible estimates we obtain of the parameter α that are reported below will bear out this supposition. When α is low, the purpose of the minimum wage is clear: it serves to offset the bargaining disadvantage searchers on the supply side of the market face. The minimum wage does this by serving as a coordination device that allows all searchers to credibly commit to not accepting a wage less than m, the stipulated minimum wage. Individual searchers in low-skill markets themselves cannot implement such a policy, since each individual bargainer has an incentive to renege on the policy and to accept a lower wage than m for some productivity values θ.[8] In terms of the choice of w in (1.1), with the government serving the role of an enforcement mechanism, the problem is solved subject to the side condition $w \geq m$.

We will look at two versions of the baseline bargaining model discussed above throughout the book. The *partial equilibrium* version of the model posits that the rate at which searchers meet potential employers is exogenously fixed, meaning that if the minimum wage is changed, the contact rate remains the same. Conversely, the *general equilibrium* version of the model allows the contact rate to adjust to market conditions, and one of these "conditions" is the minimum wage. As a result the contact rate will, in general, change with the minimum wage.

Within the partial equilibrium version of the model, all minimum wage increases result in a higher unemployment rate among labor market participants. This is consistent with most empirical evidence on the subject, though not all. It is important to note, however, that even in the face of decreasing employment, a minimum wage increase can prove beneficial to all members of the minimum wage "pool," which we can define operationally as all individuals who *could* be paid the minimum wage.[9] We will devote a substantial amount of attention to defining alternative welfare concepts for the supply side of the market. We will show that under most of them, it is possible for all members of the supply side of the market to benefit from a change in the minimum wage (typically an increase, since the level of minimum wages in the United

States is relatively low). Thus we will be able to establish that even individuals whose jobs are destroyed by minimum wage increases can benefit from the increase. For this to be the case, it will be necessary that individuals be "forward looking" and at a bargaining disadvantage (i.e., to have a low value of α). The reason is that the minimum wage changes the search environment of the unemployed (also of the employed in the model that allows for on-the-job search, as is discussed in chapter 10). The change in the value of unemployed search can be so large that the value of searching in the new environment without a job is more valuable than being employed at a low-productivity job in the absence of a minimum wage (or with a lower one).

The minimum wage, in this view, can be thought of as a reallocation mechanism, meant to compensate the supply side of the market for its relatively weak bargaining position (in terms of α). Besides transferring rents from one side of the market to the other, the minimum wage can result in an efficiency gain, if you will, even in the partial equilibrium version of the model. This gain can occur if the minimum wage increases the value of joining the labor market (as an unemployed searcher), thus inducing individuals to enter the labor market. It is even possible for the employment rate in the population (but not in the labor market) to increase as a result of a minimum wage increase.

Before proceeding, it is important to point out that our view of wage policy as "correcting" asymmetries in bargaining power should be applied symmetrically. That is, if firms were the ones to have low bargaining weights, then it is reasonable to consider a "maximum wage" policy. One can view the salary caps that are observed in a number of professional sports leagues as a response to players and their agents having too much of a bargaining advantage when negotiating contracts with team owners in the era of free agency.

When we consider the general equilibrium version of the search and bargaining model, the mechanism through which minimum wage policies can actually be "constrained" efficient becomes clearer. In the general equilibrium case the rate of contacts between workers and firms is a function of the sizes of the sets of unemployed searchers and firms with vacancies. An important paper in this regard is by Hosios (1990) who showed that an efficient equilibrium occurs whenever the share of the surplus received by unemployed searchers is equal to their marginal contribution to match formation. In our case this means that if the unemployed do not receive much of the surplus in any match they become a part of, there is little incentive for them to search. If their contribution to match formation is large, firms should be willing to give up some of the bargaining power to induce more individuals on the supply side of the market to search more intensively. If it is not possible for individual agents to control the bargaining power (α) in the market, the minimum wage is a way to change the amount of "effective" bargaining power held by the two sides. There are even situations of imbalance where the minimum wage increases can lead to increases in market output.

Of course, a more effective policy intervention would be to have the government actually set the bargaining power value α optimally. In order for the government to monitor a decree that workers should receive a portion α of the surplus, they would have to observe the output, θ, of each and every match in existence at a point in time. This is clearly not feasible. The minimum wage is a crude instrument, and the imposition of this policy has deadweight loss compared to the optimal rent division rule. Enforcing minimum wage policy requires instead access only to firm reports on wage payments to individual employees of the type that are routinely made to state and federal agencies. Given the astronomically large costs associated with enforcing an "optimal" output division policy, minimum wage laws are relatively costless to administer and still may be effective in moving the labor market toward an efficient level of output.

1.3   Brief History of Minimum Wage in the United States

In the early 1930s the Roosevelt administration attempted to establish minimum wage and maximum hours laws a number of times. The first formal attempt was included in the National Recovery Act (NRA), although the labor market restrictions in the law were declared unconstitutional in 1935. Other attempts to regulate employment conditions by the federal government suffered similar fates. One should keep in mind that states had de facto and de jure control over most labor market laws and regulations from the time of the founding of the country. The federal government's ability to intervene in commercial matters was only explicitly recognized in regard to interstate commerce. This was the rationale given by the US Supreme Court when it declared the restrictions on wages and hours in the NRA unconstitutional; that is to say, the federal government did not have the authority to intervene in labor market matters, broadly defined. Thus, aside from the normal disagreements among the business and organized labor communities regarding the costs and benefits of government restrictions of this form on the labor market, there was overlaid the issue of jurisdiction. It should be noted that a number of states already had minimum wage and maximum hours laws on the books prior to the 1930s. Federal minimum wage laws were largely cast as challenges to state's rights, and the difficulty of passing these laws cannot solely be attributed to the normal conflicts between the owners of capital and labor.

An excellent summary of the legislative history of the Fair Labor Standards Act (FLSA) can be found in Douglas and Hackman (1938, 1939). Within the Congress, the main battle lines were drawn between representatives of the northern and southern states.[10] The southern legislators noted that the largest impact of the minimum wage would be borne by their states, and that employment effects could be enormous. In fact the economies of the north and south were undeniably diverse in terms of the occupational and industrial distribution of workers, wages, the cost of living, and transportation costs, among many other things. On the basis of this diversity, the southern legislators promoted the idea of an indexed minimum wage that would vary by region. The fact that this argument was eventually rejected has important implications for the analysis conducted in this book, and so we will spend a bit of time considering the points made against it.

Perhaps the most salient point made in the debate, reflected in current concerns regarding the determination of the consumer price index, was that the prices of goods were lower in the south because the goods produced there were of inferior quality. Advocates of the position of a nonindexed minimum wage argued that by building in wage differentials, southern laborers would be locked into an effectively lower standard of living than those living in the north. Supporters of the regionally indexed minimum wage also acknowledged that the productivity of southern laborers was generally lower than that in the north, so southern manufacturers would effectively pay higher input costs than competitors in the north.

Southern manufacturers and agricultural producers who argued in favor of regional minimum wage differentials supported their point by noting that their transportation costs were much higher than the costs borne by producers in the north (for empirical evidence, see Douglas and Hackman 1938). As their opponents suggested, from a political economy perspective it would have been preferable to address this issue directly by making the transportation sector more competitive. Nonetheless, it was clear that in general, producers and consumers in the south and the north faced very different environments. A strong prima facie case was made that the impact of a common minimum wage would have had a much more disruptive effect, in the short run at least, on the southern economy.

Union interests were also ambivalent regarding minimum wage legislation. Initial legislative drafts envisaged the existence of a powerful Labor Standards Board with the ability to set minimum wages and maximum hours within finely delineated regional and industrial categories. The Board was only to be limited in its ability to determine wage and hours limits by some very "loose" caps that were to apply to the various region-industry categories. Besides strengthening these caps (and thus limiting the Board's range of choices) union leaders successfully pushed for the additional stipulation that the board should not set standards in an industrial-regional category when working conditions were already substantially determined through collective bargaining.

The mix of groups with strong and competing interests in working conditions legislation, along with the questionable legal authority of the federal government to regulate these conditions, led to the eventual abandonment of the idea of minimum wages that varied across geographic and industrial sectors but that had a substantial amount of "bite" within each. The compromise was a system without an all-powerful Labor Standards Board with the ability to fine-tune working conditions regulations in favor of one federal minimum wage rate that essentially was a "lowest common denominator" type of policy, affecting only the lowest skilled workers in the entire US labor market. So as not to effectively shut down sectors of the economy that employed this class of worker, federal minimum wages have always been kept at a lower proportion of the average wage earned in the market than is the case in other modern Western economies.

The role played by the federal minimum wage limits our ability to determine the effects that would ensue from a substantial increase in the minimum wage. No fan of state intervention in markets, Stigler (1946) made the argument that in order to consider the possibility of constructing "optimal" minimum wages, a social planner would have to take into account the particular structure of narrow industry categories, much as the Labor Standards Board was originally envisioned doing. It is interesting that not even the most strident proponent of increasing the minimum wage rate advocates a nonhomogeneous minimum wage, and in this sense minimum wages in the United States are best viewed as an antipoverty measure rather than an employment policy per se. We will speak often of the statistical and econometric difficulties

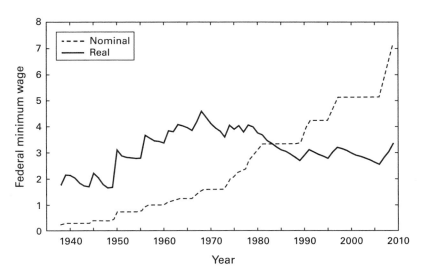

Figure 1.1
Nominal and real minimum wage levels, in 1984 dollars

of extrapolating the labor market impacts of minimum wages to levels that have not been historically observed.

Figure 1.1 presents the nominal and real (in 1984 dollars) level of the federal minimum wage from its inception through the present. The nominal value of the federal minimum wage is changed only by congressional action, and, as is well known, changes in the minimum wage have been quite infrequent over the past three decades. Most of the empirical and policy analysis reported concerns the two nominal minimum wage changes that occurred in the later part of the 1990s (both set in the same legislation); these changes took place in 1996 (when the minimum wage was increased from $4.25 to $4.75) and 1997 (when the minimum wage was increased from $4.75 to $5.15).

The path of the real minimum wage is striking. From its inception until the late 1960s the trend in the real minimum wage was clearly positive, and since then the real minimum wage has almost continually declined. The few nominal minimum wage changes that occurred during this period merely partially halted the decline for a brief period. This decline explains why fewer and fewer employees are paid at or below the minimum wage over this three-decade period. We turn to a description of these trends in the following chapter.

1.4   State Minimum Wages

In this book I focus on the impact of the federal minimum wage rate on labor market outcomes. In terms of the theoretical framework I develop, the only potentially relevant minimum wage rate that could affect market outcomes is the largest of the legally binding minimum wages impacting the market. For example, a number of southern states have minimum wage rates that are either equal to zero or that are substantially below the level of the federal minimum wage. In all such cases the federal minimum wage takes precedence for all workers covered under the FLSA. For cases where the state minimum wage is greater than the federal minimum wage for covered workers, the state minimum wage will be the binding minimum wage. Thus $m = \max\{m_F, m_S\}$, where m is the minimum wage rate that will appear in the models discussed below, m_F is the federal minimum wage, and m_S is the state minimum wage.

The empirical analyses that I report below do not include state minimum wages, which is a potentially serious omission. There are a few compelling reasons for their absence in my treatment, however. First, state minimum wages tend to exceed federal minimum wage levels when the federal rate has not been changed for a substantial period of time. In this case, especially high cost-of-living states tend to raise their minimum wage rates so as to provide something of a "living wage" to workers in their market. In the last several decades this phenomenon was particularly prevalent during long-running Republican administrations, those of Ronald Reagan and George W. Bush. Since most of our empirical analyses focus on a period around the increases in the federal minimum wage of the late 1990s, there were fewer states with higher minimum wages than the federal. This is not to say that there weren't a number of such cases, just that they were fewer in number than in the late 1980s or in 2005 (before the latest round of increases in the federal minimum wage).[11]

Second, the inclusion of state minimum wages into the empirical analysis is not unproblematic. If all states were identical, then looking at the effects of different state minimum wages on employment and wage outcomes would seem to be an ideal way to amass identifying information on the underlying parameters characterizing labor market structure. Unfortunately, it is unreasonable to believe that the states are cooperating in the analyst's quest to obtain results from a natural experiment. State labor markets are likely to differ in terms of the skill distributions possessed by agents and local demand conditions, for example. It is also clear that state labor markets are not closed economies that can be analyzed in isolation from one another. In the end, focusing on state labor markets would probably entail estimating a separate behavioral model for each one; in so doing, the econometric issues of identification and interpretation that I raise below regarding the US labor market would reappear at the state level.[12]

2 Descriptive Evidence on Minimum Wage Effects

This chapter provides some descriptive evidence on the impact of minimum wages on labor market outcomes. The purpose of the empirical exercises performed in this chapter is twofold. First, I want to focus the reader's attention on the impact of minimum wages at the disaggregate level. Card and Krueger (1995), among others, have convincingly argued that time series analyses performed at the macro level gloss over the distributional effects of minimum wage changes. In the United States, where federal minimum wages have typically been very low relative to the average wage in the market, it is not reasonable to expect that changes in the minimum wage will have significant effects on aggregate labor market or productivity statistics. However, within the segments of the population that tend to receive lower wage offers, the impact on labor market outcomes could possibly be substantial. The labor market participants most likely to be paid the minimum wage are recent labor market entrants and low-skilled laborers. However, most of the empirical analysis I report in this chapter and in the sequel will focus on young (potential) labor market participants.

My second reason for the descriptive, disaggregated analysis performed here is to set the stage for the development of the theoretical models and more highly structured empirical analyses that follow. As will be seen in chapter 5, where various equilibrium theories of minimum wage effects are discussed, these models produce different implications for the impacts of minimum wage changes on employment and unemployment rates, as well as for the wage distribution. By first considering some empirical results relevant to these comparisons, we will be in a better position to assess some of the relative strengths and weaknesses of each of these competing views of the structure of labor market equilibria. Having some faith in the appropriateness of a modeling framework is critical if we are to take at all seriously some of the policy implications it generates.

2.1 The Data Source

The data used throughout this book, with the exception of chapter 10, are taken from the Current Population Survey (CPS). It is therefore appropriate to spend some time describing these data, and the rationale for using them. The CPS is a nationally representative, monthly household survey that is primarily used to calculate timely measures of the state of the labor market (particularly the unemployment rate). Each month, roughly 50,000 households are interviewed, with approximately one-fourth of the monthly sample consisting of newly added households. Each newly added household remains in the survey for four months, and then is "rotated out" for eight months. The household rejoins the survey for another four months following this inactive period. The sampling plan is often referred to by the shorthand "4–8–4."

While it would seem that eight months of information are available for each household member aged 16 or over, for purposes of conducting labor market research this is not the case. Only in the last month of a four-month sample participation span is information on wages and salaries solicited. Households in their fourth or eighth month of participation in the sample are referred to as "outgoing" samples, and the CPS Outgoing Rotation Group (ORG) sample in a given month consists of those households in their fourth or eighth month of survey participation. While basic employment, hours, and unemployed search information is collected in every month, if one wants to examine the impact of minimum wage legislation on wage outcomes, we must limit attention to the CPS-ORG subsample. Given the large size of the CPS survey, this subsample still contains a substantial number of individuals.

The survey is a household survey, which means that information regarding all members of the household (i.e., those residing at the same physical address or who are temporarily absent at the time of the monthly interview) is collected at each of the survey points. Typically all information on the household collectively, as well as for its individual members, is reported by a single *household respondent*.[1] Labor market information is collected from the household respondent for all household members 16 years of age or older at the time of the interview. Standard demographic information, including years of schooling completed, is collected for all members at least 15 years of age.

The manner in which the CPS data are collected creates some serious measurement problems, and most of these because all the information is often collected from a single respondent. When studying the labor market outcomes of young individuals, many of whom still live with their parents, it is likely that the household respondent will be one of their parents or siblings. Further we know from validation experiments, like those involving the Panel Study of Income Dynamics (Bound et al. 1994) and the Survey of Income and Program Participation (Abowd and Stinson 2005), that even when individuals report their own earnings in these surveys, there often exist wide discrepancies between self-reported wages and earnings and the analogous information obtained from payroll, tax, or other types of administrative records. Moreover the measurement error appears to be "nonclassical." The classical model of measurement error posits that $\tilde{w} = w + \varepsilon$, where $\tilde{w}$ is the reported measure, w the "true" measure, and ε represents a realization of a random variable, which is independently and identically distributed (i.i.d.) in the population.[2] One reason that measurement error is found not to satisfy the i.i.d. assumption is the presence of heaping. While there is no canonical model of heaping, a standard representation of the phenomenon would be as follows: Suppose that there exists a set of "focal points" $\hat{W} = \{\hat{w}_1, \ldots, \hat{w}_L\}$ and a set of L nonoverlapping intervals $\hat{I} = \{\hat{I}_1, \ldots, \hat{I}_L\}$, with each of the intervals containing exactly one focal point. If $w \in I_l$, then with probability $p_l(w, \hat{w}_l)$ the respondent reports the focal point $\hat{w}_l$, and with probability $1 - p_l(w, \hat{w}_l)$ she reports the true value w. In this case the measurement error clearly is not "classical," since the distribution of the error depends on the true value w, the set of focal points $\hat{W}$, and the set of intervals $\hat{I}$. The set of focal points is often obvious given the nature of the application, and should be thought of as depending on the distribution of the true value w in the population.

Inaccuracies in individual reports of the value of some personal characteristic w are likely to exacerbated when a proxy respondent is involved. In particular, it seems plausible that a proxy respondent may be more likely to report focal values than a self-respondent, since the information on which they must base their report is more vague. If a proxy respondent is reasonably secure that another family member's w belongs to the set I_l, but has no further information regarding w, a safe response may be $\hat{w}_l$, to the extent that the respondent believes that $\hat{w}_l$ represents some type of modal value within the interval I_l.

We have engaged in a discussion of heaping because, as we will see, it is extremely prevalent in the CPS data. Table 2.1 summarizes the data

Table 2.1
Descriptive statistics of CPS-ORG for individuals aged 16 to 24

Characteristic	9/96	2/97	8/97	1/98
N	3199	3236	3117	3150
N_O/N	0.365	0.369	0.307	0.375
$N_U/(N_U + N_E)$	0.097	0.119	0.082	0.104
Female	0.505	0.522	0.518	0.510
Black and Hispanic	0.252	0.248	0.274	0.254
t_U	3.411	2.889	2.612	2.515
	(4.973)	(3.230)	(1.006)	(3.576)
w	6.932	7.016	7.254	7.513
	(3.480)	(3.874)	(4.361)	(4.178)
m	4.25	4.75	4.75	5.15
$\chi[w = 4.25\|E]$	0.053	0.022	0.013	0.002
$\chi[w = 4.50\|E]$	0.020	0.012	0.006	0.002
$\chi[w = 4.75\|E]$	0.024	0.063	0.047	0.007
$\chi[w = 5.00\|E]$	0.125	0.118	0.101	0.053
$\chi[w = 5.15\|E]$	0.002	0.002	0.010	0.075
$\chi[w = 5.25\|E]$	0.023	0.039	0.029	0.050
$\chi[w = 5.50\|E]$	0.035	0.046	0.056	0.054
$\chi[w = 6.00\|E]$	0.083	0.092	0.092	0.092
$\chi[w = 7.00\|E]$	0.062	0.061	0.069	0.060
$\chi[w = 8.00\|E]$	0.047	0.046	0.052	0.046
$\chi[w = 9.00\|E]$	0.019	0.027	0.023	0.031
$\chi[w = 10.00\|E]$	0.031	0.028	0.024	0.032
Total at these values	0.524	0.556	0.522	0.505
$\chi[w < m\|E]$	0.054	0.052	0.054	0.041

Note: Standard deviations are in parentheses.

from an estimation sample that is heavily utilized in later chapters. The data are for members of the ORG samples in the age range 16 to 24, inclusive, for months spanning the federal minimum wage changes that occurred in 1996 and 1997.

The first few rows of the table provide information on the labor market state of the sample members at the time of the interview. A large proportion of sample members were not employed or actively looking for work, described as state O—for "out of the labor force." About one-third of the sample is in this state, which is not surprising, since many of these individuals are full-time students. The proportion in state O is markedly smaller in the August 1997 sample, since many students are working or looking for summer jobs in that month.

Our main focus of interest in the table is the wage distribution. The changes in the means and standard deviations of wages across the four months are unremarkable. More interesting is the actual pattern of wage reports. We present the proportion of wage reports exactly equal to one of twelve values (i.e., to the penny) and note that the sample proportion of wage reports at one of these values hovers above one-half in every month. The set of twelve wage values that we present seem to be obvious focal points, including integers in the dense part of the wage distribution and the three values of the minimum wage in force during the four months. Fortunately for our argument, none of the three federal minimum wage levels during this period is an obvious candidate for focal point status. That is, while we do notice some slight tendency for wages to "heap" at intervals at one-quarter and three-quarters of a dollar, which is relevant when we look at the mass of reports at the minimum wages $4.25 and $4.75, the mass points at integer dollar values and one-half dollar values are significantly larger.

The largest mass points are observed at the values $5.00 and $6.00, and it is interesting to note that in the month when the minimum wage is $5.15, the largest mass is observed at $6.00, while in all other months the largest mass is at $5.00. The probability mass at the minimum wage, no matter which of the three values it takes in these months, is fourth highest. This is the case even when the minimum wage is the decidedly "non-focal" $5.15. When the minimum wage is less than $5.15, the proportion of respondents that reported this value is never more than 0.01; when $5.15 becomes the federal minimum wage, the proportion jumps to 0.075.

Our interpretation of the CPS wage distribution is that the mass at the minimum wage does exist, and we will see further evidence of this in the next section. In fact the estimates of the mass at the minimum wage may be biased downward, since we use earnings data for all wage and salary workers in constructing this table, including those not paid on an hourly basis. For employees not paid on an hourly basis, the hourly wage rate is imputed by dividing weekly wages paid on the person's main job by their usual weekly hours at that job. Even if an individual works at a job at which she is not paid on an hourly basis, but that is designed to pay the individual the minimum wage on average, measurement error and temporal variation in weekly wages and/or hours will lead to an imputed hourly wage not equal to the minimum wage. Among workers in the age range 16 to 24, approximately 80 percent are paid on an hourly basis, so this bias is probably not too severe. One of the advantages of focusing our attention on this age group is that the proportion paid on an hourly basis is much higher than in the general employed population, producing a less serious measurement problem.

I should point out that our discussion of focal points and the heaping phenomenon must be considered speculative to some extent. The reason is that the *actual* wages paid to CPS sample members are not observed by us. We do not know that firms, when choosing a compensation policy, do not tend to favor hourly wage rates that have been considered by us to be "focal points." While we might suppose that some initial wage rates were set in this manner, percentage-based wage increases seem to move wages to nonfocal values in relatively short periods of time. While we cannot completely rule out heaping as a phenomenon present in the actual hourly wage distribution, it seems unlikely to be nearly as pronounced as what we observe in the distribution of reported hourly wages.

Most of the empirical analysis in this book uses CPS-ORG data from selected months in the period 1996 through 1998, prior to the more recent changes in the federal minimum wage that began in 2007. We have just seen that a small, but quite noticeable, proportion of wage reports occur at the minimum wage, and some occur at values less than the federal minimum wage. In terms of wages lower than the minimum, while some such observations may represent noncompliance on the part of employers,[3] it must be borne in mind that minimum wage coverage does not extend to all employees. The most important exemptions occur for certain service occupations, such as those in the restaurant business whose compensation mainly consists of gratuities, in which young workers are overrepresented. We will see this pattern clearly in the next section.

The negligible direct impact of minimum wage changes on the wage distribution observed in recent decades has not always been the case, as we see in figure 2.1. The figure contains plots of the proportion of hourly wage workers paid a rate less than or equal to the minimum wage, for the entire sample of employees (reweighted to be representative of the US population) and also by sex, beginning in 1979 and ending in 2005. The dotted vertical lines in the figures appear in years for which there was an increase in the federal minimum wage. The proportions are for the entire hourly wage population of workers, not merely those

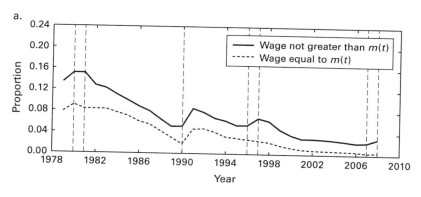

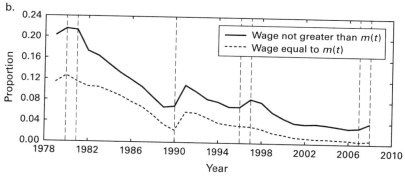

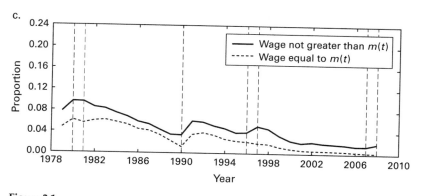

Figure 2.1
Hourly workers paid the minimum wage, 1979 to 2005: (a) All workers, (b) female workers, (c) male workers.

16 to 24 years of age, though these workers are overrepresented in the population of those paid on an hourly basis as was noted above.

The dashed lines in the figures represent the proportion of the hourly wage population paid exactly the minimum wage in the year. While the proportion of the population paid the minimum wage is never large in an absolute sense, there is a marked secular decline in the proportion of this population paid the minimum wage, with the only shifts off of the trend line occurring at points when the nominal federal minimum wage was changed. We see that over 9 percent of this population was paid exactly the minimum wage as recently as 1980, while less than 1 percent are paid $5.15 in 2005. The proportion paid less than or equal to the minimum wage follows the same pattern. In 1980, over 15 percent of hourly workers were paid an amount less than or equal to the minimum wage, with that figure declining to 2.5 percent in the year 2005. While those paid less than or equal to the minimum wage never exceeded one-sixth of hourly paid workers, which would translate into less than one-eighth of all dependent workers, this percentage has declined precipitously over the last twenty-five years.

Figure 2.1b and c illustrates the large difference between the sexes in the proportion paid at or below the minimum wage. There is little noticeable difference in the shape of the curves over this period; however, the proportion paid less than or equal to the minimum wage is always approximately twice as high in the population of female hourly wage workers. There also exists some gender difference in those paid exactly the minimum wage as a proportion of those paid at or below the minimum wage. Males are more likely to be paid the minimum wage than females in this case, which is consistent with the observation that the male wage distribution stochastically dominates the wage distribution of females.[4]

2.2 Who Are the Minimum Wage Workers?

Part of the answer to this question can be gleaned from figure 2.1. For instance, it is clear that females in the hourly wage population are greatly overrepresented in this group of workers paid the minimum wage or less. We now go on to consider other defining characteristics of this group by employing information presented in the annual report of the Bureau of Labor Statistics entitled "Characteristics of Minimum Wage Workers." The information presented here is taken from the report for 2005.

Table 2.2
Minimum wage proportions by occupational group, 2005

Occupation	Proportion		
	$w < \$5.15$	$w = \$5.15$	$w \leq \$5.15$
Management and professional services	0.03	0.02	0.05
Health care support	0.013	0.002	0.016
Protective services	0.001	0.002	0.012
Food preparation and serving	0.149	0.025	0.174
Cleaning and maintenance	0.015	0.009	0.025
Personal care	0.035	0.014	0.049
Sales and office	0.005	0.006	0.001
Farming, fishing, and forestry	0.011	0.011	0.022
Construction	0.002	0.001	0.003
Installation and repair	0.003	0.001	0.005
Production and transportation	0.005	0.004	0.009

Perhaps the most striking characteristic of minimum wage workers is their concentration within one particular service worker category, those working in "Food Preparation and Food Serving." The proportion paid at or below the minimum wage in some of the major occupational categories is presented in table 2.2. We see that 17.5 percent of hourly wage workers in that occupational category are paid at or below the minimum wage of $5.15, with 15 percent paid less than the minimum wage. Presumably the major reason for this result is the fact that a large proportion of workers in this category are not covered by the federal minimum wage of $5.15. The 1996 amendments to the FLSA set the minimum wage to employees receiving gratuities at $2.13 per hour, as long as the employee's average hourly tips were sufficient to provide total average hourly compensation at or above the "standard" minimum wage level.

Minimum wage/low-paid workers are also concentrated in part-time employment. Figure 2.2 contains a plot of the proportion of hourly wage employees with a wage rate less than or equal to the minimum wage by usual hours worked per week. (The category "0" represents employees who work varying numbers of hours.) We see a large drop off in the proportion paid the minimum wage or less at around 30 hours per week, with the lowest proportion of workers paid the minimum working "normal" full-time hours of between 40 to 45 per week. There is a slight increase in the proportion at or below the minimum wage as we

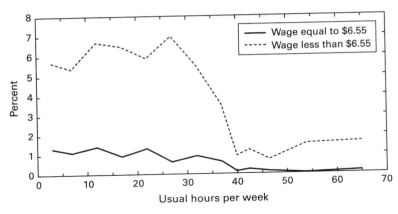

Figure 2.2
Wages less than or equal to $5.15 for all hourly workers by weekly hours, 2005

get to an extremely high number of weekly hours, though few workers fall into this category.

In figure 2.3 we graph the relationship between age and gender by the proportion paid the minimum wage or less. From the top panel, which graphs the relationship for the population, we see a strong, slightly nonlinear relationship between age and the likelihood of being paid the minimum wage or less. The highest levels, by far, are observed for individuals less than twenty-five years of age. There also exists a positive relationship between age and the probability of having one of these low-paying jobs for those who are at least 60 years of age. This may stem from retired or semi-retired individuals taking part-time jobs to top off their social security or private pension payments. The patterns by gender are similar to what we have seen in the other figures. They largely mirror the aggregate pattern, with the female proportions roughly twice as large as the male proportions at each age.

In this descriptive analysis we have seen that women, part-time employees, workers in food preparation and serving occupations, and youth are much more likely to be paid at or below the minimum wage than other dependent employees. However, perhaps the most important implication of this descriptive analysis is that the proportion of workers paid at or below the minimum wage is small in all of these groups, never exceeding one-fifth in any of them. Thus, while minimum wage work is highly concentrated, it is rare throughout the age, occupational, gender, and weekly hours distributions.

a.

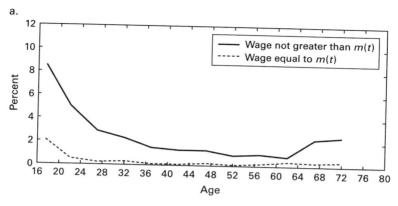

b.

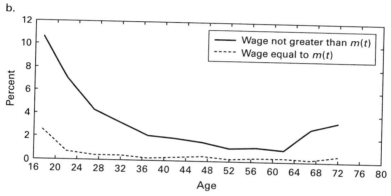

c.

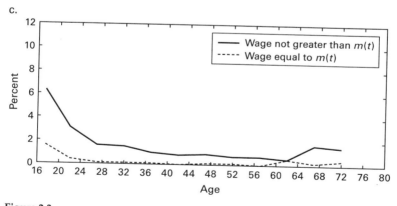

Figure 2.3
Wages less than or equal to $5.15 for hourly workers, 2005: (a) All hourly workers by age, (b) female workers, (c) male workers

2.3   Impacts of Minimum Wage Changes on Wages

From figure 2.1 it is apparent that following a change in the federally mandated minimum wage, there occurs an increase in the proportion of individuals paid at or below the minimum wage. To understand how minimum wages influence labor market decisions and outcomes, it is important to understand the mechanism that results in this change. For example, if the labor market is noncompetitive, in the sense that firms and/or workers earn rents from an employment match, a minimum wage change may simply reallocate the division of the surplus between the two parties, in a manner described in detail in the following chapters. However, if the market is competitive so that workers are each paid their marginal product, an increase in the minimum wage will result in termination of all employment matches for which the current wage is greater than or equal to the old minimum wage and less than or equal to the new one.

In this section we examine the impact of a change in the federal minimum wage on employment status and wage realizations in our target population, individuals aged 16 to 24. From the CPS-ORG subsample we can create a sequence of short panel data sets, using a household member's data from the fourth and eighth month of being in the sample, which by construction results in observations separated by approximately one year. For other labor market characteristics besides wages (e.g., unemployment, or hours at work for those employed), it is possible to form panels with eight observations per individual. But our focus, using the panel aspect of the CPS, will be on wage outcomes, so we will limit attention to the panels constructed using the CPS-ORG.[5]

Between 1990 and 2006 the federal minimum wage has been changed four times. Let τ_j be the calendar date at which the jth change occurred. Then any monthly panel that begins at a date s_j, where $\tau_j - 11 < s_j < \tau_j - 1$, will include two wage observations for the same individual that span the jth minimum wage change. The idea is to use these wage changes to investigate the impacts of the minimum wage at the most disaggregated level possible, the individual.

The goal of this analysis is to perform a before and after comparison of remuneration rates after a minimum wage change. Qualitatively, there are four types of wage and employment comparisons we would like to make, all differentiated by the wage payment at the first observation (which we will denote by w^1). Let m denote the minimum wage in effect at the time of the observation of w^1, and let $m'(>m)$ denote the minimum wage in effect at the time of the individual's second wage observation (w^2). The four groups which are of interest are

Group	Level of w^1
A	$w^1 < m$
B	$m = w^1$
C	$m < w^1 < m'$
D	$m' \leq w^1$

Group A is paid less than the minimum wage at time time 1. Essentially none of the labor market models we will propose or survey has an explicit explanation of such an outcome, other than to assert that wage reports below the binding minimum must result from measurement error.[6] Of course, there are a large number of reasons an individual could legitimately earn a wage less than the minimum, the main one being that they are performing a job not covered by the FLSA. The likelihood of this being the case is certainly substantially higher for labor market participants in the age range 16 to 24 than for older individuals. If holding a job not covered by the FLSA is the reason that $w^1 < m$, then it may be the case that a change in the minimum wage rate will have no, or little, effect on whether the individual is employed at time 2 and, if still employed, on their wage at that point in time.

Individuals in group B are an interesting case, and the implications for their fate after a minimum wage increase are different across some of the models surveyed in chapter 5. Some versions of the standard neoclassical model would imply that any member of classes B and C would face unemployment (with certainty) under a higher minimum wage. The model we develop, and others that we survey, produce more nuanced implications due to their assumption that there exist search frictions in the labor market, giving both sides of the market some degree of bargaining power. This results in wages (and profits) generally being less than the productivity of the employment relationship. As a result minimum wage changes can lead to termination of the employment relationship, or continuation of the employment relationship after a reallocation of the surplus attributable to it. In this view of the world, even workers paid the minimum wage generate some profit for their employers, and hence an increase in the minimum wage does not necessarily lead to termination. In group B we are especially interested in seeing what proportion of individuals transit into unemployment (or nonparticipation), what proportion remain employed and experience wage increases to the new minimum wage, and what proportion move to wages above the new minimum.

Group C members most closely parallel the standard textbook treatment of the minimum wage. In their situation the individuals' wages at time 1 are not constrained by the presence of a minimum wage. At time 2, however, all changes: their wage either must be raised to the new level of the minimum wage (at least), or the employment relationship must be ended. The experience of this group, which, unfortunately, is small, yields a substantial amount of information regarding the operation of the labor market, at least for relatively unskilled workers.

Group D members have wages, both before and after the minimum wage change, that exceed the new minimum wage level. In this case the changes in the minimum wage law do not require a wage change. However, it is often maintained that "a rising tide lifts all boats," which is to say, in order to preserve the relative wage structure, increases in the lowest wage may produce increases in wages above the new minimum. The formal argument behind this claim is usually missing, though some authors find empirical evidence of minimum wage "spillover" to the upper reaches of the wage distribution. The model I develop in the next chapter is capable of generating spillover, and has precise empirical implications regarding its manifestation. For this group of individuals, there is no reason to expect a significant impact on the likelihood of unemployment. However, changes in the wage received by members of group D are capable of shedding some light on the manner in which wages are determined, and whether the model developed below is consistent with these changes.[7]

From these descriptions of the groups and the impacts of minimum wage changes on them it may appear that the CPS-ORG data enables us to perform carefully controlled experiments. Of course, this is not even approximately the case. First of all, the matches between successive observations are only statistical ones, in the sense that we cannot be sure that the labor market outcomes in period 1 and period 2 are associated with the same individual. While the probability that they are is exceedingly high, it is not unity.

More problematic is our limited ability to ensure that the individual is employed at the same job at both points in time. A common underlying assumption in most models of job turnover is that the baseline productivity of an individual working at a given firm is essentially fixed. By baseline, we are referring to some initial level of productivity that may change over the duration of the match but in an essentially exogenous manner. Because of the limitations of the data used in the empirical analysis, the model developed below assumes a fixed rate of productivity over the entire life of the employment contract, one that is not affected by changes in minimum wage levels. Within such a framework we know that if an individual kept their job despite an increase in the minimum wage, then the productivity level was sufficiently high for the worker to remain employed. From a separation we would draw the opposite conclusion.[8]

Since we have no information regarding an employee's job tenure at time 2, we cannot be certain that she was employed at the same job that she held at time 1. Thus, as was the case in matching observations to individuals in a household, we must resort to a sort of statistical matching to quantify the likelihood that the individual was employed in the same job at both points in time. In particular, we use information on the major industry and occupation classification of the job at both points in time to make a probabilistic assessment of whether it is the same job or not. If these two classifications are different, we can be reasonably sure that the job is different.[9] If the two classifications are the same, then the likelihood that the job is the same increases. However, this probability clearly is far from unity.

With these caveats in mind, we can turn to the results. Table 2.3 contains the basic set of results produced using the short panels. In the top panel of table 2.3 are presented the estimated transition matrices for the samples in which the fourth month-in-sample occurred in the 11-month period between October 1995 and August 1996. By defining the sample in this way, the first observation occurs when the minimum wage is $4.25, and the second occurs when the minimum wage is $4.75. All the observations are then pooled to increase the precision of our estimates of the conditional probabilities and to smooth seasonal effects.

The first thing to note in the panel is that the conditional probability of entering unemployment is substantially larger for those paid the minimum wage than for any other initial state, even that of earning a wage less than the minimum. Those earning the minimum wage before the change have the highest probability, by far, of being paid the new minimum after the change, followed by those originally paid more than the old minimum but less than the new one. The observation that those paid less than m are not as likely as those paid m to be in the U state one year later, nor as likely to be employed at a wage equal to m' one year later, is consistent with a substantial number of individuals in this group

Table 2.3
Transition probabilities all matched individuals aged 16 to 24 (first year)

	Destination state				
Origin state	U	$w < m'$	$w = m'$	$w > m'$	N
Group 1: $m = 4.25$, $m' = 4.75$					
$w < m$	0.075	0.158	0.064	0.703	360
$w = m$	0.101	0.138	0.106	0.654	188
$m < w < m'$	0.059	0.163	0.069	0.708	288
$w \geq m'$	0.045	0.067	0.011	0.877	3639
Group 2: $m = 4.75$, $m' = 5.15$					
$w < m$	0.047	0.208	0.051	0.693	548
$w = m$	0.026	0.153	0.128	0.694	196
$m < w < m'$	0.064	0.175	0.023	0.738	515
$w \geq m'$	0.041	0.073	0.012	0.874	3370
Group 3: $m = m' = 5.15$					
$w < m$	0.052	0.149	0.021	0.779	679
$w = m$	0.049	0.091	0.037	0.823	164
$w > m$	0.045	0.065	0.008	0.882	3835

Note: Data from CPS-ORG.

being employed in jobs not covered by the minimum wage. Perhaps the major impression to take away from this transition matrix is that there is a high transition rate into jobs paying more than the new minimum wage m', no matter which initial state is occupied. From this descriptive evidence, it appears that even if minimum wage changes do have some immediate impacts on the labor force status of low-wage workers, these effects may quickly wear off in a sufficiently "dynamic" labor market environment.

The second panel in table 2.3 repeats this exercise for the minimum wage change that occurred in 1997. In this case we selected appropriately aged individuals who were in their fourth month-in-sample in the 11-month period October 1996 through August 1997. The second observation for these individuals therefore occurred after the change in minimum wage from $4.75 through $5.15.

In interpreting the transition rates in this panel, it is important to bear in mind that this change in the minimum wage occurred only 11 months after the previous increase, and that both increases were mandated in the same legislation. While it is unclear what impact these conditions might have on the estimates, the situations surrounding the minimum wage increases in 1996 and 1997 are somewhat different.

Perhaps the most striking difference between the top and middle panels is in the transition rates into the unemployment state. In contrast to the top panel, those whose wage was originally equal to $4.75 had the lowest probability of being unemployed one year later. The highest probability of being unemployed one year later was instead associated with those paid between $4.75 and $5.15, a group whose first job compensation is also clearly impacted by the minimum wage change. Although there were few transitions into the unemployment state for those paid the minimum wage in the first period, there was a high probability of receiving the new minimum wage in the second period. It is possible that these patterns are associated with the staggered change to the minimum wage of $5.15. Low-productivity jobs could have been terminated immediately when the minimum wage was increased to $4.75, with those remaining being productive enough to withstand the eventual increase to $5.15. As was true in the top panel, we see that all groups have a high probability of escaping pay at or below the minimum wage by the time of the second wage observation.

The bottom panel in the table is meant to provide a benchmark in evaluating the impact of minimum wage changes observed in the top two panels. To estimate these transition probabilities, the individuals selected were in their fourth sample months in the 11-month period beginning October 1997 and ending August 1998. There was no minimum wage change in this period. So, ignoring business cycle differences, the bottom panel roughly represents the pattern of movements we might have expected to observe in the absence of a minimum wage change. The initial wage states are the same as in the top two panels, except that there is no $m < w < m'$ category because $m = m'$ in this case.

The transition rates into unemployment are very similar across the three initial wage states, which was not the case when the minimum wage changed between labor market observations. The transition rates from wages that are at or below the minimum wage to wages above the minimum is a bit higher than was observed in the top two panels. The likelihood that an individual is observed at a minimum wage job at both interview dates when there was no minimum wage change is only 0.037, which is much smaller than the likelihood of being observed at the new, higher minimum wage in the case of a minimum wage change.[10]

The results of this simple descriptive exercise can be summarized as follows: at the aggregate level few individuals are paid the minimum wage, even in the age group 16 to 24. Increases in the nominal minimum wage, which tend to happen relatively infrequently, result in small increases in the proportion of the labor force paid the minimum wage or below, though these increased rates are quickly dissipated by inflation. Also at the aggregate level it is difficult to pick up any discernible systematic impact of increases in the minimum wage on employment or unemployment rates. This is where individual level data from the CPS has helped us observe the impacts of minimum wage changes on wage and employment outcomes.

We used statistical matching of the CPS-ORG data to create a short panel of two observations per individual. The data points were separated by approximately twelve months, and during this period a change in the legislated minimum wage occurred. We saw that there those who were paid at or below the new minimum wage at the first observation point were much likely to move to the new minimum wage or into the unemployment state at the second interview than those who were paid more than the new minimum wage initially. This gives some support to the idea that a minimum wage increase tends to result in the end of some low-productivity jobs, though some workers at jobs with low pay but sufficiently high productivity have their wages bumped up to the new minimum wage level. Because of the impossibility of knowing what happened to the individual between these two time points, including whether or not they are employed at the same job at both points in time, our interpretation must be considered highly speculative. Nonetheless, the results that we begin to develop in the following chapter are broadly consistent with this story.

Perhaps the biggest lesson to take away from the descriptive results of this chapter is that few individuals are paid the minimum wage, and that small changes in the minimum wage do not have significant impacts on labor market outcomes in the short and medium run. This is not to say that minimum wages are not capable of having large impacts on labor market outcomes and welfare; rather, they have not had an impact because they have been set at such low levels for much of the period since the enactment of the FLSA.

3 A Model of Minimum Wage Effects on Labor Market Careers

The standard model used to theoretically and empirically investigate minimum wage effects on labor market outcomes views individuals and firms operating in stochastic environments that are governed by probabilistic laws that do not change over time. This is clearly an abstraction from reality, but for purposes of examining minimum wage effects, it may not be too egregious an assumption for a number of reasons. Most individuals paid the minimum wage are young, as we saw in the previous chapter, and as a result the impacts of minimum wage laws on labor market careers are largely concentrated in the first few years of labor market activity.[1] Over such a relatively short period, the probabilistic structure of the labor market is not likely to change dramatically. Furthermore the data used in all of the empirical analysis (drawn from the Current Population Survey) except that conducted in chapter 10 are essentially static. To estimate a dynamic model using such data requires us to assume that the labor market environment does not change over time. In particular, under the assumption of stationarity (i.e., constancy of the probabilistic laws governing the economy) the rational behavior posited for all labor market participants and firms can be characterized in terms of decision rules that are invariant over time. If we were to allow the model to be nonstationary, we would be forced to specify all the conditions that individuals and firms have faced in the past and will face in the future in order to describe their decisions at any point in time. While we don't have access to data that would allow us to undertake such a modeling effort, it is doubtful that such a complex theoretical analysis would even be enlightening.

Why attempt to build such a model in the first place? The point is that it is extremely useful to have a relatively complete, equilibrium model of employment relations if we are to comprehensively summarize the impact of minimum wages on labor market outcomes and the welfare of labor market participants and firms. To make welfare valuations, it is necessary to endow each set of agents in the economy with their own set of objectives. Subject to technological and budget constraints, and given the optimizing decisions of other agents in the market, each individual or firm acts so as to maximize the value of their objective function. We will view minimum wages as constraining the actions of all labor market participants, both individuals and firms, though as we will see the minimum wage "constraint" may, under certain circumstances, increase the welfare of labor market participants, firms, or even both. In many cases only one side of the market will experience a welfare increase as a result of a given minimum wage increase (and yes, it could be employers), while minimum wage increases at extremely high levels will negatively impact both sides of the market.

The objective function with which we endow all labor market participants is one of expected wealth maximization. That is, individuals are assumed to care only about their (discounted) average earnings over their labor market careers; in particular, the variance of (realized) income flows does not favorably or unfavorably affect welfare. This is a strong assumption, and is made primarily for reasons of tractability. However, it is easy to show that when consumption decisions can be "decoupled" from earnings, as is the case when there exist perfect capital markets for borrowing and lending, expected wealth-maximization behavior in the labor market is consistent with aversion toward consumption risk on the part of individuals. While young labor market participants may not have access to perfect capital markets, transfers between parents and children may serve the same role. There is no strong reason to expect that young labor market participants will behave in ways other than those consistent with expected wealth maximization.

Perhaps less controversially, firms will be assumed to behave so as to maximize expected profits. The model employed throughout is search-theoretic. At some points in the welfare analysis we will add general equilibrium elements by incorporating a "matching function" setup (e.g., see Pissarides 2000). In this framework, firms make decisions regarding the number of vacancies to create and the contact rate is an increasing function of the number of searchers and the number of vacancies. There will be no other "general equilibrium" links between searchers and firms in our model, such as those that might occur through the public ownership of firms. The general equilibrium analysis posits an expected value of zero for all new vacancies, which occurs through the mechanism of free entry, though firms with filled jobs do earn positive profits, and the profit level is, in general, a function of the minimum wage rate. In the partial equilibrium analysis, all firms earn nonnegative profits in equilibrium. We have thus deliberately kept our model of firm behavior and the link between firms and searchers as simple as possible subject to the restriction that it possess empirical implications broadly consistent with patterns found in the CPS data that we utilize in the most of the empirical analysis.

As is clear from the description of the model so far, many phenomena that could have significant impacts on the effect of the minimum wage on labor market outcomes have been omitted. The first thing that often comes to mind is capital goods. If firms have access to production technologies that allow them to substitute capital for labor, then substantial minimum wage increases that significantly affect the price of labor, at least at the low end of the skill distribution, may lead employers to substitute machinery for human labor. Since we have no measures of capital utilization at the firms employing individuals in our the CPS data, we have no way of directly using this information to characterize the potential degree of substitutability between capital and labor in this part of the skill distribution.

Although it is common to assume the absence of capital in search-theoretic labor models, it may be preferable to allow firms to make these decisions. Over the past several decades we have seen the demand for lower skilled individuals decrease precipitously in the United States, which has given rise to a marked increase in inequality in labor market earnings. While we cannot explicitly include in the model and the empirical work a number of important factors affecting the demand for labor, our Nash bargaining formulation of the wage determination process does allow us to represent the cumulative impact of these factors in an indirect way—through the bargaining power parameter. Recently Cahuc et al. (2006) explicitly estimated bargaining power parameters for segments of the French workforce, and found that higher skilled workers tend to have more bargaining power than lower skilled workers, even after accounting for some other differences in the labor market environments that these groups face. Of course, one problem with allowing this one characteristic to represent the plethora of omitted factors is the necessity we face of assuming that it is a "primitive" parameter, that is, that it remains the same when labor market policy (the minimum wage in our case) is (even radically) altered. Since many of our policy implications flow from the estimated value of the bargaining power parameter and our assumption that it is fixed, all of our findings and welfare analyses must be interpreted cautiously.

Firms may also attempt to "work around" a minimum wage if the employment contract and working conditions are multidimensional. For example, Hashimoto (1982) suggests that in response to an increase in the minimum wage, a firm may lower the investment content of jobs held by younger workers, which would then result in a flatter wage profile over the life cycle. Similar adjustments in other nonpecuniary aspects of the job, such as whether it includes an offer of employer-provided health insurance, may also occur. The ability of firms to adjust their compensation packages along other dimensions may dampen or eliminate the impact of the minimum wage on a subset of labor market outcomes.

3.1 Characterization of the Labor Market Career

We will think of labor market events as occurring continuously in time. By this we mean that there are no natural times, say weeks or months, at which labor market events always take place. Technically speaking, we view the labor market as a continuous-time point process, which means that at any point in time an unemployed individual can receive a job offer. Furthermore at any point during an employment relationship the contract can be exogenously terminated. In more general versions of the model, discussed in chapter 10, one can allow for on-the-job search. In this case employed individuals at one firm may make contact with another that offers them an employment opportunity. As a result jobs with a given employer may end due to some exogenous separation (e.g., plant closing down or individual changing locations) or for endogenous reasons (e.g, the employee finds a job at which she is more productive and terminates her position at her current employer). We will mainly focus on the case of unemployed search only because it is more straightforward to analyze and because such a model can be estimated with CPS data, the largest and most representative US labor market data set available to us.

Individuals begin their labor market careers as unemployed searchers, eventually locating a job paying some "acceptable" wage (we will define below what we mean by acceptable). After some randomly determined period of time, that job will end, and she will once again enter the state of unemployment, where the job search process will be repeated in exactly the same manner as it was the first time around. This "cycling" continues unabated until the individual eventually leaves the market—the reason for which we will suppose is exogenous. In the language of stochastic process theory, we characterize the labor market career *as* an alternating, marked renewal process. It is *alternating* because time in the labor market is spent alternatively in unemployment and employment spells. It is a *renewal* process because we will be assuming that the individual's past labor market history plays no role in determining how long she will spend in a current spell of unemployment or employment. Finally, it is a *marked* process because when she is employed, we will not only be concerned with how long the employment spell lasts but also at what wage she is employed. The wage rate is the marker, or subsidiary characteristic, that is of interest to us over and above the timing of events.

Let us fix ideas with an example. Say that an individual begins her labor market career at time 0, an inconsequential normalization. Assuming that she will continue to participate in the market as an unemployed searcher or worker over her entire life, her labor market career can be completely characterized by the time at which she meets prospective employers, the value of the match associated with each contact, and the time at which employment matches she has accepted are (exogenously) terminated. For example, since she begins her labor market career in the unemployed search state at time 0, the first ten "events" in her labor market career might be given by the values in table 3.1.

The interpretation of the figures in table 3.1 is as follows: The individual initiated search at time 0, at which point she occupied the

Table 3.1
Hypothetical early labor market career

Event number	State	Time of event	Duration draw	Match value
1	*U*	0.891	0.891	6.243
2	*U*	3.168	2.277	4.329
3	*U*	15.554	12.386	3.871
4	*U*	15.558	0.004	10.918
5	*E*	38.921	23.363	—
6	*U*	44.236	5.315	7.891
7	*U*	56.793	12.557	12.119
8	*E*	157.421	100.628	—
9	*U*	164.772	7.351	10.145
10	*E*	322.510	157.738	—
⋮	⋮	⋮		⋮

unemployed state U. At time 0.891 she encountered her first potential employer. (Time units are arbitrary here, but it may help to think of the unit of time as the week.) When she met her first employer, the productivity of the potential match was revealed to be 6.243; this is to be thought of as the "flow" value of productivity that will be realized every moment she works for this employer. The value of this first potential match was insufficient to result in an employment contract, so the individual remained in the nonemployed state. The second potential employer was encountered at time 3.168 and the potential value of that match was 4.329, which also was deemed unacceptable. Only the fourth potential match resulted in an employment contract. This employment contract began at time 15.558 and had a flow value associated with it of 10.918. This match surplus is divided between the worker and the firm according to an idealized bargaining process, as will be described in detail below. Whatever the division, it was sufficient to induce both parties to begin the employment contract, which was terminated (exogenously) at time 38.291. This caused the individual to reenter the nonemployment state, and she immediately began to search for a new acceptable employment contract. After one unsuccessful encounter at time 44.236, she found another acceptable match with a value of 12.119 at time 56.793. This match was eventually terminated at time 157.421, and the nonemployed search process was repeated.

The events described in table 3.1 are not strictly exogenous. Some events are conditionally exogenous; for example, given the decision to begin the labor market career at time 0, the arrival of the first possible job match at time 0.891 and the total flow value of that match, 6.243, are determined strictly randomly. However, the decision to reject that possible match is a behavioral one made by the searcher and the first firm encountered. This led the individual to continue in the nonemployed state and eventually to meet her second potential match at a time that was, once again, determined randomly. Thus the labor market career is a sequence of exogenous events followed by decisions that lead to further exogenous events (conditional on the previous exogenous events and past decisions), and so on. The method of dynamic programming (DP) allows us to formalize this recursive process.

The only decision explicitly made by the searcher in this simple conceptualization of a labor market career is whether to accept a particular employment contract. Although the wage associated with a given match value is assumed to be the outcome of a bargaining procedure, this procedure is largely "black-boxed," and hence not strictly behavioral.[2]

Under the assumption that the environment is constant, the decision of whether to begin a particular employment match will be made by comparing the value of the match, denoted by θ, with a constant, θ^*. An employment contract will be initiated whenever a match value θ equals or exceeds θ^*. The parameter θ^* will be a function of all of the parameters that characterize the economic environment. From the partial labor market history contained in table 3.1 it is clear that $7.891 < \theta^* \leq 10.145$ if the individual is following our prescription for optimal behavior.

Another decision, which is particularly relevant for young (and old) individuals, is whether to participate (i.e., undertake search) in the labor market. For the moment we will ignore this decision and assume that all individuals in the population we are considering are labor market participants. We will return to a consideration of the participation decision at the end of this chapter.

3.2   The Stationary Labor Market Environment

There are a number of ways to formally characterize the stationary environment within which firms and individuals interact. Perhaps the most straightforward is in terms of the distributions of times spent in the various labor market states. We assume that there are two duration distributions, one associated with event times in the unemployment state (those are the times at which job offers are received) and the other associated with event times while employed (when the job is terminated).

The distribution of times between events while unemployed is given by $F_U(t_U)$, and it has an associated probability density function given by $f_U(t_U)$. By assuming that the labor market is "memoryless," the implication is that the rate of receiving an offer since the last time the searcher received one is independent of the length of the interval. More formally, the likelihood of receiving an offer at time t_U given that an offer has not been received before t_U is

$$h_U(t_U) = \frac{f_U(t_U)}{1 - F_U(t_U)}.$$

In our case, for the offer arrival process to be memoryless, it should be the case that the likelihood of receiving an offer is independent of how long it has been since the last offer was received, or

$$h_U(t_U) = \lambda,$$

where λ is some positive constant. A continuous distribution with a well-defined density can be equivalently represented in terms of its hazard function, and vice versa. The only continuous distribution associated with a random variable that takes positive values that possesses a constant hazard is the negative exponential, for which

$$h_U(t_U) = \lambda,$$

$$\Leftrightarrow f_U(t_U) = \lambda \exp(-\lambda t_U),$$

$$\Rightarrow F_U(t_U) = 1 - \exp(-\lambda t_U).$$

An individual who exits an unemployment spell (which requires the receipt of an *acceptable* offer, which is defined below) immediately enters an employment spell. The employment termination process is also memoryless, which implies that the hazard rate function out of employment is given by $h_E(t_E) = \eta$, where η is positive and t_E is the elapsed time since the employment spell began. The constant hazard rate assumption implies a negative exponential distribution of employment durations, with

$$f_E(t_E) = \eta \exp(-\eta t_E),$$

$$F_E(t_E) = 1 - \exp(-\eta t_E).$$

The labor market experiences of an individual can be thought of as unfolding in the following manner: As in the example, the individual begins their labor market life in the unemployment state at time 0. The individual then draws a duration of time until a first job offer is received from the distribution F_U. In our example this random draw resulted in a duration to first offer of 0.891. When the firm is contacted, another random draw is made, this time from the distribution of matches, G. The match value drawn at the first firm contact was equal to 6.243. This job offer was rejected, and another independent draw was made from the duration distribution F_U. In this case the second draw was equal to 2.277 (column 4), so the event occurred at time 3.168 from the beginning of the labor market career. The match value drawn at this contact time was 4.329, which was also rejected. All the draws of durations until events 1 through 4 are made, independently, from the distribution F_U.

The fourth match value drawn during the first unemployment spell (which consists of events 1 through 4) was accepted and an employment spell began at time 38.291. At that moment in time, a draw was made from the distribution F_E that determined the length of time the employment spell would last (23.363, in this case). Once that employment spell ended, the next unemployment spell began, and it consisted of events 6 and 7. The process proceeds until the individual exits from the labor market, which may in principle be never.

We see that the labor market proceeds as a sequence of draws from the distributions F_U, F_E, and G. In the example of table 3.1, the durations associated with events {1, 2, 3, 4, 6, 7, 9} were i.i.d. draws from F_U, while the durations associated with events {5, 8, 10} were i.i.d. draws from F_E. The match values associated with each contact in the unemployment state were i.i.d. draws from G. The endogeneity of the labor market process stems from the selection on draws made from the match distribution G, and the implications of this selection process for the rate of leaving unemployment and the observed accepted wage distribution. In the following section we characterize the acceptance rules used by searchers.

3.3   The Decision-Theoretic Model

The individuals in our model are posited to be taking actions so as to maximize their expected lifetime wealth. They can only maximize expected wealth due to the presence of "search frictions." In this case search frictions refer to the fact that individuals do not know the location of the firms with employment vacancies, and even more important, do not know the identity of the firm with which they could achieve their highest productivity level. Prior to actually contacting a given firm and learning their productivity level there, all potential employers look alike to the individual.[3] In an expectational sense, then, the individual is initially indifferent with respect to the identity of the firm that is contacted.[4] Firms are only differentiated after contact.

It is important to be clear regarding our assumption as to the manner in which an individual's productivity, θ, is determined at a randomly selected firm. We assume that this productivity value is a draw from the fixed, known distribution G. For the moment we do not distinguish individuals in terms of observable characteristics. One might suppose that schooling, for example, tends to make an individual more productive in the labor market.[5] Within our modeling framework, a generic effect of schooling could be incorporated by conditioning the match distribution, and possibly other labor market parameters as well, on schooling. In general, let x denote a characteristic or set of character-istics upon which population members are distinguished. Then the conditional matching function is $G(\theta|x)$. If x was years of schooling completed, for example, we might assume that $G(\theta|x') \le G(\theta|x)$ for all $\theta > 0$ when $x' > x$. This is a first-order stochastic dominance relation-ship so that the likelihood that any match draw is less or equal to θ for a highly educated individual is no greater than it is for a less-educated individual. Of course, a logical consequence of this is that the average match draw of the more highly-educated individual is at least as large as that of the less-educated person. Other things equal, more-educated individuals will receive higher wages, but at any given firm their pro-ductivity may be lower than that of their less-educated colleague. Given an individual's characteristics, as summarized by x, match draws across alternative employers will be independently and identically distributed according to $G(\theta|x)$.[6]

There are many other alternative formulations one could envision re-garding the manner in which worker–firm productivity is determined. One leading approach is to assume that individual i on the supply side of the market has a time-invariant productivity-determining character-istic a_i, while firm j on the demand side of the market has a time-invariant productivity-determining characteristic b_j, with the productivity of indi-vidual i at firm j being given by $\theta_{ij} = a_i b_j$. This is the setup utilized by Postel-Vinay and Robin (2002) and by Cahuc et al. (2006) in their analysis of labor market dynamics using matched French employer–employee data. They skillfully exploit these data and are able to recover esti-mates of the employee skill distribution $F(a)$ without making para-metric assumptions regarding the form of the distribution. Given a distribution of firm characteristics $Z(b)$, each individual faces their own matching distribution $Z(b) \times a$. In many ways this is more general than the matching process described in the previous paragraph in that it does not require us to specify which factors, such as schooling, should be used to differentiate workers. Nevertheless, it does place a number of undeniably strong restrictions on the distribution of match values across workers and firms.[7]

At each moment in time the individual makes decisions so as to maximize expected wealth given her current labor market state and her knowledge of the parameters that characterize the labor market en-vironment. The method commonly used to characterize her decision in such a framework is dynamic programming (DP). To illustrate the DP approach in a continuous time model like ours, we will begin by assuming that workers receive the entire value of the match. In this case the wage offer distribution is identical to the matching distribution G.

The value of being in any particular labor market state at a point in time consists of the sum of a "flow" value, which is the "current period return" (a period should be thought of as an instant in this case), and the discounted expected value of next period's problem given the current state and action taken. If the current state is denoted by s, the current choice or action by a, and next period's state is given by s', then the general formulation of the problem is

$$V(s) = \max_a R(s,a) + \beta E[V(s')|s,a], \tag{3.1}$$

where $R(s,a)$ denotes the current period return to the action a taken when the state is s, β is some positive scalar, s' denotes next period's state, and $E[V(s')|s,a]$ is the conditional expectation of the value of next period's decision problem given current state s and action a. In computing this expectation, the conditioning on s and a reflects the fact that, in general, the probability distribution of s' is not independent of the current state and the action taken (s and a, respectively).

Consider first the value of being in state U. Assume that the flow value of searching is given by the constant scalar b. This flow value of non-employment can reflect unemployment benefits, direct costs of search activity, and the value of other activities undertaken while the individual searches. Our strong stationarity assumption requires that b be time invariant and that time spent in search does not change the parameters characterizing the labor market environment of the individual. These are both clearly counterfactual, especially for young labor market participants. In the case of unemployment benefits, for example, there are limitations on the length of time they can be received (and they may not be received at all if an individual does not have the requisite employment history).[8] In addition young labor market searchers are often simultaneously investing in human capital. This investment in human capital would be expected to impact several parameters characterizing the labor market environment, such as the productivity distribution G and the rates of match arrivals and dissolutions of employment contracts. Introducing human capital accumulation into the model adds another state variable, the current level of the human capital stock, considerably complicating the analysis. The fact that human capital is not directly observable makes it necessary to rely on ad hoc assumptions concerning the nature of the human capital production function and the dependence of search parameters on the human capital stock and investment activity. For these reasons we have chosen to ignore it in the present analysis.

Another important benefit of working under a stationarity assumption is the relative simplicity of the decision rules that are associated with optimizing behavior. In particular, the decision of whether to accept a job at a newly discovered job opportunity characterized by θ will only be a function of θ and, in particular, will not be a function of the duration of the unemployment spell or previously received job opportunities. This rules out the situation in which an individual who rejects a match θ at some arbitrary time t "wishes" she would have accepted it at some later time $t' > t$. The acceptance rules we derive under stationarity imply that any newly received offer will be accepted only if it is as least as large as some constant θ^*. Thus, if the match θ was rejected at time t, it would have been rejected at any future time t' as well.[9]

Our model is set in continuous time, and therefore has no natural "periods" to distinguish the "current" from the "future." Our strategy will be to assume that there does exist a "decision period" of duration ε over which new actions are precluded.[10] That is, the individual will take an action given the state s and will reap the reward from this action over the period ε. At the conclusion of this decision period, she will take a new action given the state to which the system has then evolved. The decision period ε is in the end just an artifice, for we will define behavior and the value of the problem in the limit as $\varepsilon \to 0$.

Define the value of the unemployed search problem as

$$V_U = (1 + \rho\varepsilon)^{-1} \left\{ b\varepsilon + \lambda\varepsilon \int \max\left(V_U, V_E(w)\right) dG(w) \right.$$

$$\left. + (1 - \lambda\varepsilon)V_U + o(\varepsilon) \right\}. \tag{3.2}$$

As currently written, (3.2) includes no explicit action, since we assume that the individual has already decided to participate in the labor market. We will discuss how this decision can be formalized later in this chapter.

In terms of the correspondence between (3.1) and (3.2), note that the term in (3.2) that corresponds to the β in (3.1) is $1/(1 + \rho\varepsilon) \equiv \beta_\varepsilon$, where ρ is the discount rate. The interpretation of the term $b\varepsilon/(1 + \rho\varepsilon)$, which is the "current period return" in the state of unemployment, is as follows. Over the short period ε the individual receives b per instant. Thus the total amount received at the end of this period is $b\varepsilon$. However, since this amount is "paid" at the end of the period ε, its beginning of period value must be appropriately discounted. Applying the discount factor, the current period return in state U is $\beta_\varepsilon b\varepsilon$.

Now consider the next term. Assume that the searcher obtains exactly one job offer at wage w (= θ in the case where she obtains the entire match surplus). Her choice then will be either to accept employment at that wage or to continue searching. The value of accepting a wage offer of w is given by $V_E(w)$ and will be discussed shortly. Given the receipt of the offer w, the individual will choose the option associated with the highest value, so that the value of getting an offer of w is given by $\max(V_U, V_E(w))$. This choice is the only explicit behavior in the current setup. The expected value of getting an offer is then the expectation of $\max(V_U, V_E(w))$ taken with respect to the distribution of all possible wage offers, which is given by $G(w)$ in this case. Given the receipt of an offer, the discounted expected value is $\beta_\varepsilon \int \max(V_U, V_E(w)) \, dG(w)$. The approximate probability of getting one offer in the short interval ε is $\lambda\varepsilon$.

If no offer is received, the individual will continue to search. This is because, in a stationarity environment, if a certain action was optimal at some arbitrary time when the individual faces choices in the set C, then the same decision will be made at any other time when the individual occupies the same state and faces the same choices.[11] Thus the value of not receiving an offer by the end of the period is $\beta_\varepsilon V_U$, and the approximate likelihood of this event is $(1 - \lambda\varepsilon)$. In terms of the DP decomposition given in [3.1], the discounted expected value of future choices given search is

$$\beta_\varepsilon \lambda\varepsilon \int \max(V_U, V_E(w)) \, dG(w) + \beta_\varepsilon(1 - \lambda_\varepsilon)V_U + \beta_\varepsilon o(\varepsilon).$$

The term $o(\varepsilon)$ includes the value of all of the other events that could occur in the finite interval of time ε, such as receiving two or more offers. The likelihood of more than one event occurring is a decreasing function of the size of the interval ε. The term $o(\varepsilon)$ is defined through the following important property:

$$\lim_{\varepsilon \to 0} \frac{o(\varepsilon)}{\varepsilon} = 0.$$

This statement implies that in the limit, as the interval ε becomes arbitrarily small, the likelihood that more than one event occurs in the interval goes to 0. In our simple example, this means that in any instant the individual will, at most, receive one job offer.

Before we can analyze the problem facing the nonemployed searcher further it is necessary to examine the situation of an employed individual being paid an "instantaneous" wage of w. Since we have precluded on-the-job search, and since it was initially optimal to accept a wage of w, an employed individual who has accepted a wage of w will never quit and enter the state of unemployed search. This implies that she will simply remain at her job until such time as the employment match is exogenously terminated. Formally,

$$V_E(w) = (1 + \rho\varepsilon)^{-1}\{w\varepsilon + \eta\varepsilon V_U + (1 - \eta\varepsilon)V_E(w) + o(\varepsilon)\}, \qquad (3.3)$$

where the current period return is now given by $\beta_\varepsilon w\varepsilon$ and the expected future value of continuing to work at the job during this "period" is

$$\beta_\varepsilon \eta\varepsilon V_U + \beta_\varepsilon(1 - \eta\varepsilon)V_E(w) + \beta_\varepsilon o(\varepsilon).$$

This term is the sum of the discounted value of being dismissed during the period and thus ending the period in the unemployment state multiplied by the (approximate) probability of being dismissed ($\eta\varepsilon$), the discounted value of ending the period in the same job multiplied by the probability of not being dismissed ($1 - \eta\varepsilon$), and the discounted value of the remainder term $o(\varepsilon)$ which reflects the value and probabilities of all other events that could occur in an interval of length ε.

We determine the value of employment as follows: multiply both sides of (3.3) by $1 + \rho\varepsilon$ to get

$$V_E(w)(1 + \rho\varepsilon) = w\varepsilon + \eta\varepsilon V_U + (1 - \eta\varepsilon)V_E(w) + o(\varepsilon),$$

$$\Rightarrow V_E(w)(\rho + \eta)\varepsilon = w\varepsilon + \eta\varepsilon V_U + o(\varepsilon),$$

$$\Rightarrow V_E(w) = \frac{w + \eta V_U}{\rho + \eta} + \frac{o(\varepsilon)}{\varepsilon},$$

where the last line is obtained after dividing both sides of the second line by ε. Now taking limits, we have

$$\lim_{\varepsilon \to 0} V_E(w) = \frac{w + \eta V_U}{\rho + \eta} + \lim_{\varepsilon \to 0}\frac{o(\varepsilon)}{\varepsilon}$$

$$= \frac{w + \eta V_U}{\rho + \eta}$$

by the definition of the term $o(\varepsilon)$.

With this definition of $V_E(w)$, we can return to our consideration of V_U. First note that

$$\max{(V_U, V_E(w))} = \max\left(V_U, \frac{w + \eta V_U}{\rho + \eta}\right)$$

$$= \frac{1}{\rho + \eta} \max{(V_U(\rho + \eta), w + \eta V_U)}$$

$$= \frac{\eta V_U}{\rho + \eta} + \frac{\max{(\rho V_U, w)}}{\rho + \eta} \qquad (3.4)$$

$$= \frac{\eta V_U}{\rho + \eta} + \frac{\rho V_U}{\rho + \eta} + \frac{\max{(0, w - \rho V_U)}}{\rho + \eta}$$

$$= V_U + \frac{\max{(0, w - \rho V_U)}}{\rho + \eta}.$$

This is an important result, for it shows that for a given wage offer w the option of accepting the employment match exceeds the value of the option of continuing to search when the wage offer w exceeds the scalar value ρV_U. This result is important enough to warrant the following terminology:

Definition 1 The *reservation wage* w^* is equal to ρV_U and has the property that any wage offer $w \geq w^*$ will be accepted and any $w < w^*$ will be rejected.

The reservation wage w^* completely summarizes the single decision rule utilized in this simple search model. Since the value of search, V_U, will depend on all of the parameters that characterize the labor market environment, so does the reservation wage. Below we will see the manner in which we can solve for w^*.

Using (3.4), we can rewrite (3.2) as

$$V_U = (1 + \rho\varepsilon)^{-1} \left\{ b\varepsilon + \lambda\varepsilon \int \left(V_U + \frac{\max{(0, w - \rho V_U)}}{\rho + \eta} \right) dG(w) \right.$$

$$\left. + (1 - \lambda\varepsilon)V_U + o(\varepsilon) \right\}$$

$$= (1 + \rho\varepsilon)^{-1} \left(b\varepsilon + V_U + \frac{\lambda\varepsilon}{\rho + \eta} \int \max{(0, w - \rho V_U)}\, dG(w) + o(\varepsilon) \right).$$

Then

$$V_U(1 + \rho\varepsilon) = b\varepsilon + V_U + \frac{\lambda\varepsilon}{\rho + \eta} \int_{\rho V_U} (w - \rho V_U)\, dG(w) + o(\varepsilon)$$

$$\Rightarrow \rho V_U = b + \frac{\lambda}{\rho + \eta} \int_{\rho V_U} (w - \rho V_U)\, dG(w), \qquad (3.5)$$

where the second line is obtained after dividing the first line by ε and taking limits. Since $w^* \equiv \rho V_U$, we can rewrite (3.5) as

$$w^* = b + \frac{\lambda}{\rho + \eta} \int_{w^*} (w - w^*) dG(w) \tag{3.6}$$

In general, the expression (3.6) cannot be manipulated so as to yield a closed-form solution for w^*. However, it is not difficult to establish that there exists a unique solution w^* to this equation which is relatively straightforward to compute. For there to be a unique reservation wage, strictly speaking, we require the distribution of wage offers to be continuously differentiable on the support[12] of the distribution, so we assume that there exists a well-defined probability density function g everywhere on the support of the distribution.[13]

Given the existence of the density function g, when we partially differentiate both sides of (3.6) with respect to w^*, we see that the derivative of the left-hand side (LHS) is simply 1, while the partial derivative of the RHS is

$$\frac{\partial RHS(3.6)}{\partial w^*} = -\frac{\lambda}{\rho + \eta} \tilde{G}(w^*) < 0,$$

where $\tilde{G}(x)$, termed the *survivor function*, is defined as $1 - G(x)$. For now, assume that the support of the distribution G is the positive real line. Then the left-hand side of (3.6) is a linear increasing function of w^* that takes values on the interval $(-\infty, \infty)$, the right-hand side is a decreasing function of w^* that takes values on the interval $(b, b + \lambda E(w)/(\rho + \eta))$. This last result follows from the fact that when the reservation wage is less than or equal to 0, the right-hand side is simply $b + \lambda E(w)/(\rho + \eta)$, since all offers are accepted, while as $w^* \to \infty$, no offers are accepted and the value of the right-hand side of (3.6) goes to b. Then there exists exactly one value of w^* that solves (3.6), though that value of w^* may be negative without further restrictions on the parameters.

We next illustrate the manner in which the reservation wage can be computed. We consider an example labor market characterized by the parameter values $b = -1$, $\lambda = 0.2$, $\rho = 0.005$, $\eta = 0.02$, and we assume that the wage offer distribution facing the individual is lognormal with parameters μ and σ (>0).[14] For our example we have set $\mu = 1$ and $\sigma = 1$. Since the expected value of a log normally distributed random variable is given by $E(w; \mu, \sigma) = \exp(\mu + \frac{1}{2}\sigma^2)$, in this case we have $E(w) = 4.482$.

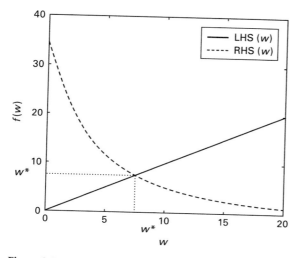

Figure 3.1
Determination of w^*

Figure 3.1 plots the LHS and RHS of (3.6) as a function of w^*. As we know, $LHS(w) = w^*$, while $RHS(w)$ is a monotone decreasing function. In our example the two lines intersect at the point $w^* = 7.439$, which is the value that completely characterizes all labor market behavior in this simple model. Note that w^* is appreciably greater than the mean wage offer in this model. In particular, we might ask what is the probability that a randomly generated wage offer will be accepted? This probability is equal to the mass of the probability density function g to the right of the point w^*, or $\tilde{G}(w^*; \mu, \sigma) = \tilde{G}(7.439; 1, 1) = 0.157$. Most offers, in this case, are rejected. The reason for the "choosiness" of the searcher we see in this particular example is due partially to the relatively low rate of discounting (with ρ "small" the value of waiting for a good offer increases), the relatively low rate of exogenous terminations (when η is small it is more worthwhile to wait for a better offer, since it will be kept longer on average), and the relatively high rate of offer arrivals, λ. We now turn to a short consideration of how comparative statics exercises can be conducted in this type of model.

Let us rewrite (3.6) in slightly different terms as

$$w^* = Q(w^*; \omega),$$

$$\Rightarrow 0 = w^* - Q(w^*; \omega) \tag{3.7}$$

where Q is the RHS of (3.6) and ω is a vector containing all of the parameters that characterize the labor market in this model. We assume that Q is a differentiable function of all of the elements of ω,[15] which means that we can totally differentiate (3.7) as follows:

$$0 = \left(1 - \frac{\partial Q(w^*;\omega)}{\partial w^*}\right) dw^* - \frac{\partial Q(w^*;\omega)}{\partial \omega_i} d\omega_i$$

(3.8)

$$\Rightarrow \frac{dw^*}{d\omega_i} = \frac{\partial Q(w^*;\omega)/\partial \omega_i}{1 - [\partial Q(w^*;\omega)/\partial w^*]},$$

where ω_i denotes the ith element of the parameter vector ω. Because $\partial Q(x;\omega)/\partial x$ is negative, the denominator of (3.8) is always positive so that

$$\text{sgn}\left(\frac{dw^*}{d\omega_i}\right) = \text{sgn}\left(\frac{\partial Q(w^*;\omega)}{\partial \omega_i}\right),$$

where sgn(X) denotes the sign of the expression X.

Consider, for example, the flow cost of job search, b. Since $\partial Q(x;\omega)/\partial b = 1$, an increase in b results in an increase in the reservation wage, a result that is intuitive. Similarly, since

$$\frac{\partial Q(x;\omega)}{\partial \lambda} = \frac{1}{\rho + \eta} \int_{w^*} [w - w^*] \, dG(w),$$

$$> 0,$$

an increase in λ increases the reservation wage. From inspection of (3.6) it is obvious that $\partial w^*/\partial \rho$ and $\partial w^*/\partial \eta$ are both negative. It is not difficult to demonstrate that, under the lognormality assumption regarding G, $\partial w^*/\partial \mu$ and $\partial w^*/\partial \sigma$ are both positive.

The search model we have described is simply a dynamic model of individual choice in a stationary environment. In this case choice is limited to whether to accept an offered wage when one arrives. Such a model is inadequate for studying minimum wage effects on labor market outcomes. Imagine that a minimum wage is imposed by the government, and that the imposition of this minimum wage, m, has no effect on any other parameters of the model. Let $w^*(\omega)$ be the original reservation wage, which by assumption was optimally chosen by the individual given her labor market environment ω. If the minimum wage is set at a value no greater than the reservation wage, namely $m \leq w^*(\omega)$, then there is no effect on choices or outcomes. If $m > w^*(\omega)$, then clearly the individual is worse off than before. The reason is that certain wage offers that were previously acceptable, those w in the interval $[w^*(\omega), m)$, are now precluded. Since the individual was free to choose a reservation wage equal to m previously but chose not to, she cannot be better off under this law. Thus in a "partial–partial" equilibrium search model the imposition of minimum wages cannot be beneficial for labor market participants.[16]

For minimum wage laws to possibly have beneficial effects for searchers, the imposition of a minimum wage must change the search environment in some positive way from the perspective of the searcher. For minimum wages to alter the labor market environment requires, at a minimum, a partial equilibrium model of the interaction between the supply and demand sides of the market. The bargaining framework we now describe provides an acceptable context from this point of view.

3.3.1 Nash-Bargained Employment Contracts

As opposed to the case we have just considered, in which match values and wage offers were equal due to the worker having all of the bargaining power, we now consider the more realistic case in which the worker does not appropriate all of the match value. The flow revenue from a match to the firm is given by θ (we normalize the product price to unity without loss of generality). The instantaneous profit to the firm is given by $\theta - w$, where w is the instantaneous wage payment to the employee. By defining match-specific profits in this manner, it is clear that we have assumed that the only factor of production is labor and that there are no other costs of employment. These assumptions are important in the derivation of the bargaining equilibrium we provide.

When a searcher meets a potential employer, the (flow) value of the match is assumed to be immediately observed. If the two parties enter into an employment contract, this contract will specify a time-invariant instantaneous wage rate w. It is important to realize that the productivity value θ is *specific to the match* and not attributable to either the worker or the firm. In that sense, both have have a valid claim to it. How is it to be divided?

There are a variety of forms of "bargaining power" that we might consider in defining the surplus division problem. First is the notion that each individual should receive at least in compensation what he or she could earn from pursuing the next best option available to them. Under the assumptions that we have made about the search technology and the labor market environment, a searcher who does not receive an acceptable job offer will continue to search. Thus the value of the next best option available to a potential employee bargaining over her share of θ is V_U. For the moment assume that the next best option available to a potential employer has a value of V_V, which denotes the value of holding onto a vacancy.

Bargaining results in a division of the flow value of the output produced. Given her wage payment w, the individual is indifferent regarding the actual value of the match.[17] In other words, the value of an employment pair $\{w, \theta\}$ to the individual is given by $V_E(w, \theta) = V_E(w)$. It then follows that the value of the surplus of the employment contact that pays w to the individual is $V_E(w) - V_U$. This difference is the rent that accrues to the worker from the employment contract.

The value of the employment match to the firm requires a little more discussion. In Pissarides's general equilibrium model of search and bargaining in a stationary environment, which we will examine in more detail below, a firm must create a job vacancy in order to search for an employee. This vacancy is costly to hold while the firm searches for an acceptable match. Since there is a large population of potential firm owners who could create a vacancy, a free entry condition (FEC) applies in which the expected value of creating a vacancy is driven to zero. We will assume that such a condition holds, so that $V_V = 0$. This value serves as the firm's outside option in contract negotiations with the worker.

Let the firm's value of an employment contract in which an employee has an instantaneous output level of θ and an instantaneous wage rate of w be given by $V_F(\theta, w)$. Then the solution to the generalized Nash bargaining problem is given by

$$w^*(\theta; \omega, \alpha) = \arg\max_{w} (V_E(w) - V_U)^\alpha (V_F(\theta, w) - 0)^{1-\alpha}, \tag{3.9}$$

where $\alpha \in [0, 1]$ is termed the *bargaining power* parameter (in this case it measures the bargaining power of the individual, while $1 - \alpha$ is the bargaining power of the firm) and where ω contains all of the parameters describing the labor market environment with the exception of α. Note that $V_E(w) - V_U$ measures the gain from participating in the employment contract paying a wage of w with respect to the next best alternative, which is to continue searching. As we argued in the last paragraph, the next best alternative to the firm, which is continuing to hold the vacancy open, has an associated value of 0. As a result the surplus of the firm is simply equal to $V_F(\theta, w)$. Note that $V_F(\theta, w) > 0$ in general, since if firms are induced to create costly vacancies they must be rewarded with some positive profits when the vacancy is filled.

To determine $V_F(\theta, w)$, we will assume that firms have the same discount rate as individuals, ρ. If an employment contract lasts for duration t, the ex post value of the contract is

$$\int_0^t (\theta - w) \exp(-\rho u) \, du = \frac{(\theta - w)}{\rho} (1 - \exp(-\rho t)).$$

Since the probability density function of completed employment contracts is given by $\eta \exp(-\eta t)$, the expected value of an employment contract $\{\theta, w\}$ is given by

$$
\begin{aligned}
V_F(\theta, w) &= E_t \frac{(\theta - w)}{\rho} (1 - \exp(-\rho t)) \\
&= \frac{(\theta - w)}{\rho} \int (1 - \exp(-\rho t)) \eta \exp(-\eta t) \, dt \\
&= \frac{(\theta - w)}{\rho} [1 - \eta \int \exp(-(\rho + \eta)t) \, dt \\
&= \frac{(\theta - w)}{\rho} \left[1 - \frac{\eta}{\rho + \eta} \right] \\
&= \frac{\theta - w}{\rho + \eta}.
\end{aligned}
$$

We use this expression for $V_F(\theta, w)$ to explicitly solve the bargaining problem.

In concluding this section, it is appropriate to say a few words about α, a parameter that will figure prominently in the theoretical, econometric, and empirical work that follows. As was stated previously, there are essentially two aspects of bargaining advantage. One is the value of the next best option available to each of the two bargainers. The "threat point" of the firm, V_V, has been fixed at 0 under the FEC, while the outside option of the individual has been set at V_U and is an *endogenously* determined value. Clearly, the larger is the value of V_U the higher the wage payment required for the individual to enter into any given employment contract.

The second aspect of bargaining advantage is the parameter α. When α is equal to 1, the individual is assumed to have all of the bargaining "power" and extracts all of the surplus from the match. The case $\alpha = 1$ corresponds exactly to the simple search problem that we considered in the previous section, for in this case the matching distribution G and the wage offer distribution are identical. At the other extreme, when $\alpha = 0$, firms possess all of the bargaining power. In this case the wage payment is independent of the match value θ, so that all employees are paid the same wage. If all employees are paid the same wage, then there is no motivation for further search, and all offers will be accepted. If the value of nonparticipation is fixed at 0, for example, and assuming that the instantaneous return associated with the search state $b < 0$, then it is not difficult to show that the common wage paid all workers will be

$$\hat{w} = -\frac{(\eta + \rho)}{\lambda \tilde{G}(\hat{w})} b.$$

In this regard, firms will earn instantaneous profit of $\theta - \hat{w}$ on all matches $\theta \geq \hat{w}$.

In general, the bargaining power parameter α is not equal to 0 or 1. It then indicates the relative "strength" of the two parties in bargaining, *conditional* on their threat points. This parameter is admittedly difficult to interpret.[18] We think of it as constituting a type of summary statistic of the labor market "position" of a particular group. For example, the match value distribution for low-skilled workers may be stochastically dominated by the match value distribution for high-skilled workers, but low-skilled workers may be at a further disadvantage due to their having little bargaining power. Their low bargaining power may derive from there being many substitutes for them in the production process, for example. In this sense, the parameter cannot be really thought of as "primitive"; significant policy changes—such as a large increase in the minimum wage—may result in participation effects or substitution responses by firms which change the labor market "position" of the group, and hence change the bargaining power parameter. Thus comparative statics exercises and policy experiments performed with the estimates obtained from this model will only be valid locally, that is, for small changes in policy variables.[19] This limitation is not unique to this parameter or this model, since any empirically based policy prescription based on counterfactual analysis becomes more suspect as the prescription increases in distance from previously observed choices.

3.3.2 The Search-Bargaining Model without Minimum Wages

We are now ready to combine the search and bargaining aspects of the model. Since $V_E(w) = (w + \eta V_U)/(\rho + \eta)$, the individual's surplus with respect to the alternative of continued search is

$$V_E(w) - V_U = \frac{w + \eta V_U}{\rho + \eta} - V_U$$

$$= \frac{w - \rho V_U}{\rho + \eta},$$

so that the solution to the bargaining problem is given by

$$w(\theta, V_U) = \arg\max_w \left(\frac{w - \rho V_U}{\rho + \eta}\right)^\alpha \left(\frac{\theta - w}{\rho + \eta}\right)^{1-\alpha}$$

$$= \arg\max_w [w - \rho V_U]^\alpha [\theta - w]^{1-\alpha}$$

$$= \alpha\theta + (1 - \alpha)\rho V_U$$

$$= \alpha\theta + (1 - \alpha)\theta^*.$$

Put another way, the wage is a weighted average of the match value and the reservation match value, $\theta^* \equiv \rho V_U$.

We can now compute the value of nonemployment. Instead of writing the value of employment as a function of the wage, we write it as a function of the "primitive parameters," θ and V_U. Rewriting (3.5), we have

$$\rho V_U = b + \lambda \int_{\rho V_U} [V_E(w(\theta, V_U)) - V_U] dG(\theta). \tag{3.10}$$

Since

$$V_E(w(\theta, V_U)) = \frac{\alpha\theta + (1 - \alpha)\rho V_U + \eta V_U}{\rho + \eta}$$

$$= \frac{\alpha\theta - \alpha\rho V_U}{\rho + \eta} + V_U,$$

we have

$$V_E(w(\theta, V_U)) - V_U = \frac{\alpha\theta - \alpha\rho V_U}{\rho + \eta}. \tag{3.11}$$

Then the final (implicit) expression for the value of search is

$$\rho V_U = b + \frac{\lambda\alpha}{\rho + \eta} \int_{\rho V_U} [\theta - \rho V_U] dG(\theta). \tag{3.12}$$

We see that this expression is identical to the expression for the reservation value in a model with no bargaining when θ is the payment to the individual, except for the presence of the factor α. This is not unexpected, since when $\alpha = 1$, the entire match value is transferred to the worker, and thus search over θ is the same as search over w.

We can now summarize the important properties of the model. The critical "match" value θ^* is equal to ρV_U, which is defined by (3.12). Since at this match value the wage payment is equal to $w^* \equiv w(\theta^*, V_U) = \alpha\theta^* + (1 - \alpha)\theta^*$, it follows that $w^* = \theta^*$. The probability that a random encounter generates an acceptable match is given by $\tilde{G}(\theta^*)$. The rate of leaving unemployment is $\lambda\tilde{G}(\theta^*)$. As we can see from (3.12), since θ^* is an increasing function of α, the likelihood of exiting a spell of unemployment is lower the larger is the worker's bargaining power. This is the first indication we have that lower rates of leaving unemployment do not necessarily imply that the worker's welfare level is low.

The observed wage density is a simple mapping from the matching density. Since

$$w(\theta, V_U) = \alpha\theta + (1 - \alpha)\theta^*$$

$$\Rightarrow \tilde{\theta}(w, \theta^*) = \frac{w - (1 - \alpha)\theta^*}{\alpha},$$

where $\tilde{\theta}$ is the value of the match that corresponds to an observed wage w given the critical match value of θ^*. The probability density function of observed wages, $f(w)$, is given by

$$f(w) = \begin{cases} \frac{\alpha^{-1}g(\tilde{\theta}(w,\theta^*))}{\tilde{G}(\theta^*)}, & w \geq \theta^*, \\ 0, & w < \theta^*. \end{cases} \tag{3.13}$$

An Example To fix ideas, let us take a close look at the computation of decision rules and the characterization of equilibrium for a very simple labor market environment. We will work with simple functional forms so as to make the computational steps as clear as possible. In the empirical work that we will encounter in later chapters, functional forms will be used that produce results more in line with empirical observation.

Let us assume that the matching distribution $G(\theta)$ is uniform, with the support of the distribution equal to the interval $[0, 10]$. Thus

$$G(\theta) = \begin{cases} 0 \Leftrightarrow \theta < 0, \\ \theta/10 \Leftrightarrow 0 \leq \theta \leq 10, \\ 1 \Leftrightarrow 10 < \theta, \end{cases}$$

and

$$g(\theta) = \begin{cases} 0 \Leftrightarrow \theta < 0 \text{ or } 10 < \theta, \\ 1/10 \Leftrightarrow 0 \le \theta \le 10. \end{cases}$$

In addition we will assume that $\lambda = 0.5$, $\eta = 0.02$, $\rho = 0.01$, and $b = -1$. These values imply that offers arrive to unemployed searchers every two time periods on average (recall that in continuous time a "period" is just a normalization that we use to express frequencies of events, and that events can occur at any time), jobs last for 50 periods on average, and searchers are "strongly" forward looking (i.e., the value of ρ is close to 0). We will characterize the equilibrium of the model for two values of α, $\alpha = 0.3$ (low bargaining power of searchers) and $\alpha = 0.6$ (high bargaining power).

Under our distributional assumption regarding G, (3.12) becomes

$$\theta^* = b + \frac{\alpha\lambda}{\rho+\eta} \int_{\theta^*}^{10} [\theta - \theta^*] \frac{1}{10} d\theta. \tag{3.14}$$

$$\Rightarrow 0 = \frac{a}{20}(\theta^*)^2 - (1+a)\theta^* + (b+5a), \tag{3.15}$$

where

$$a \equiv \frac{\alpha\lambda}{\rho+\eta}.$$

This is a quadratic equation in θ^*, and given the parameter values we have chosen, there exists a unique solution in the interval $(0, 10)$.

The labor market equilibrium in terms of equilibrium wage functions is represented in figure 3.2. In figure 3.2a we have graphed the population density of match draws, which is equal to 0.1 on the interval $[0, 10]$. Figure 3.2b plots the wage functions corresponding to the two values of α we consider. We note that the reservation match value θ^* is considerably higher when $\alpha = 0.6$. The reason is intuitive. Since the searcher gets to keep more of the surplus generated by the match, it is worthwhile holding out for a high draw. Since the exit rate from unemployment is $\lambda \tilde{G}(\theta^*)$, the unemployment spells will last longer on average when α is high.

The wage densities ($f(w)$) corresponding to the two values of α are graphed in figure 3.2c and d. Because the distribution of θ is uniform and because the wage function is a linear mapping from θ to w, the wage distributions are both uniform as well. The support of the wage

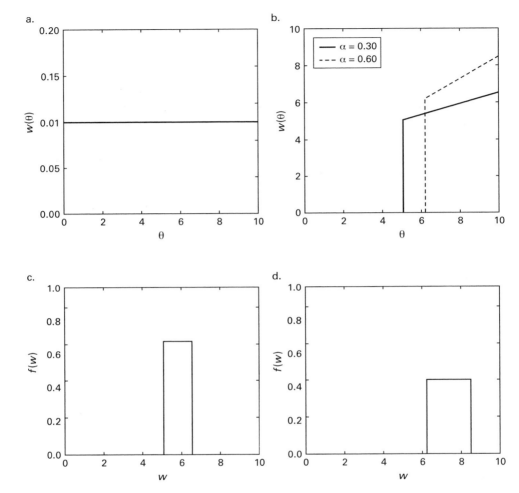

Figure 3.2
(a) Match value density, (b) equilibrium wage functions, (c) wage density $\alpha = 0.3$,
(d) wage density $\alpha = 0.6$

distribution associated with $\alpha = 0.3$ begins to the left of the other distribution and is more concentrated. Thus low α not only reduces the average accepted wage in this example, it also reduces the variance of accepted wages.

3.4 Bargaining with a Minimum Wage Constraint

The introduction of minimum wages into the search-bargaining framework is accomplished in a fairly straightforward manner. We assume that the labor market environment is exactly as described above, with the exception that a "side constraint" is imposed on the worker–firm bargaining problem (3.9). This constraint is that any employment contract must yield a wage payment of at least m to the worker no matter what is the value of θ. The minimum wage is assumed to be set by the government and applies to all potential matches. This assumption represents the US case fairly well, since the minimum wage applies to virtually all employment contracts in the labor force, with a few notable exceptions.[20]

The modified bargaining problem we develop is then represented by

$$w^*(\theta, m) = \arg \max_{w \geq m} (V_E(w) - V_U(m))^\alpha \left(\frac{\theta - w}{\rho + \eta} \right)^{1-\alpha}, \tag{3.16}$$

where $V_U(m)$ denotes the value of search given a minimum wage of m. If we define $\rho V_U(0) = \theta_0^*$, which is the reservation match value when there is no minimum wage, it is clear that any $m \leq \theta_0^*$ has no effect on the behavior of applicants or firms and thus would be a meaningless, or "slack," constraint. Therefore we consider only the effects of an imposition of $m > \theta_0^*$.

The first thing to note concerning the effect of the constraint on behavior is that since the value of the employment contract to the firm is proportional to $\theta - w$, no employment contract will be formed for which the match value $\theta < m$; clearly, in this case the firm would lose money continuously over the course of the match. If there is no opportunity cost to the firm of forming a match, then any match for which it doesn't lose money will be acceptable to it. Since $\theta^* < m$, this implies that fewer encounters between searchers and firms will result in employment contracts, which will result in an increase in the unemployment rate, other things equal. In a model with a fixed set of labor market participants, this implies that the employment rate necessarily must decrease. This loss of employment effect is consistent with that predicted by the simplest static competitive labor market models. Later we will investigate the extent to which this prediction is robust with respect to alterations in modeling assumptions.

The effect of the addition of the minimum wage "side constraint" on the solution to the bargaining problem is relatively intuitive. If we ignore the minimum wage constraint and solve (3.16) using $V_U(m)$, we will get the wage offer function

$$\tilde{w}(\theta, V_U(m)) = \alpha\theta + (1-\alpha)\rho V_U(m). \tag{3.17}$$

Under this division of the match value, the worker would receive a wage of m when $\theta = \hat{\theta}$, where

$$\hat{\theta}(m, V_U(m)) = \frac{m - (1-\alpha)\rho V_U(m)}{\alpha}.$$

Then, if $\hat{\theta} \leq m$, all "feasible" matches would generate wage offers at least as large as m. When $\hat{\theta} > m$, this is not the case. When θ belongs to the set $[m, \hat{\theta})$, the offer according to (3.17) is less than m. However, when confronted with the choice of giving some of its surplus to the worker versus a return of 0, the firm pays the wage of m for all $\theta \in [m, \hat{\theta})$. Wages for acceptable θ outside of this set (i.e., when $\theta \geq \hat{\theta}$) are determined according to (3.17).

We can now consider the individual's search problem given this wage offer function. We use the ε interval formulation to write the value of search under a binding minimum wage constraint as

$$V_U(m) = (1+\rho\varepsilon)^{-1} \left[b\varepsilon + \lambda\varepsilon \left\{ \int_m^{\hat{\theta}(m,V_U(m))} \left[\frac{m + \eta V_U(m)}{\rho + \eta} \right] dG(\theta) \right. \right.$$

$$\left. + \int_{\hat{\theta}(m,V_U(m))} \left[\frac{\alpha\theta + (1-\alpha)\rho V_U(m) + \eta V_U(m)}{\rho + \eta} \right] dG(\theta) + V_U(m)G(m) \right\}$$

$$\left. + (1 - \lambda\varepsilon)V_U(m) + o(\varepsilon) \right],$$

$$\Rightarrow (1+\rho\varepsilon)V_U(m) = b\varepsilon + \lambda\varepsilon \left\{ \int_m^{\hat{\theta}(m,V_U(m))} \left[\frac{m + \eta V_U(m)}{\rho + \eta} \right] dG(\theta) \right.$$

$$\left. + \int_{\hat{\theta}(m,V_U(m))} \left[\frac{\alpha\theta + (1-\alpha)\rho V_U(m) + \eta V_U(m)}{\rho + \eta} \right] dG(\theta) + V_U(m)G(m) \right\}$$

$$+ (1 - \lambda\varepsilon)V_U(m) + o(\varepsilon)$$

The integrand in the first integral on the right-hand side of these expressions is the value of a job at a firm where the match productivity lies in the interval $[m, \hat{\theta})$, which we know pays a wage of m and has a total value of $(m + \eta V_U(m))/(\rho + \eta)$. The integrand of the second integral is the value of a job when the match value is greater than $\hat{\theta}$, and $V_U(m)$ is the value of encountering a firm where the match value is less than m, which we know results in no job and continued search. The probability of this event is $G(m)$.

After subtracting $V_U(m)$ from both sides, we get

$$\rho \varepsilon V_U(m) = b\varepsilon + \lambda \varepsilon \left\{ \int_m^{\hat{\theta}(m, V_U(m))} \left[\frac{m + \eta V_U(m)}{\rho + \eta} - V_U(m) \right] dG(\theta) \right.$$

$$+ \int_{\hat{\theta}(m, V_U(m))} \left[\frac{\alpha\theta + (1-\alpha)\rho V_U(m) + \eta V_U(m)}{\rho + \eta} - V_U(m) \right] dG(\theta)$$

$$+ G(m)(V_U(m) - V_U(m)) + o(\varepsilon),$$

$$\Rightarrow \rho \varepsilon V_U(m) = b\varepsilon + \lambda \varepsilon \left\{ \int_m^{\hat{\theta}(m, V_U(m))} \left[\frac{m - \rho V_U(m)}{\rho + \eta} \right] dG(\theta) \right.$$

$$+ \int_{\hat{\theta}(m, V_U(m))} \left[\frac{\alpha\theta + (1-\alpha)\rho V_U(m) - \rho V_U(m)}{\rho + \eta} \right] dG(\theta) + o(\varepsilon).$$

After dividing both sides by ε and taking limits as $\varepsilon \to 0$, we arrive at

$$\rho V_U(m) = b + \frac{\lambda}{\rho + \eta} \{ (m - \rho V_U(m))(G(\hat{\theta}(m, V_U(m))) - G(m))$$

$$+ \alpha \int_{\hat{\theta}(m, V_U(m))} (\theta - \rho V_U(m)) dG(\theta) \}. \tag{3.18}$$

It is important to note a fundamental difference between the value $\rho V_U(m)$, which we might want to refer to as the "implicit" reservation wage in the presence of a binding minimum wage constraint, and $\rho V_n(0)$, the corresponding "explicit" reservation wage (and reservation match) value when no minimum wage constraint is binding. The value of $\rho V_U(0)$ is an acceptance value; that is, it completely characterizes the decision of whether an employment contract is struck. When a binding minimum wage is present, employment contacts are formed whenever $\theta \geq m$. The value of $\rho V_U(m)$ is only instrumental in determining the equilibrium wage contract and wage distribution. Put another way, when there is no binding minimum wage constraint, the smallest possible observed wage will be equal to $\rho V_U(0)$, and the distribution of wages will be continuous as long as G is. When there is a binding minimum wage, the smallest observed wage will be given by m, and in this case we know that $\rho V_U(m) < m$. The observed wage distribution will consist of a mass point at the minimum wage, whose size is given by $(G(\hat{\theta}(m, V_U(m))) - G(m))/\bar{G}(m)$, while the distribution of wages immediately above m will be continuous (once again, as long as G is). In the presence of a binding minimum wage, the observed wage distribution is given by

$$f(w) = \begin{cases} \frac{\alpha^{-1}g(\bar{\theta}(w,V_U(m)))}{\bar{G}(m)}, & w > m, \\ \frac{G(\hat{\theta}(m,V_U(m)))-G(m)}{\bar{G}(m)}, & w = m, \\ 0, & w < m. \end{cases}$$

An Example (continued)   In the same search environment as before, we want to determine the impact of the imposition of a minimum wage of 7 on the equilibrium wage distribution. Recall that in the previously part of this example, we computed the wage distribution under a low and high value of α, 0.3 and 0.6. We noted that without a minimum wage, the acceptance match value was an increasing function of α. Previously the critical match value when $\alpha = 0.6$ was equal to 6.204, so a minimum wage of 7 was binding for both values of α.

As we noted above, when the underlying population match distribution is continuous, the imposition of a binding minimum wage results in a mixed discrete–continuous equilibrium wage distribution in which there exists a mass point at the value m with a continuous distribution of wages beginning immediately "to the right" of m. To represent a random variable w that does not have a density everywhere on its support, we must plot the cumulative distribution function instead of the density function (as was done in figure 3.2). Figure 3.3a exhibits the c.d.f. of the match distribution. The equilibrium wage function with the binding minimum wage of 7 is shown in figure 3.3b. In this case, since the minimum wage is binding for both values of α, the lower bound of the support of both distributions is the same. However, we see that for $\alpha = 0.3$, *all* positive wage offers are equal to the minimum. This is due to the bargaining power of searchers being low and the minimum wage being high relative to the upper bound of the support of the distribution of θ. Instead, when $\alpha = 0.6$, there is significant clustering of wages at m though most wages observed will be greater than m. The critical value

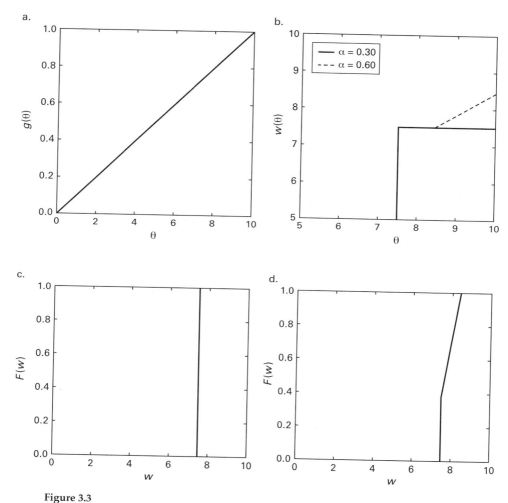

Figure 3.3
(a) Match value c.d.f., (b) equilibrium wage functions, (c) wage c.d.f. $\alpha = 0.3$, (d) wage c.d.f. $\alpha = 0.6$

we have defined as $\hat{\theta}(m)$, which is the highest value of θ that will yield a wage payment of m, is equal to 7.557 for $\alpha = 0.6$ (as opposed to 10 when $\alpha = 0.3$).

Figure 3.3c and d displays the wage distributions for the two values of α. The wage is a degenerate random variable in the case of $\alpha = 0.3$; that is, it assumes the constant value $m = 7$ for all employees. In the case of $\alpha = 0.6$, while there is a considerable mass point at $w = 7$, about 82 percent of all wage observations are greater than 7. The conditional distribution of wages greater than 7 is uniform.

3.5 The Labor Market Participation Decision

We now consider some generalizations of the basic model. The phenomena we discuss are of obvious importance when attempting to evaluate the impact of a minimum wage policy on labor market outcomes, and are not intended to make the model more elegant or complete. In this section we continue with the assumption of an exogenously determined rate of contacts among searchers on both sides of the market but now give individuals on the supply side of the market the power to decide whether to actively participate in it.

Individuals out of the labor market have a number of activities to pursue, including leisure, home production, and investment in human capital. We assign a flow value, ρV_O, to being out of the formal labor market for every individual on the supply side of the market. We do not study the determinants of this value, but assert that it is continuously distributed in the population, with c.d.f. L and p.d.f. l.

Individuals who are out of the labor force (OLF) and choose to enter must begin their labor market activity in the unemployment state. The flow value of this state, given the possibility that a binding minimum wage is in place, is denoted by $\rho V_U(m)$. Define $d = 1$ when the individual is a labor market participant, and let $d = 0$ when this is not the case. Then the decision rule of an agent with an "outside option" value of ρV_O is

$$d = \begin{cases} 1 & \text{if } \rho V_O \leq \rho V_U(m), \\ 0 & \text{if } \rho V_O > \rho V_U(m). \end{cases}$$

It follows that under the minimum wage m, the labor market participation rate is

$$\ell \equiv p(d = 1 | m) = L(\rho V_U(m)). \tag{3.19}$$

We see immediately from (3.19) the manner in which the minimum wage can affect the participation rate. A minimum wage increase alone has no direct effect on participation. Any effect on participation will be of the same sign as the impact of the minimum wage on the value of unemployed search.

3.6 Endogeneity of the Rate of Contacts

We adopt the standard setup (in the macroeconomics literature) for modeling firms' decisions to create vacancies. At any moment in time any firm can create a vacancy, which is a precondition for adding a worker to its staff. Think of it as setting up the workplace in advance. One rationale for why this activity has to be accomplished in advance is that a potential employee must be evaluated in this setting to determine her match value θ at that particular job. As is standard in this literature, we assume that there exists a constant returns to scale (CRS) matching technology,

$$M(\tilde{u}, v) = vq(k),$$

where $k \equiv \tilde{u}/v$, $\tilde{u}$ is the size of the set of unemployed searchers, and v is the size of the set of vacancies. The contact rates differ depending on which side of the market the agent is on. On the supply side of the market the contact rate is the average number of matches (per unit time) per unemployed searcher, or

$$\lambda = M(\tilde{u}, v)/\tilde{u}$$

$$= \frac{vq(k)}{\tilde{u}}$$

$$= \frac{q(k)}{k}.$$

From the vacancy holder's point of view, the contact rate is

$$\frac{M(\tilde{u}, v)}{v} = \frac{vq(k)}{v}$$

$$= q(k).$$

Assuming that there exists a population of potential (firm) entrants with an outside option value of 0, firms create vacancies until the point at which expected profits are zero. Let the flow cost of creating a vacancy be given by $\psi > 0$. Then the expected value of creating a vacancy is given by

$$\rho V_V = -\psi + q(k)\tilde{G}(r)(J - V_V),$$

where r denotes the acceptance match value (which is equal to the maximum of $\rho V_U(m)$ and m), $q(k)\tilde{G}(r)$) is the rate at which a firm fills a vacancy, $q(k)$ is the rate at which it meets job applicants, $\tilde{G}(r)$ is the probability that the match value drawn is greater than the lowest acceptable value, r, and J is the expected value of a filled vacancy (where the expectation is taken with respect to the distribution of acceptable matches, which are those for which $\theta \geq r$). By setting r to the maximum of $\rho V_U(m)$ and m, we allow for the possibility that the minimum wage m is not binding. To close the model, we assume that firms keep creating vacancies up to the point at which the expected value of a vacancy is 0—this is the free entry condition (FEC) that was discussed in the course of deriving the Nash-bargained wage contract). Imposing $V_V = 0$, we have

$$0 = -\psi + q(k)\tilde{G}(r)J. \tag{3.20}$$

We can solve for the equilibrium number of vacancies given the expected value of a filled vacancy and the size of the set of unemployed searchers using (3.20) and other pieces of the model. As we will see in chapter 4, in the steady state the probability that a labor market participant is unemployed is given by

$$p(u|m, d = 1) = \frac{\eta}{\eta + \tilde{G}(r)q(k)/k}.$$

Given the proportion of labor market participants ℓ, the size of the set of unemployed searchers (relative to the entire population) is

$$\tilde{u} = u\ell$$

$$= \frac{\eta\ell}{\eta + \tilde{G}(r)q(\tilde{u}/v)/(\tilde{u}/v)}. \tag{3.21}$$

With endogenous contact rates, a labor market equilibrium in the presence of a minimum wage (which may or may not be binding) is characterized by the vector of values $(\ell, u, v, \rho V_U(m))$ that is solely a function of the parameters $(\rho, b, \eta, \alpha, G, Q, q, \psi)$ and the minimum wage rate m. An equilibrium, if one exists, can be constructed by first fixing a value of the contact rate (from the searching individual's perspective), λ. Let $x \equiv \rho V_U(m)$. Then given λ, equation (3.18) determines $x(\lambda)$. The participation rate is then determined as $\ell(\lambda) = L(x(\lambda))$. From (3.21) we have $\tilde{u}(\lambda) = \ell(\lambda)\eta/(\eta + \lambda\tilde{G}(\max\{x(\lambda), m\}))$. So we use $\tilde{u}(\lambda)$ and $J(\lambda)$ with (3.20) to determine $v(\lambda)$. Then we let $T(\lambda) \equiv q\left(\frac{\ell(\lambda)u(\lambda)}{v(\lambda)}; \omega\right)\Big/\left(\frac{\ell(\lambda)u(\lambda)}{v(\lambda)}\right)$. There exists a unique equilibrium if and only if there exists a unique value λ^* such that $\lambda^* = T(\lambda^*)$. In general, without further restrictions on the parameter space and the functional forms of q, G, and L, there may exist no equilibrium or multiple equilibria. For example, if we restrict the outside option flow value ρV_O to be positive for all individuals, and if we fix all other parameters aside from b at some given values for which the model is well defined[21], then there will exist sufficiently negative values of b for which no one participates in the market.

Given existence, multiple equilibria can arise depending on specific properties of the distribution functions L and G. In performing the empirical exercises and policy simulations reported below, we assumed particular functional forms for q, L, and G. When performing the policy simulations, in which m is varied over some range of values, we have found a number of cases of nonexistence. However, when an equilibrium existed we found it to be unique in the sense that $\lim_{n\to\infty} T^n(\underline{\lambda}^0) = \lim_{n\to\infty} T^n(\overline{\lambda}^0) = \lambda^* \in [\underline{\lambda}^0, \overline{\lambda}^0]$, where $\underline{\lambda}^0$ and $\overline{\lambda}^0$ are the smallest and largest starting values of λ used in the iterative updating process for finding a fixed point λ^*.

To illustrate some of the properties of a labor market equilibrium with and without a binding minimum wage, we have the following examples. Due to the fact that the existence of an equilibrium, and its computation, is a more challenging problem in this general equilibrium setting, we will change some of the underlying assumptions used in the partial equilibrium settings we have considered to this point.

Example 2   Assume that ρV_O is normally distributed with mean 5 and variance 4 in the population, and that $\ln\theta$ is normally distributed with mean 5 and variance 0.25. The discount rate, in "monthly" units, is $0.05/12$, the exogenous dismissal rate (η) is 0.038, the utility flow in unemployment (b) is -20, and the flow cost of holding a vacancy (ψ) is equal to 120. The matching production function M is given by

$$M(\tilde{u}, v) = \tilde{u}^\gamma v^{1-\gamma}, \tag{3.22}$$

where the Cobb–Douglas parameter $\gamma \in (0, 1)$.

Table 3.2 presents equilibrium outcomes under these assumptions for various combinations of the bargaining power parameter (α), the

Table 3.2
Equilibrium outcomes with endogenous contact rates

Environment	Parameters			Equilibrium			
	α	γ	m	u	l	v	$\rho V_U(m)$
1	0.2	0.2	0	0.039	0.390	0.015	3.442
2	0.2	0.2	5	0.076	0.313	0.012	3.027
3	0.2	0.5	0	0.036	0.492	0.023	3.962
4	0.2	0.5	5	0.048	0.509	0.023	4.046
5	0.2	0.8	0	0.037	0.472	0.028	3.861
6	0.2	0.8	5	0.045	0.533	0.028	4.168
7	0.4	0.2	0	0.081	0.298	0.009	2.940
8	0.4	0.2	5	0.117	0.217	0.007	2.438
9	0.4	0.5	0	0.064	0.639	0.019	4.710
10	0.4	0.5	5	0.065	0.666	0.021	4.857
11	0.4	0.8	0	0.059	0.797	0.023	5.659
12	0.4	0.8	6	0.062	0.805	0.026	5.716
13	0.6	0.2	0	0.146	0.110	0.002	1.545
14	0.6	0.2	5	0.189	0.070	0.002	1.053
15	0.6	0.5	0	0.094	0.639	0.012	4.710
16	0.6	0.5	5	0.092	0.684	0.015	4.956
17	0.6	0.8	0	0.080	0.899	0.015	6.550
18	0.6	0.8	7	0.084	0.911	0.020	6.690

Cobb–Douglas matching function parameter (γ), and various values of the minimum wage. The equilibrium is first solved for all nine combinations of $\alpha \in \{0.2, 0.4, 0.6\}$ and $\gamma \in \{0.2, 0.5, 0.8\}$ with no minimum wage constraint imposed. Equilibrium outcomes for each pair of α and γ are computed under a binding minimum wage. The minimum wage is set equal to 5 except in two cases when 5 would not have been a binding constraint on the Nash-bargaining problem.

Let us begin by considering environment 1, where workers have very low bargaining power (0.2) and make minimal contributions to creating matches through their search effort ($\gamma = 0.2$). With no minimum wage, the unemployment rate u, which is the proportion of labor force *participants* who are not employed, is relatively low at 0.039. However, the participation rate is only 0.39 in this case, and the vacancy rate is equal to 0.015. The reservation match value (θ^*) is 3.442.

Environment 2 is identical to the first except for the presence of a binding minimum wage of 5. When we discuss welfare measures of minimum wage impacts in the next chapter, we will see that one important indicator of welfare for individuals on the supply side of the market is the "implicit" reservation wage, $\rho V_U(m)$. Although individuals have a relatively low value of search in environment 1, the imposition of a minimum wage of 5 leads to an equilibrium outcome that is worse on several dimensions. First, the unemployment rate almost doubles in the new steady state equilibrium. Second, the implicit reservation wage registers a significant decline. Since the participation rate l is a monotone increasing function of $\rho V_U(m)$, fewer individuals are in the market. With fewer individuals searching, the number of vacancies decreases as well. Taken together, this example clearly illustrates that minimum wages may not lead to improvements in equilibrium outcomes for individuals on the supply side of the market.

Sometimes minimum wages can improve the position of searchers. This is the case in environment 5, where searchers have very little bargaining power ($\alpha = 0.2$) but make a large contribution to match formation ($\gamma = 0.8$). The imposition of the binding minimum wage (environment 6) results in a small increase in the unemployment rate, but large increases in the value of search and the participation rate in the economy. The vacancy creation rate is not affected. Under the welfare metrics we will propose in chapter 4, the welfare of searchers is increased even though the unemployment rate increased. The value of unemployed search is an important determinant of all the welfare measures we will consider. Since the participation rate is an increasing function of the value of search under our simple specification of the participation decision, while the unemployment rate is not, a quick check of the impact of any minimum wage change on the welfare of searchers should involve a comparison of participation rates, not solely unemployment rates or employment rates.

By comparing the appropriate rows, we see numerous cases where the imposition of a minimum wage, at the arbitrary level chosen, results in increases in the value of unemployed search and the labor market participation rate. In one such case, exhibited in environments 15 and 16, the imposition of a minimum wage of 5 results in an increase in the participation rate *and* a decrease in the unemployment rate due to a nonnegligible increase in vacancy creation. In chapter 4 we will provide a discussion of the conditions under which a binding minimum wage can lead to welfare increases for the entire economy.

4 Labor Market and Welfare Impacts of Minimum Wages

The model developed in the previous chapter is put to work in this chapter, allowing us to examine the manner in which a change in the statutory minimum wage affects equilibrium in the labor market, as well as on the welfare of agents on the supply and demand sides of the market. As is traditional in the minimum wage literature, we will be most concerned with how minimum wage changes affect employees and those looking for work. We begin this chapter by looking at how shifts in the minimum wage affect the unemployment rate and the accepted wage distribution. This is followed by a section in which we develop and motivate a number of welfare measures within a Benthamite social welfare framework.

4.1 Minimum Wages and Labor Market Status

As we saw in chapter 3, the imposition of a (new) minimum wage has potentially important effects on the unemployment rate (defined with respect to all labor market participants or the population), the labor market participation rate, and the accepted wage distribution. Unlike the situation that prevails when there is no binding minimum wage, the minimum wage produces a "spike" in the accepted wage distribution at m, even when match productivity θ is continuously distributed.[1] In the basic model, where the participation decision is fixed and contact rates are exogenously determined, an increase in the minimum wage leads to an increase in the unemployment rate (and, conversely, a decrease in the employment rate). We will see whether this implication withstands the introduction of endogenous labor market participation decisions and contact rates.

4.1.1 Minimum Wages and Unemployment

We first consider the case where there is no labor market participation decision and a fixed rate of contact (λ) between searchers and firms. Recall that the acceptance match value is given by $r = \max\{\rho V_U(m), m\}$, where $V_U(m)$ represents the equilibrium value of search when there is a minimum wage of m. When there is no binding minimum wage, there is no "wedge" between the acceptance wage r and the reservation match value $\theta^*(m) = \rho V_U(m)$. When the minimum wage is binding, then $m - \rho V_U(m) > 0$, and there is a strictly positive wedge between the minimal acceptable match value m, at which an employment contract is struck, and the "implicit" reservation wage.

In stationary point process models like the one analyzed here, the proportion of labor market participants who are unemployed (in the steady state) can be derived as follows. When an individual enters the unemployment state, we think of the duration of the unemployment spell, t_U, as being determined by a draw from some fixed distribution F_U. When the unemployment spell is complete, the individual transits into a job, which is characterized by a wage w and an employment duration t_E. When there is no on-the-job search, then w and t_E are independently distributed. We let the distribution of t_E be given by F_E. All draws of unemployment and employment durations are assumed to be independent of any previous draws, thus making the model a special case of an alternating renewal process.

We can think of a labor market "cycle" as consisting of a complete spell of unemployment followed by a complete spell of employment. A given cycle lasts for a duration of $t_U + t_E$, where t_U and t_E are independent draws from the distributions F_U and F_E. The average length of a cycle is simply the sum of the average lengths of unemployment and employment spells, since $E(t_U + t_E) = \int t_U dF_U(t_U) + \int t_E dF_E(t_E) = E(t_U) + E(t_E)$. Then we ask, in an average cycle, what proportion of time is spent in the unemployment state? This is simply $E(t_U)/(E(t_U) + E(t_E))$. Therefore, if we sample a labor market history at some random point in time, the probability that we will find any individual in the unemployment state is

$$p(U) = \frac{E(t_U)}{E(t_U) + E(t_E)}.$$

If there are a large number of (ex ante identical) labor market participants, the proportion unemployed at any arbitrary moment in time will be $p(U)$ as well.

Under stationarity, all duration distributions are of the negative exponential form. Therefore the cumulative distribution function of unemployment duration is

$$F_U(t_U) = 1 - \exp\left(-\lambda \tilde{G}(r) t_U\right),$$

with probability density function

$$f_U(t_U) = \lambda \tilde{G}(r) \exp\left(-\lambda \tilde{G}(r) t_U\right).$$

The distribution of employment spell durations is also negative exponential, so that

$$F_E(t_E) = 1 - \exp\left(-\eta t_E\right)$$

with probability density function

$$f_E(t_E) = \eta \exp\left(-\eta t_E\right).$$

If the random variable X has a negative exponential distribution, so that $F_X(x) = 1 - \exp\left(-ax\right)$, then the mean of X is a^{-1}. Thus

$$E(t_U) = (\lambda \tilde{G}(r))^{-1}$$

and

$$E(t_E) = \eta^{-1}.$$

We can write the steady state probability of unemployment as

$$p(U) = \frac{(\lambda \tilde{G}(r))^{-1}}{\eta^{-1} + (\lambda \tilde{G}(r))^{-1}}$$

$$= \frac{\eta}{\eta + \lambda \tilde{G}(r)}.$$

The steady state probability that a randomly selected individual will be unemployed is always a function of the separation rate, η, the contact rate, λ, and the distribution of match values G. When there exists a binding minimum wage, these parameters and m determine the unemployment rate. When the minimum wage is not binding, then $r = \theta^*$, and θ^* is a function of all of the parameters that describe the labor market environment.

The United States has had a "binding" federal minimum wage since the 1930s, so, when investigating the impact of a minimum wage change it is most relevant to consider the change in the steady state unemployment rates when moving from m to m', where $m' > m$. It is important to note that we are considering differences in *long-run* unemployment rates after the change. We know that immediately after a change in the minimum wage, some already existing matches will be dissolved, namely those for which $m \leq \theta < m'$. Consequently the proportion of unemployed individuals will be high and not consistent with its long-run equilibrium value (at the new minimum wage). Over time the labor market will adjust to its new equilibrium level. As the transitional dynamics to the new equilibrium in the presence of endogenous contact rates are extremely difficult to characterize, we will focus our attention on the comparison of long-run unemployment rates under the old and new minimum wage levels.

The change in the steady state unemployment rate is given by

$$p(U|m') - p(U|m) = \frac{\eta}{\eta + \lambda \tilde{G}(m')} - \frac{\eta}{\eta + \lambda \tilde{G}(m)}$$

$$= \frac{\eta \lambda [\tilde{G}(m) - \tilde{G}(m')]}{[\eta + \lambda \tilde{G}(m')][\eta + \lambda \tilde{G}(m)]}$$

$$> 0.$$

The size of the increase clearly depends on the Poisson parameters λ and η that describe the rate of arrival of job contacts and dismissals, as well as probability mass in the matching distribution G between the old and the new minimum wages. As long as this mass is positive, and given the strict positivity of λ and η, the increase in the steady state unemployment rate must always be nonnegative. It is important to bear in mind, however, that given the low levels (relative to average wages, say) at which the minimum wage has historically been set in the United States, it is quite possible that $\tilde{G}(m) - \tilde{G}(m')$ is small, thus yielding negligible impacts on unemployment rates. We will return to this point when discussing our empirical results and their policy implications.

As was argued in the previous chapter, the majority of empirical studies of minimum wage effects on employment and unemployment have found small, but generally statistically significant, negative impacts of minimum wage increases on the employment rate of "at risk" groups. However, in a number of cases no significant employment effects have been found, and in a few event studies of the minimum wage, prominently featured in Card and Krueger (1995), there were indications of positive employment effects. We now consider whether minimum wages can have more "beneficial" impacts on employment and unemployment probabilities when we consider a more general version of the labor market environment.

Fixed Contact and Endogenous Participation Rates We first consider the impact of a change in the minimum wage on unemployment and employment outcomes when the contact rate is fixed but labor market participation is endogenously determined. The impact of an increase in the minimum wage in this case is dependent on whether the rates are computed relative to the population of individuals in the labor market population or the entire population. Letting $\ell(m)$ denote the proportion of the *population* in the labor market when the minimum wage is m, the unemployment rate defined with respect to the total population is

$$p(\tilde{U}|m) = p(\ell U|m)$$

$$= \ell(m)p(U|m);$$

the impact of an infinitesimal change in the minimum wage on the unemployment rate in the population is then given by $\partial \ell(m)p(U|m)/\partial m = \ell'(m)p(U|m) + \ell(m)\partial p(U|m)/\partial m$. The sign of the second term on the right-hand side is unambiguously positive, as we saw above,[2] while the first term can be positive or negative. Given our assumption regarding the nature of the participation decision, we have

$$\ell(m) = Q(\rho V_U(m)),$$

$$\Rightarrow \ell'(m) = Q'(\rho V_U(m))\rho V'_U(m).$$

A necessary condition for an increase in the minimum wage to lead to a lower proportion of unemployed in the population is that the value of search decreases, or $V'_U(m) > 0$.

Since the population employment rate is $\tilde{E}(m) = \ell(m)(1 - U(m))$, it follows that an increase in $\tilde{E}$ requires that the value of search be increasing in m. Combining these two necessary conditions, we note that the fact that the population employment and unemployment rates are multiplicatively separable in the participation decision and a function of the unemployment rate among labor market participants implies that a minimum wage increase cannot simultaneously yield an increase in the employment rate and a decrease in the unemployment rate. Minimum wage hikes always involve a trade-off between unemployment and employment (in the population) when λ is fixed.

Fixed Participation and Endogenous Contact Rates We now return to the case of a fixed participation rate where ℓ is independent of m, but we allow for an endogenous contact rate $\lambda(m)$. We again consider the unemployment rate within the set of labor market participants,[3] so that

$$\frac{\partial p(U|m)}{\partial m} = \frac{p(U|m)}{D(m)}(\lambda(m)g(m) - \lambda'(m)\tilde{G}(m)),$$

where $D(m) \equiv \eta + \lambda(m)\tilde{G}(m)$. We have seen that when λ is a primitive, parameter $\lambda'(m) = 0$ for all m, and $\partial p(U|m)/\partial m$ is unambiguously positive. With an endogenous contact rate, for the minimum wage to decrease the unemployment rate requires that

$$\frac{\lambda'(m)}{\lambda(m)} > \frac{g(m)}{\tilde{G}(m)}, \tag{4.1}$$

where the right-hand side of (4.1) is the hazard rate of the matching distribution evaluated at m.

We can say more about this condition if the matching function is Cobb–Douglas, a leading case in the matching function literature. Then we have

$$\lambda(m) = \frac{(p(U|m)\ell)^\delta v(m)^{1-\delta}}{p(U|m)\ell}$$

$$= \left(\frac{v(m)}{p(U|m)\ell}\right)^{1-\delta},$$

where $v(m)$ is the measure of vacancies at the minimum wage m and δ is the Cobb–Douglas matching function parameter. The free entry condition (FEC) under the minimum wage implies that

$$\psi = \left(\frac{v(m)}{p(U|m)\ell}\right)^{-\delta} \tilde{G}(m)J(m),$$

where $J(m)$ is the value of a filled vacancy given a minimum wage m, or

$$v(m) = A(m)^{1/\delta}p(U|m)\ell,$$

where

$$A(m) = \frac{\tilde{G}(m)J(m)}{\psi}.$$

Then

$$\lambda(m) = A(m)^{(1-\delta)/\delta}.$$

After some simplification, we find that for a minimum wage increase to decrease the unemployment rate requires that the following inequality holds:

$$\frac{J'(m)}{J(m)} > \frac{1}{1-\delta}\frac{g(m)}{\tilde{G}(m)}.$$

A necessary condition for this to occur is $J'(m) > 0$. By the definition of $J(m)$, a necessary condition for this to occur is that $V'_U(m) < 0$, so that the unemployment rate can only decrease if the value of search decreases. The decreasing value of search condition is the same as the one that we found for the case of fixed λ and variable participation. Because the size of the set of labor market participants is fixed in the current case, the employment rate increases only when the unemployment rate decreases, so a necessary condition for employment gains is a decrease in the value of search. Deceases in the value of search increase the size of the surplus that firms can claim during the bargaining process, and leads them to create more vacancies.

Endogenous Participation and Contact Rates As in the preceding section, we will confine our attention to the case of a Cobb–Douglas matching function. If we measure the unemployment rate as a proportion of the population in the unemployment state, then

$$\frac{\partial \ell(m)p(U|m)}{\partial m} = l'(m)p(U|m) + l(m)\frac{\partial p(U|m)}{\partial m}.$$

From the preceding section, a necessary condition for $\partial p(U|m)/\partial m < 0$ is $V'_U(m) < 0$. Under this condition, we have $l'(m) < 0$. If $V'_U(m) > 0$; then $\partial p(U|m)/\partial m > 0$ and $l'(m) > 0$. Thus $V'_U(m) < 0$ is necessary for a decrease in the population unemployment rate $\ell(m)p(U|m)$.

In contrast, the proportion of the total population employed, $\ell(m)p(E|m)$, can increase even with $V'_U(m) > 0$ through the participation effect. While the proportion of individuals in the labor market in the employed state will decrease in this instance, the positive participation effect will counterbalance it. When instead $V'_U(m) < 0$, the participation rate decreases even though the employment rate in the labor market increases. Thus a decrease in the value of search can lead to a decrease in the population unemployment rate and an increase in the population employment rate. An increase in the value of search leads to an unambiguous increase in the population unemployment rate and has an ambiguous effect on the population employment rate.

Discussion   We have seen that increases in the minimum wage do not necessarily lead to increases in the unemployment rate, measured as a proportion of the population or of the set of labor market participants. The condition required for this to be the case is that the value of unemployed search be decreasing in the minimum wage, which means that the welfare level of a set of individuals (at least those in the unemployment state) must decrease for unemployment to decrease as well. This result foreshadows the discussion to come later in this chapter regarding the welfare effects of minimum wages. Within the context of the model we are considering, minimum wage impacts on unemployment rates can be expected to be small, but negative, for minimum wage changes of the size we have witnessed over the history of the law. While policy makers may well be concerned with increases in unemployment due to the increased demand for unemployment insurance benefits and tied transfers from other programs, we will argue that minimum wage increases may be welfare-enhancing for all labor market participants, both on the supply and demand side of the market, even given increases in the unemployment rate.

4.1.2   The Impact of Minimum Wage Changes on Wage Distributions
In this section we look at the impact of a minimum wage increase on the steady state accepted wage distribution. The accepted wage distribution is altered for two reasons. Obviously there is a new truncation point m' for the accepted wage distribution that is greater than the previous truncation point m. But not so obviously, the Nash bargaining posited to take place between employer and employee is altered by the new minimum wage. We can think of the new minimum wage producing a new search environment, with a modified wage offer distribution and different "acceptable" offer arrival rate, and these changes lead to a change in the value of search from $V_U(m)$ to $V_U(m')$. Since the value of continued search is the searcher's threat point when negotiating with the firm, an increase (decrease) in V_U leads to an improvement (deterioration) in the searcher's bargaining position.

For simplicity, we will investigate the relationship between the minimum wage and the accepted offer distribution under the assumption that the contact rate is exogenously determined and constant.[4] We assume that immediately upon the imposition of the new minimum wage, all current surviving matches are renegotiated under the new minimum wage and given the new value of search. If the new minimum wage increases the value of unemployed search, then employees have a higher outside option in the Nash bargaining framework, and as a result extract more of the surplus from any given match θ (at least when the negotiated wage exceeds the minimum wage). If the new minimum wage results in a decreased value of search, then the bargaining position of employees is weakened. In chapter 3 we found that the wage distribution under the minimum wage of m is given by

$$p(w|m) = \begin{cases} \dfrac{\alpha^{-1}g(\tilde{\theta}(w,V_U(m)))}{\tilde{G}(m)}, & w > m, \\[2mm] \dfrac{G(\hat{\theta}(m,V_U(m))) - G(m)}{\tilde{G}(m)}, & w = m, \\[2mm] 0, & w < m. \end{cases}$$

When the new minimum wage m' is imposed, then the accepted wage distribution becomes

$$p(w|m') = \begin{cases} \dfrac{\alpha^{-1}g(\tilde{\theta}(w,V_U(m')))}{\tilde{G}(m')}, & w > m', \\[2mm] \dfrac{G(\hat{\theta}(m',V_U(m'))) - G(m')}{\tilde{G}(m')}, & w = m', \\[2mm] 0, & w < m'. \end{cases}$$

With $m' > m$, the new distribution of accepted wages shifts out as the lower bound increases from m to m'. The difference in the size of the mass points at the new and old value of the minimum wage is

$$\frac{G(\hat{\theta}(m',V_U(m'))) - G(m')}{\tilde{G}(m')} - \frac{G(\hat{\theta}(m,V_U(m))) - G(m)}{\tilde{G}(m)}$$

$$= \frac{G(\hat{\theta}(m',V_U(m')))}{\tilde{G}(m')} - \frac{G(\hat{\theta}(m,V_U(m)))}{\tilde{G}(m)}.$$

The sign of this difference obviously depends on the pairs of values $(m, V_U(m))$ and $(m', V_U(m'))$.

In general, there is overlap between the continuous portions of the old and new probability distribution of wages above the new minimum wage value of m'. At any given wage value $w > m'$, we see that the ratio of the new to the old density is

$$\frac{[\alpha^{-1}g(\tilde{\theta}(w, V_U(m'))/\tilde{G}(m')]}{[\alpha^{-1}g(\tilde{\theta}(w, V_U(m))/\tilde{G}(m)]} = \frac{\tilde{G}(m)}{\tilde{G}(m')} \frac{g(\tilde{\theta}(w, V_U(m'))}{g(\tilde{\theta}(w, V_U(m))}, \qquad w > m'.$$

Once again, the ratio of the densities above m' also depends on the pairs of characteristics, $(m, V_U(m))$ and $(m', V_U(m'))$. The changes in the wage distribution can be summarized in terms of these four scalar values, a fact that we will exploit in chapter 6 when we attempt to determine whether the two most recent minimum wage changes improved welfare in a particular sense. For now we will simply note that the mapping between the distribution function of wages under m and the distribution function of wages under m' is determined by the two scalar values $V_U(m')$ and $V_U(m)$, in addition to m and m', of course. While the mapping itself is relatively complicated, the analysis of a minimum wage change on the accepted wage distribution hinges solely on these two values.

4.2   Welfare Measures

4.2.1   General Welfare Criteria

We begin by describing a fairly general framework that will enable us to define a few (hopefully) compelling welfare measures. Because the model is stationary, we will for the most part focus our attention on the long-run welfare impact of minimum wage changes. This is consistent with the approach taken by Hosios (1990), which will serve as an important guide in interpreting the policy implications of our model. At any point in time, any individual agents who are (potentially, at least) on the supply side of the market will be (1) nonparticipants, (2) unemployed searchers, or (3) employed at an acceptable match value θ and earning a wage of w. On the demand side of the market, firms will be deciding whether to create vacancies. Given our constant returns to scale assumption, the model delivers no implication regarding the distribution of employment or vacancy creation across firms. From the point of view of defining and interpreting the welfare function, it is simplest if we think of firms as potential or existing positions that can be occupied by at most one worker. Then a potential position may be in one of three states at any moment in time: (1) dormant, meaning that the position is unfilled and there is no active search going on to fill it; (2) vacant, meaning that the position is unfilled but with an active search under way to fill it; or (3) filled, in which case it is currently occupied by an employee whose match value with the position is θ and whose wage is w.

We will assume that the minimum wage is the only policy instrument available to a social planner, and that the planner's objective can be expressed as a Benthamite social welfare function, defined as follows:

$$S(m;a) = a_1(T_1(m))\overline{V}_O(m) + a_2(T_2(m))V_U(m) + a_3(T_3(m))\overline{V}_E(m)$$
$$+ a_4(T_4(m))\overline{J}(m), \tag{4.2}$$

where $T_1(m)$ is the size of the set of individuals who are out of the labor force under minimum wage m and $\overline{V}_O(m)$ is their average welfare level, $T_2(m)$ is the proportion of the population unemployed (all unemployed individuals have the same welfare level $V_U(m)$), and $T_3(m)$ is the proportion of the population who are employed in the steady state with $\overline{V}_E(m)$ denoting their average welfare level. On the demand side of the market, we have ignored the welfare contribution of agents who have chosen not to create a vacancy and those currently holding a vacancy, since the free entry condition implies that the welfare of firms (or potential firms) in either of these cases is zero. Thus the only nonzero welfare contribution from the demand side is associated with firms with a filled vacancy. The size of this set is denoted by $T_4(m)$ and the average value of a filled vacancy to the firm is $\overline{J}(m)$.

While it may seem natural to specify total welfare in terms of group-weighted averages, we have allowed for slightly more generality by specifying weight functions a that depend on group size. This additional flexibility facilitates the discussion of one welfare measure developed below. In general, however, we will be considering welfare weights of the form

$$a_i(T_i(m)) = a_i^0 T_i(m),$$

where $T_i(m)$ is the size of the set of individuals to which the scalar weight a_i^0 is applied.

First consider the size of the set of individuals who do not participate in the market. Given an equilibrium outcome of $\rho V_U(m)$, we have

$$T_1(m) = 1 - Q(\rho V_U(m)) \equiv \tilde{Q}(\rho V_U(m)).$$

We assume that ρV_O is continuously distributed in the population so that T_1 is a monotonically decreasing function of $V_U(m)$. Any minimum wage change that results in an increasing value of search leads to a decrease in T_1. Whether or not this group contributes to social welfare decreases is ambiguous, however, since the mean welfare level of nonparticipants is a decreasing function of the participation rate.

The size of the set of searching participants is given by the participation rate multiplied by the steady state probability of unemployment
(given participation). Thus

$$T_2(m) = Q(\rho V_U(m)) \times \frac{\eta}{\eta + \lambda(m)\tilde{G}(r)},$$

where $r = \max\{\rho V_U(m), m\}$ and $\lambda(m)$ signifies that the contact rate (from
the searching individual's perspective) depends on the equilibrium participation and vacancy creation decisions, which are a function of m
(when m is binding, or $r = m$). Defining the minimal acceptable θ in this
way, that is, by r, allows for the possibility that the minimum wage m
is not binding.

The size of the set of employed individuals is defined in a similar way,

$$T_3(m) = Q(\rho V_U(m)) \times \frac{\lambda(m)\tilde{G}(r)}{\eta + \lambda(m)\tilde{G}(r)}.$$

The size of the set of filled vacancies is equal to the size of the set of
employed agents by definition, so

$$T_4(m) = T_3(m).$$

4.2.2 Specific Welfare Measures

We now discuss some particular welfare measures of interest that are
special cases of (4.2). Before doing so, it is important to note that two
"welfare measures" commonly employed, at least implicitly, in the
empirical literature on minimum wages are not derivable from (4.2).
These are the unemployment rate of labor market participants and the
population employment rate. Given the definitions of specific welfare
weights developed above, the steady state unemployment rate is simply $T_2(m)/(1 - T_1(m))$, while the steady state employment rate among
population members is $T_3(m)$. These numbers are simple to compute
but have a problematic welfare interpretation. Their deficiencies as welfare measures stem from the fact that the size of these particular sets is
not necessarily informative regarding the distribution of welfare among
members of the set(s), and they contain even less information regarding
the distribution of welfare of other agents in the population who are not
employed or unemployed. The welfare measures we briefly consider
below all explicitly take into account the distribution of welfare in at
least some of the population classes.

Rawlsian Criterion   Under this criterion the welfare impact of a minimum wage is measured by its impact on the worse-off members of the population. For this to be an interesting exercise we must ignore the demand side of the market, since under the FEC the least well-off agent has a value of 0 no matter what the value of m. Thus we restrict attention to the supply side of the market only when considering this welfare measure.

On the supply side of the market, the lowest welfare value at a moment in time belongs to those agents who are in the labor market and unemployed. Thus our Rawlsian criterion is represented by a choice of welfare weights

$a_1 = 0,$

$a_2 = 1,$

$a_3 = 0,$

$a_4 = 0.$

As a result the (supply side) Rawlsian welfare measure is equal to $V_U(m)$.

In a model without a labor market participation decision, that is, one in which it is assumed that all individuals begin to participate in the market at some exogenously determined time, $V_U(m)$ is the ex ante value of the labor market career at the time of labor market entry. Under this interpretation, $V_U(m)$ is common to all individuals on the supply side of the market at the moment in time at which a cohort enters the labor market.

We will be interested in the conditions for minimum wage changes to improve welfare under all of the criteria we define. For this Rawlsian criterion, the conditions for a welfare improvement are particularly easy to state.

Proposition 3   A minimum wage m is better than a minimum wage m' in a Rawlsian sense if and only if $V_U(m) > V_U(m')$.

This is a simple condition to check. Since V_U is a continuous function of m, it may also prove possible to determine an optimal minimum wage, one that maximizes the welfare of the least well-off agents on the supply side. In a model where all agents participate in the market, that minimum wage also maximizes the expected value of the labor market career.

Total Welfare (*TW*) The focal point of our analysis will be social welfare, broadly construed, in which each agent's welfare is equally weighted. In this case we have

$a_1^0 = 1,$

$a_2^0 = 1,$

$a_3^0 = 1,$

$a_4^0 = 1.$

For convenience we will define $S(m; a)$ in this case by $TW(m)$. In this situation the weights attached to the expected value of being in each of the qualitatively distinct states are simply equal to the size of the set of agents in that state in the steady state. There is no simple way to characterize an optimal choice of the minimum wage in this case.

Participants' Welfare (*PW*) In his seminal study of the conditions for efficient labor market equilibria, Hosios (1990) explicitly considered only the welfare of labor market participants. This would be consistent with $TW(m)$ if we were to make an analogous free entry condition for the supply side of the market by normalizing the value of the nonparticipation state to 0 for all population members. Since we don't want to impose such a condition, we will define a separate welfare measure that applies only to market participants (on both the supply and demand side). The weighting scheme in this case is

$a_1^0 = 0,$

$a_2^0 = 1,$

$a_3^0 = 1,$

$a_4^0 = 1.$

This measure will be the focus of our analysis in what follows, both because we can relate optimization of this social welfare function to the Hosios (1990) analysis and because our specification of welfare of nonparticipants on supply side of the market is highly arbitrary. We now consider the applicability of his results concerning the maximization of PW to our problem.

Discussion Within a relatively general bargaining framework (broadly consistent with ours in the absence of a binding minimum wage) and using a constant returns to scale matching technology, Hosios (1990) showed that the maximization of the aggregate welfare criterion PW required that the effects of search externalities be appropriately recognized in the allocation of surplus shares to the unemployed searchers and vacancy creators. Thus the policy variable of his analysis was α.

Given that we will only be able to estimate (or calibrate) extremely simple matching functions given the data available to us, we consider the implications of this result when the matching technology is Cobb–Douglas,

$$M(\ell p(U), v) = (\ell p(U))^{\zeta} v^{1-\zeta}.$$

The Cobb–Douglas parameter ζ is the elasticity of the matching function with respect to search input from the supply side of the market. The Hosios condition[5] for efficiency is

$$\alpha = \zeta.$$

When this condition holds, there is no scope for a minimum wage to increase aggregate welfare as defined by $PW(m)$. In this case social welfare of labor market participants is optimized by setting $m = 0$, or at least to a level that is not binding.

The discussion in Hosios (1990) treats α as a policy variable that can be set by the social planner when designing an optimal compensation scheme. Our perspective is decidedly different, in that we consider α to be set by market forces, preference characteristics, and the generic bargaining environment, all of which are considered to be beyond the purview of the social planner.[6] In the econometric analysis below, a substantial amount of effort is devoted to the identification and estimation of α and ζ using the Current Population Survey data and information taken from the aggregate economy or a private-sector firm. Our estimates suggest that $\alpha \neq \zeta$.[7] If $\alpha < \zeta$, a minimum wage may improve welfare, as measured by PW or TW, by increasing the "effective" bargaining power of searchers on the supply side and inducing them to increase their participation rate to approach what it would be under $\alpha = \zeta$. This increased participation rate can have positive impacts on all market participants by increasing the size of the employed population (which is equal to the size of the set of filled vacancies).

From this perspective the minimum wage can be viewed as an instrument to increase total welfare of labor market participants or the entire society. It is crude in the sense that its performance will not be as beneficial as setting α to equal ζ. In its favor is the relative ease of implementation. We should note that the minimum wage can properly be viewed as a part of a larger policy that entails truncating the wage distribution, whether from below or above. Thus, if it is found that vacancy creators get too low a share of the surplus relative to $(1 - \zeta)$, an efficiency-enhancing wage truncation policy could result in wage caps.

While we do not derive explicit propositions concerning the conditions under which minimum (or maximum) wages will be welfare-enhancing under our three welfare measures, we do analyze optimal policy choices given our estimates of the parameters characterizing the labor market. Generally, we find that the welfare impacts of the minimum wage depend critically on the endogeneity of the contact rate, λ.

Ex post Welfare (Short-Run Welfare)   We conclude this chapter by considering a welfare enhancement criterion that is not nested within (4.2), but which we feel is a particularly interesting one from the vantage point of the political economy of the minimum wage. The social welfare function approach to policy analysis and implementation is "black-boxed" in the sense that the origin of the welfare weights is unexplained, as is the social planner's power to implement her policy choices. The criterion we examine now is particularly instructive in understanding the impact of minimum wage changes on the supply side of the market.

Consistent with our focus on the supply side, we assume that all model parameters are invariant with respect to the minimum wage, which rules out the endogeneity of contact rates. The situation we envision is one where a minimum wage m is currently in place, and at an arbitrary point in time a new minimum wage $m' > m$ is implemented. We will assume for simplicity that the minimum wage change is unanticipated, and when implemented, all agents are fully informed as to the new value m'.

Under any given minimum wage rate m and labor market environment described by the parameter vector ω, we can assign a unique labor market value to each θ, $\theta \in R_+$, and we will denote this value by $S(\theta; m)$. In defining this value, we exclude all individuals who do not participate in the market at a minimum wage m, that is, those for whom $V_O > V_U(m)$. For labor market participants with (hypothetical) draws of $\theta < m$, the value of the state is that of continued search. For those with draws of θ greater than or equal to m and less than $\hat{\theta}(m)$, the value of the state is that of employment at a wage of m, and for all values $\theta \geq \hat{\theta}(m)$, the value of the state is that associated with being employed at a wage $w(\theta, \rho V_U(m)) = \alpha\theta + (1 - \alpha)\rho V_U(m)$. To summarize, among labor market participants, we have

$$
S(\theta; m) = \begin{cases} V_U(m) \Leftrightarrow \theta < m, \\ V_E(m; m) \Leftrightarrow m \leq \theta < \hat{\theta}(m), \\ V_E(w(\theta, \rho V_U(m)); m) \Leftrightarrow \hat{\theta}(m) \leq \theta. \end{cases}
$$

The formal definition of Pareto improvement is then given by:

Definition 4 (SRW) The minimum wage m' Pareto dominates the minimum wage m in labor market environment ω if and only if $S(\theta; m') \geq S(\theta; m)$ for all $\theta \in R_+$ and $S(\theta; m') > S(\theta; m)$ for a measurable subset of values of θ.

Definition SRW is stated in terms of Pareto-improving minimum wage changes, but when interpreting this criterion within the context of our model, it is important to bear in mind that it does not refer to individuals but rather to labor market states. The condition requires that for any labor market state any agent may occupy at any moment in time, the change to the binding minimum wage m' will either improve her welfare at that moment in time or will at least leave her indifferent between facing the binding minimum wage m' or the minimum wage m. Note that either m or m' could be chosen to be nonbinding, so this criterion can be used to compare situations where in either state of the world there is a binding minimum wage or where there is a binding minimum wage in only one state of the world.

While the criterion refers only to improvements in the current values of participating in the labor market—on the assumption that the population is homogeneous (in the sense that all individuals face the same labor market environment ω)—there is a strong dynamic consistency to this criterion as well. Since each individual will occupy all labor market states at some point in their (infinitely long) labor market career, the condition states that the individual will also be at least as well off in every future labor market state they can occupy under the minimum wage m' as they would be in the absence of a binding minimum wage. It is perhaps surprising that such a seemingly strong condition can be satisfied for "reasonable" values of the labor market environment ω and choices of m'.

When a binding minimum wage m exists, the necessary and sufficient condition for a Pareto improvement in switching to m' is given by:

Proposition 5   The imposition of a new minimum wage m' in a labor market that currently has a binding minimum wage m is welfare-improving under *SRW* if and only if

$$V_U(m') \geq \begin{cases} V_U(m) + \frac{\alpha(m' - \rho V_U(m))}{\rho + \eta}, & \hat{\theta}(m) \leq m', \\ V_U(m) + \frac{m - \rho V_U(m)}{\rho + \eta}, & m < m' < \hat{\theta}(m). \end{cases} \tag{4.3}$$

The proof of this proposition promotes a deeper understanding of the mechanics of the model, and is sketched below. First note that the two expressions on the right-hand side of (4.3) both carry the implication that $V_U(m') > V_U(m)$. In the top expression, since $m' > m > \rho V_U(m)$, because m is a binding minimum wage, then

$$\frac{\alpha(m' - \rho V_U(m))}{\rho + \eta} > 0,$$

$$\Rightarrow V_U(m') > V_U(m).$$

In the case of the bottom expression, we know that m was a binding minimum wage, so

$$m > \rho V_U(m).$$

From our previous discussion of the Rawlsian welfare criterion, we know that for individuals unemployed before and after a minimum wage change, their welfare change will be $V_U(m') - V_U(m)$. For this set of individuals to be no worse off requires that this difference be non-negative. Thus this condition is required for any Pareto-improving minimum wage change.

Before discussing the impact of the minimum wage on the employed population (under m or m', or both), let is consider the welfare impact on the nonparticipants. Since participation is an ex ante decision, the welfare of nonparticipants does not depend on specific values of $S(\theta; m)$. The welfare of individuals who were not participants under both m and m' remains at V_O throughout. But say an individual is a participant under m but not under m'. The only way for this to occur is when $V_U(m') < V_U(m)$. In this case the individual's welfare has decreased, since $V_U(m) > V_O$ and $V_O > V_U(m')$. If instead $V_U(m') > V_U(m)$, the participation rate will increase, as we have seen. The individuals who enter the market have a value $V_U(m') > V_O > V_U(m)$. Thus all these individuals experience a welfare gain. The same condition that is required for all unemployed participants to be better off after the minimum wage change works for the set of nonparticipants (under m) as well; that is, $V_U(m') > V_U(m)$.

Now we look at the employed agents, and consider the requirements for welfare improvement for each possible value of θ in the feasible set, defined with respect to both m and m'. Since we have already seen that $V_U(m') > V_U(m)$ is a necessary condition for a Pareto improvement to occur on the supply side of the market, we will limit our attention to this case. We then know that $\hat{\theta}(m') > \hat{\theta}(m)$, and we will begin by looking at the improvement in $S(\theta; m)$ for $\theta \geq \hat{\theta}(m')$ when switching to minimum wage m'.

For all $\theta \geq \hat{\theta}(m')$, the minimum wage constraints under m and m' are not directly binding, in the sense that the individual would be paid a wage greater than m under minimum wage m and a wage greater than m' under minimum wage m'. The value of being in such an employment state under minimum wage j is given by

$$V_E(\theta, j) = (\rho + \eta)^{-1}(\alpha\theta + (1 - \alpha)\rho V_U(j) + \eta V_U(j)).$$

This function is increasing in $V_U(j)$, so $V_U(m') > V_U(m) \Rightarrow S(\theta; m') > S(\theta; m)$ for $\theta \geq \hat{\theta}(m')$.

Figure 4.1 depicts the case where the new minimum wage m' exceeds the value of $\hat{\theta}(m)$. The strategy in demonstrating the necessity and sufficiency of the condition for Pareto optimality is to look for the individual match value θ that will gain the least when the minimum wage increases to m', given that $V_U(m') > V_U(m)$. Since the wage is increasing in θ, clearly the match value that gains the least is that value ε to the left of m', where ε is an arbitrarily small positive number. Such an individual will enter the unemployment state after the minimum wage increase, and the value of that state will be $V_U(m)$. Now the value of $\theta = m' - \varepsilon$ under the old minimum wage was (approximately)

$$S(m' - \varepsilon, m) \doteq (\rho + \eta)^{-1}(\alpha m' + (1 - \alpha)\rho V_U(m) + \eta V_U(m)).$$

For an individual with a match value slightly less than m' no worse off unemployed under m' requires

$$V_U(m') \geq (\rho + \eta)^{-1}(\alpha m' + (1 - \alpha)\rho V_U(m) + \eta V_U(m))$$

$$\Rightarrow V_U(m') \geq V_U(m) + \frac{\alpha(\theta - \rho V_U(m))}{\rho + \eta}, \tag{4.4}$$

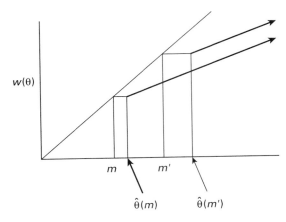

Figure 4.1
Wage functions under two minimum wages

as claimed above. When the new minimum wage m' is less than $\hat{\theta}(m)$, so that the wage under the match value $\theta = m'$ is equal to m in the initial minimum wage regime, the condition for no decrease in welfare is slightly modified to

$$V_U(m') \geq (\rho + \eta)^{-1}(m + \eta V_U(m))$$
$$\geq (\rho + \eta)^{-1}((m - \rho V_U(m) + \rho V_U(m) + \eta V_U(m))$$
$$\geq V_U(m) + \frac{(m - \rho V_U(m))}{\rho + \eta}.$$

Since individuals at the match value $\theta = m' - \varepsilon$ are the least well-off of all individuals at all match values $\theta \in R_+$ given that $V_U(m') > V_U(m)$, the condition given in the proposition is both necessary and sufficient.

We will summarize the Pareto welfare comparison results with the aid of figure 4.1. The horizontal axis is divided into five sets of values of θ. Set A consists of match values in $(0, m]$, set $B = (m, \hat{\theta}(m)]$, set $C = (\hat{\theta}(m), m']$, set $D = (m', \hat{\theta}(m')]$, and set $E = (\hat{\theta}(m'), \infty)$. Set A contains θ values that would not be accepted under either minimum wage, since for all of these values $\theta < m$, and with $m < m'$, none of them could possibly yield nonzero flow profits to a firm. The value of drawing any value of θ in this set under either minimum wage is then simply the value of continued search. If $V_U(m') > V_U(m)$, then the value of drawing any of these values when encountering an employment opportunity is greater under m' than under m.

Values of θ in set B result in employment under the minimum wage m but are not acceptable under minimum wage m'. The value of accepting one of these values under m is simply

$$\frac{m + \eta V_U(m)}{\rho + \eta},$$

whereas the value under the minimum wage m' is just the value of continued search, $V_U(m')$. Thus for m' to yield better outcomes for every point in B requires that $V_U(m') > (\rho + \eta)^{-1}(m + \eta V_U(m))$.

Set C also contains values of θ that are not acceptable under m' but are acceptable under m. The only difference from the set B comparison is that the wage function under m is increasing on the set C. We have already derived the necessary and sufficient condition for improvements under m' for all points in set C; see (4.4).

All values of θ contained in set D are acceptable under both minimum wages. The wage function is strictly increasing on this set under m, while under m' all θ values in this set yield the minimum wage m'. The value of a match on set D under m' is

$$\frac{m' + \eta V_U(m')}{\rho + \eta},$$

while the *best* outcome on this set under m has a value equal to

$$\frac{w(\hat{\theta}(m'), m) + \eta V_U(m)}{\rho + \eta}$$

$$= \frac{\alpha\{[m' - (1 - \alpha)\rho V_U(m')]/\alpha\} + (1 - \alpha)\rho V_U(m) + \eta V_U(m)}{\rho + \eta}$$

$$= \frac{m' + (1 - \alpha)\rho(V_U(m) - V_U(m')) + \eta V_U(m)}{\rho + \eta}.$$

Then every point in D has a higher value under m' then under m if

$$(1 - \alpha)\rho(V_U(m') - V_U(m)) + \eta(V_U(m') - V_U(m)) > 0.$$

Since $(1 - \alpha)\rho$ and η are both positive, the necessary and sufficient condition for improvement on this set is

$$V_U(m') > V_U(m).$$

On set E, both wage functions are increasing at the rate α in θ. The only difference in the lines is the "intercept" term, which is $(1 - \alpha)\rho V_U(j)$ for minimum wage j. Then the state value of a $\theta \in j$ is given by

$$\frac{\alpha\theta + (1-\alpha)\rho V_U(j) + \eta V_U(j)}{\rho + \eta},$$

and once again, the necessary and sufficient condition for all match values in E to have a higher value under m' than under m is $V_U(m') - V_U(m) > 0$.

In summary, in cases where individuals occupy the same state under m and m', the necessary and sufficient condition for m' to be better than m for all values in the sets A, D, and E is for $V_U(m') > V_U(m)$. When $m < m'$, there is a set of points, B and C in this case, where the individual will be unemployed under m' but employed under m. To obtain superior payoffs over all points in these sets under m' requires a stronger condition than $V_U(m') > V_U(m)$.

The proposition is particularly interesting in that it gives us a formal condition for the switch from m to m' to deliver a universal welfare improvement on the supply side of the market. This Pareto improvement requires (1) an increase in the labor market participation rate and (2) an *increase* in the unemployment rate.

While checking conditions for a Pareto-optimal improvement or to find a social welfare function optimizing value of the minimum wage, estimates of all parameters characterizing the labor market environment are required. However, as our previous discussion has emphasized, a critical necessary condition for Pareto improvement is that $V_U(m') > V_U(m)$. In chapter 6 we will explore the manner in which observed unemployment rate and wage distribution changes occurring after a minimum wage change can be used to infer the sign of the change in the value of search. While the value of search undoubtedly has its limitations as an overall welfare measure, the advantage of the approach we outline in that chapter is that estimates of primitive parameters are not required, and neither are the arbitrary distributional assumptions required to completely characterize the model. In the remainder of the book, we will consider how data can be used to form consistent estimators for the parameters of the model, ω, and how the estimates obtained can be used to conduct wide-ranging comparative statics exercises and policy experiments.

5 Minimum Wage Effects on Labor Market Outcomes: A Selective Survey

In this chapter we have two goals. The first is to explore, in a very general way, the large volume of empirical research devoted to examining minimum wage impacts on labor market outcomes. After considering four of the surveys of the empirical literature on minimum wages, we will proceed to a reasonably detailed analysis of five studies. These studies were selected either because they focus on large or persistent changes in minimum wage rates at the national or regional level, or because they employ an innovative methodology in performing the empirical analysis.[1] In all cases the findings of the studies or the methods used are evaluated with respect to the implications of our modeling framework.

The second objective is to compare and contrast our behavioral model of minimum wage impacts with other theory-grounded empirical investigations of minimum wage effects on labor market equilibria. Any model of interrelated phenomena as complex as wage setting, job mobility, and unemployment must, of necessity, be based on a number of strong assumptions in order to be analytically tractable. But beyond standard assumptions regarding the distributions of random variables appearing in the model, whether or not individuals are risk averse, and so forth, models are distinguished in terms of assumptions regarding the manner in which searchers and firms interact and how employment contracts are formed and broken. In the second portion of the chapter, we will examine how variations in model assumptions affect the role of minimum wages in attaining better market outcomes for at least one side of the market. We will also consider the implications of the models regarding observable market outcomes, such as employment and unemployment rates, mobility rates across jobs, and wage distributions. This will aid in distinguishing which type of market structure assumption may be most appropriate in a particular environment.

5.1 Surveys of Empirical Studies of Minimum Wage Effects

We will not attempt to survey the vast empirical literature on the relationship between labor market outcomes, particularly employment and
unemployment rates, and the level of the minimum wage. There have
been at least four excellent surveys of the empirical literature that
have been published over the past twenty-five years. The first is that
of Brown et al. (1982). In their survey, the authors clearly delineate the
large discrepancies between the findings of time series studies of minimum wage effects, which employ aggregated data, and those that are
based on smaller sampling units, typically the individual. Virtually all
minimum wage studies, then and now, have focused exclusively on
employment and unemployment outcomes. Time series studies tend
to consistently find evidence of negative employment effects, but the
question is whether these effects arise spuriously. The argument for this
claim rests on the fact that since few labor market participants seem to be
"directly" affected by the minimum wage, time series analyses of their
employment impacts on large subpopulations should not be expected
to yield large effects of any type. If they do, some other factors must be
at play.

Card and Krueger (1995) focus on this point, and claim that minimum wage effects on employment should ideally be examined using
microdata sources and a type of "natural experiment"methodology. In
a series of studies (e.g., Card 1992; Card and Krueger 1994) they looked
at state-level changes in minimum wages and used controls to isolate
employment impacts. Based on this work, they claim that even reasonably substantial increases in minimum wage rates may have no, or even
positive, effects on employment levels. Needless to say, these claims
have generated a substantial amount of debate in academic and policy
circles. Their book not only serves as a survey but takes a particularly
hard line in questioning those studies that consistently found negative
employment effects, as is the case for most of the literature.

While sometimes more on the strident side, Card and Krueger's book
does an admirable job of discussing methodological problems encountered in performing minimum wage analysis in the US context.[2] The
main problem, as we saw in the descriptive analysis presented in chapter 2, is that minimum wages are set at such low levels that their labor
market impacts are difficult to discern. The authors argue that only by
focusing on the substantial changes in the minimum wage that have

occurred in local labor markets from time to time can the empirical impact of the minimum wage on labor market outcomes be assessed.

While such "natural experiments" are undoubtedly of interest, there are limits to what can be learned from these types of analyses. The most obvious issue has to do with extrapolating results from studies of local labor markets to the national level. Another problem lies in the difficulty of interpreting estimates obtained using empirical frameworks not explicitly derived from a behavioral model of the labor market. A good example is the interpretation of a finding of positive employment effects as a "good thing." While in a standard monopsonistic model (with no search frictions) that would be the case, it can also be a sign of a welfare decrease experienced on the supply side of the market according to the model we have developed in the previous two chapters. The point being made is simply that the interpretation of parameter estimates is always made within the context of some modeling framework, whether explicitly or implicitly part of the empirical analysis. Virtually all theoretical models of the labor market generate some unique implications for the distribution of the data available to researchers. By iterating theoretical development, empirical work, and econometric analysis, the hope is that gradually a consensus may be reached as to the appropriate modeling framework for an analysis of minimum wage effects in a given labor market context, as well as the appropriate values of the primitive parameters that characterize the favored model.

Brown (1999) presents an excellent, balanced survey of the literature since the 1982 Brown et al. paper. A similarly complete survey has more recently been published by Neumark and Wascher (2008), themselves authors of numerous notable empirical analyses involving federal and state minimum wages. This survey is highly recommended, as it also brings more of the theoretical literature on minimum wages into play, and discusses the pluses and minuses of the various modeling approaches that have been taken to the analysis of minimum wages in a very even-handed way.

5.2   Empirical Studies of "Large Impacts" and Methodological Innovations

5.2.1   Pereira (2003)

Pereira (2003) performs a very interesting empirical analysis that looks at the labor market impacts of the change in Portugal's minimum wage

law in 1987. On January 1 of that year, "full" minimum wage entitle-
ment was extended to 18- and 19-year-old employees; before that date
this group's minimum wage was set at 75 percent of the "adult" value.
She mentions three reasons why this change can be considered significant. One, the minimum wage was equal to 56 percent of the average
wage in the Portuguese economy in 1996, in contrast to the US value of
less than 40 percent in the same time period. Second, a large share of
workers in the directly impacted group were paid wages close to the
old-minimum wage, and hence a large number of employees would
be directly impacted by the 25 percent increase in the minimum wage.
Third, the fact that Portugal is a small, open economy implies a limited
scope for output price increases to cushion the increased cost of labor
that resulted from the minimum wage increase.

She uses information from employer-based national surveys to look
at annual changes in age-specific employment levels and wages over
the five-year period, 1985 to 1989. The age groups examined are (1)
18- and 19-year-olds; (2) 20 to 25-year-olds; and (3) 30- to 35-year-olds.
The sample is a repeated cross section of firms; in particular, individuals cannot be followed over time. The methodology employed is that of
an event study. Specifically, Pereira utilizes the employment and wage
experiences of the 30- to 35-year-old group over the period as a control, and measures the impact of the large minimum wage change on
wages and employment of the younger groups relative to the control.
The results on both the wage and employment sides are striking. In particular, the minimum wage change was found to result in the average
wage growth of the youngest workers being 7 percent higher than in
the control group. The minimum wage increase brought a substantial
decline in the employment of 18- to 19-year-olds, with an estimated elasticity of employment with respect to the minimum wage in the range
−0.2 to −0.4 for this group. Especially interesting was the finding of
substantial substitution toward the presumably close substitutes in the
20- to 25-year-old group.

This large minimum wage change, directed toward a particular group
of low-wage workers, had substantial earnings and employment effects.
Are they consistent with the predictions of the model developed in
chapter 3? If so, can anything be said about the welfare impacts of
the change, in terms of the welfare metrics described in the previous
chapter?

For the first question, the answer is clearly in the affirmative. As would
be true in the simplest textbook analysis of minimum wage effects in

competitive markets, the wage of the 18- to 19-year-old group increased. In our model the higher lower bound on wages might seem to imply that average wages must increase, but this would only be strictly true if the wage offer distribution was exogenous. Of course, this is not the case here. If the new higher minimum wage increased the bargaining position of employees, by increasing the value of continued search, then the average wage must increase. If the minimum wage was "too high," in the sense of decreasing the value of search for young participants, then the average wage may rise or fall depending on other parameters characterizing the market. These types of effects and comparisons will be spelled out in more detail in conjunction with our welfare analysis of the 1996 and 1997 minimum wage changes in the United States that follows in chapter 6.

The employment effects are clearly consistent with our model, particularly in the simplest case of exogenous contact rates. As noted previously, any increase in a binding minimum wage necessarily results in a decrease in the employment rate among labor market participants. Also recall that in the general equilibrium case with endogenous contact rates, it is theoretically possible for the employment rate to increase after a minimum wage change, though one suspects that the conditions for such an outcome are unlikely to be present in actual labor markets. We should note that a simple, static monopsony model of the labor market for 18- to 19-year-olds would imply an increase in both wages and employment. This is clearly not what occurred.

Based on these findings, can we say anything about the impact of the minimum wage change on the welfare of 18- to 19-year-old labor market participants in Portugal? As we saw in the previous chapter, a decrease in the employment rate of labor market participants does not indicate a drop in welfare under any of the welfare metrics we considered. Neither does an increase in the average wage of employees necessarily indicate an increase in welfare under any of the metrics. There are two ways to evaluate welfare effects empirically. One is to develop some conditions on equilibrium distributions before and after minimum wage changes that allow one to determine whether a particular welfare measure increased or decreased as the result of the change. This is the method utilized in chapter 6. The other method is to directly estimate the parameters characterizing the labor market, and to use these estimates to determine whether the value of a particular welfare measured increased as the result of an observed minimum wage change. This is the technique developed and implemented in chapters 7 through

9. One of these approaches must be used if we are to say anything about the welfare effects of a given minimum wage change.[3]

5.2.2 Bell (1997)
Bell (1997) is a nice example of a non-event type of minimum wage analysis, namely one that is not tied to examining the impact of one particular minimum wage change on labor market outcomes. She employs both firm- and household-supplied information on employment and wages from Colombia and Mexico to look at some detailed features of the earnings distributions in the two countries in an attempt to determine the impact of minimum wage policy on earnings outcomes. In both of these developing countries there are large numbers of workers employed in the "informal" sector and in agriculture, where minimum wage coverage and enforcement is spotty or nonexistent. In this case minimum wage impacts are expected to be observed, if anywhere, in the formal sector of the economy, with minimum wage changes also potentially impacting the distribution of workers across sectors and total employment.

In Mexico minimum wages are set at the regional level, though the number of regions decreases substantially over the sample period she analyzes, 1981 to 1987. The main difference in these two countries is in terms of how much the minimum wage "bites." Examining the estimated earnings distributions for the two countries, she notes a substantial spike in the Colombian distribution around the minimum wage level, while for Mexico there is no discernible probability mass around the relevant region-specific minimum wage. Using firm-level panel data for the two countries, she then estimates a number of labor demand functions (all linear in the parameters), where labor is differentiated in terms of skilled and unskilled status. The demand for labor of skill status s is modeled as a linear function of the prices of productive factors, including the prices of skilled and unskilled labor, as well as the minimum wage level. All prices, and the minimum wage, are divided by an output price deflator.

The most credible estimates of the demand functions are obtained using a fixed effect specification (in which firms are taken to have permanent differences in their labor demand function intercept terms). She finds that the coefficient associated with the real minimum wage is not statistically significant for Mexico but has a statistically and economically significant effect in Colombia. Moreover the size of the impacts on the employment of unskilled workers with respect to the real minimum wage in Colombia are roughly in agreement with those found using time series methods with US data, with an elasticity in the range of -0.33 to -0.15, while the elasticity is considerably smaller in absolute value for skilled workers.

With regard to our model, the approach used in this analysis has some advantages and some disadvantages. The main advantage is that the model explicitly allows for substitution between unskilled workers, those whose wages are most impacted by minimum wage laws, and other factors of production, most important, skilled labor and capital equipment. Our model has no such allowance for explicit substitution possibilities, and an important assumption underlying all of the analysis is that the output of a firm is simply the sum of the outputs of all employees. In this way the contractual outcome between a firm and a worker can be analyzed independently of the contracts and productivity characteristics of other employees at the firm. On the plus side, our modeling framework could be used to analyze within-firm heterogeneity in wages in a more natural way then is possible with Bell's aggregated-data (at the firm level) regression methods.

As the model of chapter 3 makes clear, there is a very direct connection between the minimum wage and the average wage paid by firms in the economy given the primitive parameters that characterize the market. Viewed from this perspective, it is clear that treating average labor factor prices and the minimum wage level as separate arguments in a input demand system is not totally satisfactory. In Mexico, where minimum wages are argued not to bind, the average wage paid to employees will not be a function of the minimum wage rate. However, in Colombia, where the minimum wage does bind, changes in the minimum wage level can be expected to have significant impacts on the average price of labor. Within the demand system specification estimated by Bell, this results in minimum wage changes having both direct and indirect effects (through the average price of labor) on employment. But the more basic and telling point is that without using an explicit model of behavior in which the minimum wage appears as a constraint on the firm's employment and wage setting behavior, the addition of a minimum wage variable to an otherwise standard factor demand system must be ad hoc.

5.2.3   Campolieti et al. (2005)

Campolieti et al. (2005) use a modified event analysis approach to assess the impact of minimum wage changes on the probability of unemployment following the change. The setting is Canada, where minimum wages are set at the province level. Moreover, within provinces, minimum wages seem to have more bite than they do in the United States, with approximately 4.3 percent of employees paid at the minimum wage level for their province. As is true in the United States, minimum wage jobs are disproportionately held by teenagers and those working part-time.

Over the sample period, there exist twenty-four minimum wage changes at the province level. Within a province that experienced a minimum wage change in a given year, the treatment group was defined as the set of employees in the province who were paid a wage greater than or equal to the old minimum wage and less than the new minimum wage in the previous period. Control groups were defined as those individuals living in provinces without a minimum wage change over the same period, and who were paid a wage greater than or equal to the reference province's minimum wage rate and less than the province specific minimum wage and a positive value x, where the lowest value of x is 0.25 Canadian dollars. As $x \to \infty$, all employees paid at or above their province-specific minimum wages living in provinces without a minimum wage change in the reference year would be considered the control group. The authors refer to this as the "broad" comparison group. The trade-offs in selecting a given value of x for making the comparison are (1) sample size in the control group grows as $x \to \infty$ and (2) heterogeneity in the control group grows as $x \to \infty$. The authors argue that a value of x equal to 1 Canadian dollar is a good compromise.

The authors limit their analysis to the study of the impact of the minimum wage change on the likelihood of remaining employed (at whatever wage) in the following year. They estimate linear probability models, and find that the impact of being in a province with a minimum wage change on employment continuation probabilities depends to a great extent on the level of x used to define the comparison group. When x is set to only 0.25, the effect is small and insignificant. As one allows x to increase, the negative impact of the minimum wage change increases in absolute value, but this result also stems from the impact of adding large numbers of high-wage workers with stable employment patterns to the comparison group. At a value of $x = 1$, those living in a province with a minimum wage increase have a 0.04 lower probability of remaining employed than do those in the comparison group. The coefficient is not significantly different from 0, however.

The innovation of the paper is to allow differentiation among employees in the treatment group by allowing differential risk of leaving employment as a function of the gap between their wage in the previous period and the new minimum wage, or $g = m' - w$, $m \le w < m'$, where m' is the new minimum wage, m the current minimum wage, and w the treatment group member's wage rate in the period before the minimum wage change. They re-estimate the linear probability model with the dummy variable for experiencing a minimum wage change replaced by g, and find statistically significant, negative impacts of g on the probability of employment in the period following the minimum wage change. They also estimate a variant of the "gap" methodology that produces similar results. After performing a number of adjustments to the coefficient estimates to allow comparison with the usual types of minimum wage elasticities often computed in the empirical literature, they find negative employment effects consistent with those typically found.

The findings from the gap specification of minimum wage effects on employment continuity can be easily rationalized using our model. The discrete time specification used in their empirical work makes direct comparisons difficult, unless we were to solely consider the likelihood that a current match is terminated as the result of a minimum wage change from m to m'. In our model, the only matches that lead to employment contracts under a binding minimum wage of m are those for which $\theta \ge m$. We know that in the original equilibrium, the one associated with the minimum wage of m, all wages greater than m were determined according to the linear function $w^*(\theta, \rho V_U(m)) = \alpha\theta + (1-\alpha)\rho V_U(m)$. When the minimum wage change is made to m', all match values $\theta < m'$ are terminated. In terms of the previous wage, then, all matches with a previous wage less than

$$\hat{w}(m', \rho V_U(m)) = \alpha m' + (1-\alpha)\rho V_U(m)$$

would be terminated. This strict ordering property is what makes the gap variable specification work. For large values of the gap, g, the wage w is low and the job will be terminated with probability one. When $w \ge \hat{w}(m, \rho V_U(m))$, the gap is low, and the job survives the minimum wage change with probability 1. One reason why we wouldn't expect the pre-change wage rate to perfectly predict employment in the following period is that there exist a number of events that can occur between the two employment measurements that are not related to this particular selection process.[4]

5.2.4   Machin et al. (2003)

In April 1999 Britain instituted an economywide minimum wage, with some differentiation across subpopulations. Machin et al. (2003) perform an event study of the effects of this law in one particular sector of the economy, the nursing home industry. Wages paid to staff in this industry are generally low, so the pre-introduction of the minimum wage could be expected to have a large impact. That is exactly what the authors found. Wage levels rose significantly in the sector, while employment levels sank. The results are interesting because of the nature of the data collected, the focus on a particular industry, and the fact that the event studied is a dramatic one—moving from no minimum wage to one that severely impacts a number of low-wage industries in the economy.

The authors demonstrate considerable resourcefulness in data collection. Having identified a sector of interest, they sent surveys to the operators of all nursing homes in the United Kingdom before and after the imposition of the national minimum wage. They asked for detailed information on hours, wages, and duties for each of the nursing home's employees. The response rate was 20 percent (the authors argue that this is a reasonable rate for a mail survey), and the authors provide some evidence that the respondents are fairly representative of the firms operating nursing homes during the period. To serve as a benchmark, the authors use data collected earlier (in 1993), when a national minimum wage was part of the Labor Party's election platform. Labor lost the election, and the minimum wage was never implemented, but they have information regarding pre- and post-hypothetical minimum wage change to compare with changes when the minimum wage was actually implemented.

In studying the nursing home sector, the authors repeatedly stress the nongeneralizability of their results to the labor market at large. We have made much of the spike in the wage distribution at the minimum wage produced by our model. Nine months following the implementation of the minimum wage law in April 1999, firms in the sample reported that 30 percent of their employees were paid the minimum wage. In the language of the model, the minimum wage allowed a large number of workers to gain a larger share of their productive value in the sector. As the authors note, however, the potential response of nursing home operators to the increase in labor costs is limited due to the fact that (1) public regulations regarding staffing requirements and (2) the price of nursing home services is set contractually. The first restriction would seem to limit the ability of operators to reduce their staff sizes, assuming that they were operating near or at the minimally required staffing levels, while the second constraint would likely lead to pressures to reduce staff, since there was limited scope for price increases. The authors found that there were substantial negative minimum wage impacts on employment in this sector, with some indication that nursing homes with lower pre-change wages experienced larger decreases in employment.

While the large wage gains as a result of the imposition of the minimum wage are not unexpected given the industry studied, the significant negative employment effects are notable due to the staffing restrictions the operators face, both from regulators and by the limited substitution possibilities in the provision of care services. Other studies of general employment effects in the low-wage population stemming from the 1999 minimum wage law in Britain found little evidence of their existence (Stewart 2004). This study demonstrates, once again, that though the general employment effect of minimum wages set at low levels with respect to the average wage in the market may be small, certain subsets of the populations of firms and labor market participants may experience major disruptions to their economic activities as a result of a minimum wage change.

5.2.5 Dinardo et al. (1996)

Many readers may be aware of the Oaxaca (1973) decomposition of mean differences between groups using a linear regression model. Using this approach, one estimates a linear regression model separately for each of two (usually) distinct subpopulations. The question addressed using the method is to what extent the overall difference in group means on the dependent variable of interest is due to differences in the mean values of the covariates within the groups as opposed to there being a different covariance pattern between the covariates and the dependent variable within the groups, resulting in different estimated coefficients.

The demographic method of "standardization" has much the same aim. For example, when comparing the total fertility rate between two countries, demographers recognize that the age distribution, particularly of the female population, will have a major impact on the overall fertility rate. Standardization may then be imposed with respect to the age distribution of the female population. Let π_a^j denote the age-specific fertility rate of women in age group a in country j. Then the overall fertility rate in country j is simply

$$\bar{\pi}^j = \sum_a \pi_a^j f_a^j,$$

where f_a^j is the proportion of the female population in country j in age group a. If we use the female age distribution in country j as the base, then the "standardized" fertility rate in country j' is just

$$\bar{\pi}^{j'}(f^j) = \sum_a \pi_a^{j'} f_a^j.$$

The difference $\bar{\pi}^j - \bar{\pi}^{j'}(f^j)$ is the standardized difference in total fertility, holding the age distribution fixed at that of country j.

Both techniques are typically used to compare mean values of some characteristic. The contribution of Dinardo et al. (1996) to this type of counterfactual analysis is to consider the entire distribution of a characteristic, not only its mean value. This is a particularly noteworthy idea given the large changes we have seen in the degree of wage dispersion over the last several decades, and the degree of professional interest in advancing explanations for the changes. We are particularly interested in this paper for its focus on the impact of changes in the real value of the minimum wage over the three decades of data examined on the increasing variance in wages observed over the period.

The focus of their analysis is hourly wage rates, and they use the CPS-ORG data throughout. The idea is relatively straightforward. Let the density of wages at time t be given by

$$f_t(w) = \int f(w|z, t_w = t, m_t) dF(z|t_z = t) \tag{5.1}$$

$$\equiv f(w; t_w = t, t_z = t, m_t),$$

where $f_t(w)$ is the actual density of wages at time t, z is a vector of conditioning variables, which may be continuous or discrete, and m_t is the minimum wage in effect at time t. The terms t_w and t_z indicate to which period the conditional wage density belongs (t_w) and which period the covariate distribution represents (t_z). The authors provide an example, which we repeat here. Say that one wanted to determine what the distribution of wages would have been in 1988 if the distribution of covariates had been what it was in 1979, with the minimum wage remaining fixed at its 1988 value. Assuming that the conditional distribution of wages given z does not depend on the distribution of z, they write the counterfactual as

$$f(w; t_w = 88, t_z = 79, m_{88}) = \int f(w|z, t_w = 88, m_{88}) dF(z|t_z = 79)$$

$$= \int f(w|z, t_w = 88, m_{88}) \psi(z; 79, 88) dF(z|t_z = 88),$$

where

$$\psi(z; 79, 88) = \frac{dF(z|t_z = 79)}{dF(z|t_z = 88)}.$$

The ψ is just a reweighting term, where the standardization (in demographers' language) is with respect to the 1979 distribution of the characteristics comprising z. If the distribution of z happens to be the same in the two years, then clearly $\psi = 1$ for all values of z. The difference between the fertility example given above and this more general method is that for a given age, there is one age-specific fertility rate, which is an average over all women in given age group. The Dinardo et al. method, in that application, would consider the object of interest to be the entire distribution of fertility within the given age group and in the (sub) population.

The authors report a number of interesting findings using this methodology. Most relevant for our purposes is the finding that declines in the real minimum wage that occurred over the three decades of data examined were associated with substantial increases in wage dispersion, with essentially the "bottom falling out" of the distribution.

As is clear from (5.1), the authors allow the minimum wage to play a different role in shifting the marginal wage distribution than other "generic" covariates included in the vector z. This is due to their reasonable supposition that the minimum wage can be expected to have particular effects on the wage distribution due to its targeting of the lower tail of the distribution. To analyze minimum wage impacts, the authors make three reasonably strong assumptions regarding how minimum wage changes impact labor market outcomes.

One assumption deals with wages below the minimum, about which our model has nothing to say. The assumption most clearly at odds with the implications of our model is their assumption 1, which states that a change in the minimum wage from m to m' has no effect on the wage densities above m' in both years. In our model the wage densities above m' will change, in general, as a result of changes in the value of search. In the analysis in the next chapter we construct tests for changes in the wage distributions above m' as a way to detect changes in the value of search.

The other assumption made (assumption 3) that is at odds with our model implications is that changes in the minimum wage have no employment effect. Except in the case of the general equilibrium version of the model, for the minimum wage to have significant effects on the wage distribution, there must be employment effects. It should be pointed out that this assumption is consistent with the implications of some equilibrium search models, however, such as the one of Burdett and Mortensen (1998).[5]

Even though we may take issue with some of the assumptions on which the empirical analysis is based, the authors do provide convincing evidence that erosion in the real value of the minimum wage over the last 30 years is partially responsible for the increased wage inequality that is observed over the period.

5.3   Alternative Behavioral Frameworks

In this section we discuss a few notable attempts to estimate explicit behavioral models of minimum wage effects on wage distributions and employment rates. Almost all of the applications described below are based on some type of equilibrium search model, although, in their original incarnations as strictly theoretical explorations, none were primarily concerned with the examination of minimum wage effects on labor market outcomes. A paper by van den Berg (2003) focuses on minimum wages as an equilibrium selection device. While the paper includes no empirical application, the idea is sufficiently compelling, and the possibility of application not so far-fetched, that it warrants discussion in this section. We commence with the description of an early econometric model of minimum wage effects on wage distributions and employment probabilities that is not built on an explicit equilibrium model of the labor market. Nonetheless, since the econometric framework is sufficiently similar to the one used here, and since the econometric contribution is an important one, it is most appropriately discussed at this point.

5.3.1   Meyer and Wise (1983a, b)

Meyer and Wise (1983a, b) estimated a model of minimum wage effects using individual-level data that allowed them to infer what the wage distribution and employment level would have been in the absence of a minimum wage. Their model was both original and suggestive. They started from a standard ln wage equation specification

$\ln w_i = X_i \beta + \varepsilon_i,$

where the disturbance term is assumed to be independently and identically distributed (i.i.d.) as a normal random variable with mean 0 and variance σ_ε^2. They assume that this equation specifies the "baseline" wage determination process in the model in the absence of minimum wages, without justifying the assumption through any formal model of labor market behavior. The minimum wage, or logarithm of the minimum wage in this case, $\ln(m)$, perturbs the population distribution in the following manner: For an individual with characteristics X_i, take a draw from the (normal) distribution of ε. If the draw $X_i\beta + \varepsilon_i \geq \ln(m)$, then the wage rate is not affected by the minimum wage and is observed with probability 1. If instead $X_i\beta + \varepsilon_i < \ln(m)$, then with probability P_1, which is common to all population members, the subminimum wage rate is maintained; however, with probability P_2, it is raised to the legal lower bound, $\ln m$, and with probability $1 - P_1 - P_2$, it is simply lost. This censoring mechanism produces a spike at the minimum wage rate whenever $P_2 > 0$. For an individual with characteristics X_i, the likelihood that they are paid the minimum wage would be given by $p(\ln w_i = \ln m | X_i) = \Phi[(\ln m - X_i\beta)/\sigma_\varepsilon]P_2$. Given this censoring mechanism, the wage distribution is continuous below $\ln m$, with positive density as long as $P_1 > 0$, is continuous to the right of $\ln(m)$, and has a single mass point at $\ln m$. The shape of the wage distribution above $\ln m$ cannot change as a result of the imposition of a minimum wage.[6]

Given the censoring mechanism, the minimum wage tautologically results in employment losses, but these are all low paying jobs, as in the model we have developed. This built-in negative employment effect has drawn criticism from a number of researchers, particularly those arguing for the possibility that small minimum wage increases may actually result in employment gains. These researchers also tend to criticize the excessive reliance on parametric assumptions in obtaining maximum likelihood estimates of the wage and employment effects.[7] These criticisms seem somewhat overdrawn, given that most credible studies of minimum wage increases estimate negative or no employment effects, and given the agreement between the estimated censored $\ln w$ model and the observed $\ln w$ distributions. From our perspective the main criticism of the Meyer and Wise model is its lack of explicit behavioral underpinnings, which results in an inability to use the model to perform welfare and policy analysis.

5.3.2   Van den Berg (2003)

There is a large literature in empirical macroeconomics in which matching functions of the type described in section 3.8 are estimated. Recall
that the equilibrium matching framework posited the existence of a
matching function

$$M(U, V),$$

where U was the number of unemployed searchers and V the number of firm-created vacancies. The inputs into the production function
of matches create a number of matches M. The rate of contacts for an
unemployed searcher is just the average product measured with respect
to the input U, or

$$\lambda = \frac{M(U, V)}{U}.$$

In the standard matching function setup, it is assumed that M is a constant returns to scale production function. If this is not the case, then the
model can easily generate multiple equilibria. Much of the empirical literature having to do with the estimation of matching functions focuses
on testing for the CRS property.[8] While the CRS property is often not
statistically rejected, for a number of countries and time periods, it is.
This suggests that the phenomenon of multiple equilibria may be an
important one to consider when designing labor market policies.

Van den Berg's point is that the minimum wage may serve as an
equilibrium selection device. A simple and compelling example is the
following: Say that the function M and other primitive labor market
characteristics are such that there exist two possible stable equilibria in
the market. In equilibrium A all individuals on the supply side of the
market and all firms on the demand side have payoffs that exceed their
payoffs in equilibrium B. In particular, assume that both equilibria are
characterized in terms of unique wage rates, and that $w_A > w_B$. A minimum wage m set in the interval $(w_B, w_A]$ will serve to produce a unique
equilibrium, the one that Pareto dominates the inferior equilibrium B.

The case for a minimum wage serving as a beneficial equilibrium
selection device is obviously strongest when the equilibria can be Pareto
ranked, with the Pareto-optimal equilibrium in the set being associated
with the highest wage rate. One can also imagine cases where this would
not be true. In that case the social planner should impose bounds on permissible wages that would lead the economy to select the Pareto-optimal

one. In the case where the wage associated with the Pareto-optimal equilibrium was the lowest in the set of equilibrium wages, the social planner would implement a maximum wage policy.

The argument advanced by van den Berg is compelling in that it allows minimum wage policies that can potentially benefit both sides of the market. It also demonstrates a manner in which minimum wages can be "binding," in an extremely strong sense, even though no individual in the market is actually paid the minimum wage. The model we developed in chapters 3 and 4 clearly utilizes the probability mass in the wage distribution at m as an indicator of the direct impact of the minimum wage, and most of the empirical work that looks for minimum wage effects using detailed earnings data has the same focus. Perhaps minimum wage rates have an impact on the nature of the equilibrium selected, but within the given equilibrium that is selected, they may also serve as a constraint on the wage bargaining process.

5.3.3   Eckstein and Wolpin (1990)

There are two major frameworks used in the equilibrium search literature. The first, due to Albrecht and Axell (1984), is based on the idea that there exists a population of potential firms in the market, differentiated in terms of their potential productivity, along with a population that consists of individuals of equal productive ability but differentiated in terms of their valuation of leisure. Firms encounter potential employees randomly, and make a fixed wage offer. They cannot observe the job applicant's leisure valuation type. If the reservation wage of the individual is below the firm's offer, they take the job; otherwise, they refuse. In the case of two types of searching individuals, Albrecht and Axell show that low-profitability firms that participate in the market will make low wage offers to all searchers they encounter, while high-productivity firms make a higher wage offer.

The high-wage offer made is just sufficient to induce all searchers to accept it, that is, it is the reservation wage of the high valuation of leisure types. The low wage offered in equilibrium corresponds to the reservation wage of those searchers who have a low valuation of leisure, and hence a low reservation wage. Since any searcher who encounters a high-wage offering firm will accept it, in the steady state these firms, which have higher productivity, will have a larger number of employees. Low-wage offering firms will only attract those with a low valuation of leisure, and will be smaller as a result.

Eckstein and Wolpin (1990) extend the Axell and Albrecht framework in two ways. The first is to allow for more than two population types (in terms of leisure valuation). The second is to make the probability of receiving an offer a function of the size of the set of active firms. The main generalization of importance when considering the imposition of a minimum wage in this framework has to do with the offer probability. In both Albrecht and Axell and Eckstein and Wolpin, the distribution of profitability among potential firms, p, was continuously distributed on the finite interval $[0, \bar{\lambda}]$. In the Albrecht and Axell case, when the probability of receiving an offer is unaffected by the size of the set of firms in the market, the efficient, optimal minimum wage, would be $m = \bar{\lambda}$. This yields only one firm type in the market, the most productive, and transfers all of the surplus from the firm to the workers. In the Eckstein and Wolpin case, instead, high minimum wages, by reducing the size of the set of active firms in the market, reduce the steady state employment rate, offsetting the beneficial composition effect on the distribution of p.

The goal of their empirical analysis was to estimate the (extended) Albrecht and Axell model and, using the estimated parameters, to determine whether there existed an optimal minimum wage that was binding. They used individual level data from the National Longitudinal Survey of Youth (NLSY79) along with a maximum likelihood estimator to obtain point estimates of the primitive parameters of the model. One problem they faced was to obtain a representation of the wage distribution generated by the model that was at all consistent with the wage data. The model was predicated on there being a relatively small number of individual types (which were differentiated in terms of their reservation wage rates), with firms offering a number of different wages no larger than the number of searcher types. To gain a correspondence between the large number of different wage values observed in the data and the predictions of the model, the authors assumed that each wage was measured with error.[9] This gave them the wage distribution flexibility they needed.

The results of the estimation were judged to be disappointing by the authors. Their estimates revealed essentially two unobservable types in the population, one that accepted all offers and the other that accepted virtually none. While the model could fit the duration of unemployment distribution well, the wage distribution was poorly fit, with essentially all variability attributed to measurement error instead of being generated by the model itself. The implication of their estimates was that the optimal minimum wage was zero, but they didn't take this implication very seriously given the failure of the model to fit the data to a reasonable degree.

5.3.4 Van den Berg and Ridder (1998)

The other main framework used in the equilibrium search literature is that of Burdett and Mortensen (1998). It is somewhat more elegant than the Albrecht and Axell setup, in that it is able to generate a nondegenerate equilibrium wage distribution even when all firms and searchers are homogeneous in an ex ante sense. The model requires the existence of on-the-job search, and the basic model takes the rates of contact between unemployed searchers and firms, λ_U, and between employed searchers and firms, λ_E, as exogenously determined. All workers are equally productive at all firms. In equilibrium all firms make acceptable offers to all unemployed searchers so that the average duration of an unemployed search spell is just λ_U^{-1}. When employed at a wage w, any new potential employer the individual meets who offers a wage $w' > w$ will gain the services of the individual. It is assumed that employers precommit to a fixed wage offer strategy and, in particular, do not respond to offers made by other firms to their current employees. This is an important, and somewhat controversial, assumption.[10]

The reason that the equilibrium can support a continuous distribution of wage offers stems from the trade-off between instantaneous profitability (the model is formulated in continuous time) and the expected duration of the match. Say that each match produces an instantaneous revenue equal to θ. A firm that offers a wage of w to each of its employees then earns a flow profit of $\theta - w$ on each of its employees. In equilibrium there will be a distribution of wages across firms that is absolutely continuous, with a cumulative distribution function given by $F^*(w)$. A firm offering a wage of w loses an employee via a quit at a rate given by $\lambda_E(1 - F^*(w))$, where λ_E is the rate at which employees encounter other potential employers and $1 - F^*(w)$ is the probability that a randomly encountered potential employer would offer a wage greater than the firm's wage of w. Then the expected value of an employment contract at a wage w, given an equilibrium distribution of wage offers F^*, is

$$(\theta - w)l(w, F), \tag{5.2}$$

where $l(w, F^*)$ is the steady state proportion of employees at a firm offering a wage w. l is increasing in w. A high-wage offer reduces the instantaneous profit, as noted above, but increases the expected length of the match through the term $1 - F^*(w)$.

This model is extremely elegant but produces (at least) one counterfactual implication, which is that the density of wages, $f^*(w)$, is increasing in w.[11] Since most empirical wage distributions, including those constructed from CPS samples and utilized in the empirical work reported below, exhibit a rather pronounced positive skew, this implication is greatly at odds with empirical evidence. The authors add heterogeneity in firm profitability to deal with this issue. In our notation the assumption is that θ is randomly distributed in the population of firms in a given market. An important emphasis of the model lies in decomposing wage and employment outcome variability into portions due to observable heterogeneity, unobservable heterogeneity, and measurement error. To this end the authors segment markets in terms of observable characteristics, such as age, education, and occupation, and assume that market-specific primitive parameters are parametric functions of these characteristics. For firm productivity levels the authors assume that within a labor market segment there is additional (unobserved) heterogeneity in firm profitability levels, so that $\theta = v \exp(x\beta)$, where x is a vector of dummy variables reflecting membership in the various observable categories and v is a random variable with a three-point distribution. By allowing for both observed and unobserved heterogeneity (in terms of firm profitability), the model is capable of generating a more standard-looking population wage distribution. While within any labor market "segment," defined by a combination of observed and unobserved heterogeneity values, the equilibrium accepted wage density exhibits an increasing density on its finite support, when we "integrate out" the heterogeneity, the marginal population distribution of wage offers exhibits, generally speaking, the typical positive skew.

The minimum wage plays an interesting role in this model with heterogeneity. In the Burdett and Mortensen (1998) framework a legislated minimum wage that is binding merely shifts the support and shape of the wage offer and steady state wage distributions. For example, say that within a homogeneous model, in the absence of a minimum wage, the lowest minimum wage offered in equilibrium is r. If the (fixed) flow productivity of the match is θ, then any minimum wage m such that $r < m \leq \theta$ will result in no employment losses. The new equilibrium wage offer distribution will have a lower support equal to m instead of r. The minimum wage in this case simply transfers some of the surplus generated through employment from firms to workers.

The situation changes dramatically when the minimum wage is set above θ, naturally, for then no firm can generate nonnegative profits.

The market shuts down, and the unemployment rate is 100 percent. With heterogeneity in the distribution of θ, more intermediate types of unemployment effects can be produced. In this case a minimum wage greater than $\theta(x, \nu)$ for a given sector (defined in terms of x, ν) will be shut down. Individuals in that sector will be permanently unemployed. All other sectors will experience no change in their employment situations. Conversely, our model with matching heterogeneity implies that there exist no individuals who will become permanently unemployed as a result of a wage change. However, any randomly selected individual from the population will, in general, spend more time in the unemployment state as the minimum wage increases.

The data used in the estimation of the model are drawn from a large-scale household labor market survey conducted in the Netherlands in the late 1980s. There are some differences between the specification and estimates of van den Berg and Ridder and those associated with our model. First, the Burdett and Mortensen equilibrium search framework strictly requires the possibility of on-the-job search. Following most of the search literature, the authors allow for the rates of arrival of job offers to differ depending on whether the searcher is currently unemployed or employed. Virtually all estimated search models find that the rate of contacts for employed searchers is substantially below that of unemployed searchers, varying anywhere from 30 to 10 percent of the unemployed contact rate. Instead, van den Berg and Ridder's estimates yield approximately equal contact rates.

More important, the authors find no evidence of a spikes in the accepted wage distribution at the minimum wages.[12] This is important for claiming that the Burdett and Mortensen (1998) is an appropriate equilibrium framework to use in looking at minimum wage effects on the labor market. Our claim is that even with exceedingly low minimum wage rates, there is evidence for a spike at the minimum wage in the accepted wage distribution, and so our framework may be more appropriate to examine minimum wage effects on the labor market in the US context.

6 Assessing the Welfare Impacts of Actual Changes in the Minimum Wage

Using a formal model, such as the one we developed in chapter 3, allows the analyst to determine whether actual minimum wage changes result in welfare increases or decreases under a given welfare metric. The modeling choices made under our framework capture certain features of the wage distribution under a binding minimum wage constraint, and, most important, allow us to assess whether minimum wage changes have actually improved welfare.

How can we can use information on observed labor market outcomes before and after minimum wage changes to determine the welfare impacts of these changes? There are two ways to approach this question. One is to make functional form assumptions regarding the match distribution G, the matching function technology q, and the distribution of outside options L, and then to estimate the model after pooling observations from the CPS data that are drawn from some month(s) before the change and some month(s) after the change. Some welfare measures can be directly estimated in this way, such as the value of search before and after the minimum wage change. These estimated values can then directly be compared. Estimation of the parameters characterizing the labor market environment also can be used to perform counterfactual policy experiments. These types of exercises will occupy our attention in chapter 9.

The benefits associated with having point estimates of the parameters characterizing the labor market environment (ω) come at a cost, of course. As has been appreciated since Flinn and Heckman (1982), in general, partial or general equilibrium search models are only estimable after making parametric assumptions on the wage offer (in the partial-partial equilibrium case) or match value distribution. Most disturbingly, variations in these untestable assumptions can produce wide swings in the results of policy experiments conducted using the estimated model. For instance, consider the direct estimation of the effect of a minimum wage change on unemployed search that was discussed in the previous paragraph. The actual estimates of these values will typically change depending on the assumption made regarding the functional form of the match distribution G. Under one assumption on the form of G, we may find that there is a significantly positive impact on the value of search, while under a different assumption on G, the difference in the estimates might be insignificantly different from zero. Since in the model we have developed there is no way to test the distributional assumption directly, we can never have a great degree of confidence that the results of our policy experiments are robust with respect to significant changes in the specification of G or other functions that appear in the behavioral model.[1]

In this chapter we consider the relatively limited question of whether it is possible to infer something about the welfare effect of an observed minimum wage change solely by comparing available data on labor market outcomes before and after the minimum wage change. Since we work with CPS data throughout, the data available to us are essentially comprised of the duration of ongoing unemployment spells and the accepted wage distribution. By the arguments given in chapters 3 through 5, we believe that little information about changes in the welfare of labor market participants can be gleaned from the comparisons of unemployment or employment rates (or, equivalently, the average length of ongoing unemployment spells). As a result we turn our full attention to determining what types of changes in the accepted wage distribution, given our model structure, could lead us to conclude that a beneficial or detrimental welfare impact had occurred.

Many of the welfare criterion we discussed in chapter 4 are complex functions of the values of a continuum of states. It is unrealistic to expect that we can learn something about how the values of these functions change solely by looking at changes in accepted wage distributions. However, an important component of *all* of the welfare measures we defined was the value of unemployed search, $V_U(m)$. In addition to being the expected value of the labor market career at its onset or the minimum welfare level for those on the supply side of the market, it is instrumental in defining the lower bound of the welfare of nonparticipants, and through the bargaining procedure, has a potentially large impact on the value of being employed at any given match value.

Consequently we will be considering what particular types of changes in accepted wage distributions could lead us to infer increases or decreases in V_U that result from a minimum wage change. All the tests we conduct in this chapter do not rely on estimates of any model parameters, nor do they require assumptions regarding the functional forms of distributions. Thus any welfare implications we are able to draw from these tests are completely robust given the general structure of our model. It will be helpful to assume that contact rates are fixed exogenously in interpreting the tests and results presented below. As we develop the tests, we will provide a fairly complete characterization of the impacts of minimum wage changes on the complete accepted wage distribution under our modeling assumptions.

6.1 Results Using Unconditional Wage Distributions

Within the model the effects of imposing a minimum wage on the accepted wage distribution are complex. The minimum observed wage will always increase in response to the imposition of a binding minimum wage or when a binding minimum wage is increased.[2] While intuition might lead one to expect that comparing wage distributions associated with the same labor market environment ω and different minimum wage levels in terms of first-order stochastic dominance (FOSD) criteria might be a reliable guide to underlying welfare levels, this is not typically the case. Using the welfare criterion that is our focus of interest, we have the fact that the wage distribution under the new (higher) minimum wage does *not* first-order stochastically dominate the old one is informative about welfare but the converse is not. We begin with a formal definition of first-order stochastic dominance:

Definition 6 Probability distribution A first-order stochastically dominates distribution B if $B(x) \geq A(x)$ for all x and $B(x) > A(x)$ for some x.

Graphically speaking, first-order stochastic dominance implies that the cumulative distribution function (c.d.f.) of the dominated distribution, which is B in the definition given above, never lies below the c.d.f. associated with A and sometimes is strictly above it. If the expected value of X exists under both A and B, then this implies that the mean and median of X will be greater under A than B. The fact that A stochastically dominates B does not generally allow us to rank moments of the distributions other than the mean, however.

Under our model we have the following necessary and sufficient condition for first-order stochastic dominance:

Proposition 7 Let the c.d.f. of wages under the minimum wage j be given by F_j. Then $F_{m'}$ first-order stochastically dominates F_m if and only if

$$\frac{\tilde{G}(m)}{\tilde{G}(m')} \geq \frac{\tilde{G}\{[z-(1-\alpha)\rho V_U(m)]/\alpha\}}{\tilde{G}\{[z-(1-\alpha)\rho V_U(m')]/\alpha\}} \qquad \forall\, z \geq m'. \qquad (6.1)$$

This condition involves all the primitive parameters of the problem as well as the two minimum wage rates. We note that as m' approaches m from above, the left-hand side of the expression converges to 1. In this case we will observe stochastic dominance as long as $V_U(m') > V_U(m)$ for all $m' > m$. Thus, heuristically speaking, the link between first-order stochastic dominance and improvement in V_U is one-to-one for very small changes in m. In reality, however, minimum wage changes are discrete, and the stochastic dominance condition is not sufficient for us to infer an improvement in V_U. The following two propositions summarize the nature of the relationship between stochastic dominance and the value of search:

Corollary 8 If $V_U(m') \geq V_U(m)$, $m' > m$, then $F_{m'}$ first-order stochastically dominates F_m.

The corollary states that when the change in the minimum wage leads to an increase in the value of search, the new equilibrium wage distribution must stochastically dominate the old one. Unfortunately, this result is not of much practical significance because $V_U(m') \geq V_U(m)$ is only a sufficient condition for stochastic dominance of $F_{m'}$ with respect to F_m and is not a necessary one. For testing and inferences purposes, the following restated version of the result is a more useful representation.

Corollary 9 (Restated) If $F_{m'}$ does not first-order stochastically dominate F_m, then $V_U(m') < V_U(m)$.

These results suggest that observed wage distributions before and after minimum wage changes can reveal whether the minimum wage increase worsened welfare, but cannot be used to infer whether or not welfare increased. The asymmetry essentially stems from the higher truncation point of the accepted wage distribution caused by the new minimum wage. Because of this phenomenon, since $F_{m'}(x) < F_m(x)$ for all $x \in [m, m']$, the distribution F_m can never FOSD the distribution $F_{m'}$.

Essentially the distribution of $F_{m'}$ begins with an unfair advantage over F_m in the FOSD race due to this truncation effect. This edge can mask even a welfare decrease, in terms of V_U, when moving from m to m'.

Obviously a variety of features of the two distribution functions could prevent $F_{m'}$ from first-order stochastically dominating F_m. Our model specification places restrictions on the way in which FOSD can fail. In particular, if $F_{m'}$ does not FOSD F_m, there must exist some x^* such that $F_{m'} \leq F_m$ for all $x \leq x^*$ and $F_{m'} > F_m$ for all $x > x^*$. That is, the c.d.f.s should intersect either never (in which case $F_{m'}$ first-order stochastically dominates F_m) or once and only once (in the case of failure of FOSD). Multiple crossings of the c.d.f.s could be produced by sampling variability or model misspecification, phenomena outside the purview of our modeling framework.

As these results make clear, it is difficult to assess welfare impacts from changes in wage distributions. We now turn our attention to another characteristic of the relationship between the pre- and post-change wage distributions that may yield some informative value and to which it is possible to give a reasonably intuitive and yet precise definition of the notion of *spillover*.

6.2 Results for Conditional Wage Distributions

Consider a wage rate w such that $w > m' > m$. Under either minimum wage rate the density of the accepted wage offer distribution is strictly positive, provided that the underlying matching distribution is absolutely continuous on the positive real line and that $\alpha > 0$. We then consider the ratio of the wage density at w under m and m', or

$$
r(w; m, m') = \frac{\alpha^{-1}(g(\tilde{\theta}(w, V_U(m')))/\tilde{G}(m')}{\alpha^{-1}(g(\tilde{\theta}(w, V_U(m)))/\tilde{G}(m)}
$$

$$
= \frac{\tilde{G}(m)}{\tilde{G}(m')} \times \frac{g(\tilde{\theta}(w, V_U(m')))}{g(\tilde{\theta}(w, V_U(m)))},
$$

(6.2)

where

$$
\tilde{\theta}(w, V_U) = \frac{w - (1 - \alpha)\rho V_U}{\alpha}.
$$

The function $\tilde{\theta}(w, V_U)$ determines the unique value of θ that generates the wage w given the value of search, V_U. If, as is generally the case, the value of search changes as a function of the minimum wage, then the value of the θ corresponding to a wage w will be different under two distinct binding minimum wages. The function r is otherwise known as a likelihood ratio, being the ratio of two densities evaluated at the same argument, w.

The likelihood ratio (6.2) is the product of two terms. The first term, $\tilde{G}(m)/\tilde{G}(m')$, we might refer to as the *truncation effect* of the respective minimum wages. Since $\tilde{G}(m) > \tilde{G}(m')$, this term is always greater than 1 and is independent of the particular value of $w > m'$ at which the function r is evaluated. The second term we refer to as the *spillover effect*, so that

$$S(w; m, m') = \frac{g(\tilde{\theta}(w, V_U(m')))}{g(\tilde{\theta}(w, V_U(m)))}.$$

It will be convenient to work with the log of the likelihood ratio, since

$$\ln r(w; m, m') = \ln \frac{\tilde{G}(m)}{\tilde{G}(m')} + \ln S(w; m, m').$$

In terms of the log likelihood ratio, the two effects are additively separable. It is also important to note that only the spillover effect involves w. Our main interest will be in determining the manner in which the shape of the wage density above m' changes when changing minimum wage rates. We will assess this by looking at the manner in which $\ln r$ varies in w above m', which is given by the partial derivative

$$\frac{\partial \ln r(w; m, m')}{\partial w} = \frac{\partial \ln S(w; m, m')}{\partial w}.$$

Definition 10   The quantity $\partial \ln S(w; m, m')/\partial w$ is the *shape perturbation* at w associated with the minimum wage increase from m to m'. This quantity is denoted $SP(w; m, m')$.

In general, any increase in the minimum wage from m to m' produces a spillover effect; that is, $SP(w; m, m') \neq 0$ for some $w > m'$. In Flinn (2002) we present two formal conditions for there to be no spillover effect associated with a minimum wage change. One condition for the matching distribution not to exhibit any spillover, even when $V_U(m') \neq V_U(m)$, is for the distribution of match values to be negative exponential so that the density is given by

$$g(\theta; \tau) = \tau \exp(-\tau\theta), \tag{6.3}$$

where τ is a positive parameter. The other, more interesting, condition for there to be no spillover is that $V_U(m) = V_U(m')$. It is obvious that there will be no spillover in this case, since $\tilde{\theta}(w, V_U)$ will be the same under m and m', and we will have $\ln S(w; m, m') = \ln 1 = 0$ for all $w > m'$, implying $SP(w; m, m') = 0$ for all $w > m'$.

When there is no spillover, the two wage densities for wages greater than m' are proportional, or

$$f_m(w) = \delta(m, m')f_{m'}(w) \qquad \forall w > m' > m, \tag{6.4}$$

where

$$\delta(m, m') = \frac{\tilde{G}(m')}{\tilde{G}(m)}.$$

The factor of proportionality is only a function of G, m, and m'.

The next formal property is used in constructing tests for changes in the value of search using wage observations above the largest minimum wage:

Lemma 11 Let $f(w; m) = \delta f(w; m')$ for all $w \in S$, where $S = (a, b)$. Then $F_m(w|w \in S) = F_{m'}(w|w \in S)$.

Using this result, we derive a testable implication for the absence of a change in the value of search:

$$F_m(w|w > m') = F_{m'}(w|w > m') \qquad \forall w > m'. \tag{6.5}$$

If the empirical evidence on the conditional accepted wage densities leads us to reject (6.5), it is important to recognize that this only implies that the value of search *has* changed, and does not yield direct evidence on the sign of the change. To determine the sign of the change requires the use of additional empirical evidence, or even fully estimating the model after making a series of additional assumptions regarding model structure.

This last point is an important one to bear in mind, for a number of researchers have provided empirical evidence that minimum wage changes benefit many employees other than the small minority receiving wages in the neighborhood of the minimum wage (see especially DiNardo et al. 1996 and references contained within). The message of this section is that these "ripple" effects are evidence that there is a link between constraints placed on wage setting at the bottom of the distribution with the remuneration received by all employees. However, we cannot be certain that these ripple effects benefited those not in the left tail of the distribution without further empirical evidence and the use of an explicit welfare criterion.

6.3   Results Using Matched Data

The most direct link between changes in V_U and changes in wage distributions occurs for individuals working at the same job (i.e., the same match productivity θ) before and after the change in the minimum wage, and who are paid more than the prevailing minimum wage at both points in time. Let this population of individuals be denoted by I, and consider an individual i from this set. Let her wages before and after the minimum wage change be denoted by w_i and w_i'. Then

$$w_i = \alpha\theta_i + (1-\alpha)\rho V_U(m), \qquad \theta_i > \hat{\theta}(m, V_U(m))$$

$$w_i' = \alpha\theta_i + (1-\alpha)\rho V_U(m'), \qquad \theta_i > \hat{\theta}(m', V_U(m'))$$

so that

$$w_i' - w_i = \rho(1-\alpha)(V_U(m') - V_U(m)). \tag{6.6}$$

The next result follows immediately from (6.6):

Proposition 12   Given that $\alpha < 1$, the minimum wage change is improving in the sense of V_U if and only if $E_I(w' - w) > 0$, where E_I denotes expectation over the population of individuals in I.

This is clear, since the wage change is proportional to the change in the value of search, with the factor of proportionality given by the policy invariant $\rho(1-\alpha)$. Because the constant is the same for all members of this population, we have the following strong implication:

Corollary 13   The wage differences $(w_i' - w_i) = (w_j' - w_j)\ \forall i, j \in I$.

This result implies that the variance in wage changes in the population I is 0. Thus the distribution of wage changes in population I has a mean given by the right-hand side of (6.6) and variance equal to 0. Of course, the distribution of wage changes in the general population does not have zero variance because it includes individuals who change jobs and, as a result includes changing values of θ.
    The model places an additional restriction on the magnitude of the increase in the average wage for members of the population I, our reference group, that can result solely from a change in the statutory minimum wage. This restriction is developed in the following two results:

Proposition 14   Let m be a binding minimum wage. Then

$$\frac{d\rho V_U(m; \omega)}{dm} \le 1.$$

This result implies, among other things, that any nominal minimum wage greater than $\rho V_U(0)$ must be binding. For example, let $\rho V_U(0)$ be equal to 4. Setting a minimum wage m at any value greater than 4 will imply that it is binding, and will never alter the underlying "core" value of the reservation match value in the absence of a minimum wage. The result above essentially guarantees that raising the statutory minimum wage cannot result in the higher minimum wage being nonbinding.

Corollary 15 Let m and m' be two binding minimum wages in the labor market environment characterized by ω, with $m < m'$. For an individual at the same job under m and m', and for whom $w > m$ and $w' > m'$,

$$w' - w \leq m' - m.$$

The change in wage rates for members of set I can never exceed the change in the minimum wage rates. As we have seen, if the new minimum wage decreases the value of search, the change in wages will be negative, while if the change is positive, the change in minimum wages is given by

$$w' - w = (1 - \alpha)(\rho V_U(m') - \rho V_U(m))$$
$$\leq (1 - \alpha)(m' - m)$$
$$\leq (m' - m),$$

where the second line follows from the previous proposition and the last line from the fact that $\alpha \in (0, 1)$.

6.4 Welfare Impacts of the 1996 and 1997 Statutory Minimum Wage Increases

We use the results developed above to investigate, in a nonparametric manner, whether the federal minimum wage changes that occurred in the late 1990s had a salutary effect on the welfare of young labor market participants. After developing the requisite hypothesis tests, we utilize (cross-sectional) Current Population Survey data to determine whether the value of search increased between a month before the change to a month after the change, where the months chosen are centered on the date of the change in the minimum wage level. The results of these tests are generally in accord with the results obtained from estimation of the equilibrium labor market model that are discussed in the sequel. This gives us some confidence in both methodologies as well as the basic framework chosen to investigate minimum wage impacts.

To summarize, we derived three main theoretical results above:

1. If $F_{m'}$ first-order stochastically dominates F_m for $m' > m$, then we can draw no conclusion regarding the relationship between $V_n(m')$ and $V_n(m)$. If $F_{m'}$ does not first-order stochastically dominate F_m, then $V_U(m') < V_U(m)$.

2. If $F_{m'}(\cdot\,|w > m') = F_m(\cdot\,|w > m')$, then there is no spillover. No spillover indicates no difference in $V_U(m')$ and $V_U(m)$ as long as the matching density g is not negative exponential (6.3). If we find no evidence of spillover, then it is possible to test that the density g is not of this form; if we find that this is the case, then we can conclude that there was no change in the value of search.

3. From wage observations before and after the minimum wage change for individuals who worked at the same job at both points in time, $E(w' - w|w' > m', w > m) > 0$ if and only if $V_U(m') > V_U(m)$.

6.4.1 Test Utilizing Cross-sectional Wage Distributions

The implications concerning the comparisons of entire conditional or unconditional distributions call for tests of equality and first-order stochastic dominance. The general statement of the testing problem is as follows: Consider two distributions $A(x)$ and $B(x)$, which could either be conditional or unconditional c.d.f.s. Assume that we have two independent random samples drawn from each distribution, X^A and X^B, with the number of draws from each given by n_A and n_B respectively. Let the empirical distribution of each be defined by

$$\hat{A}_{n_A}(x) = n_A^{-1}\sum_{i=1}^{n_A}\chi[X_i^A \le x], \quad \hat{B}_{n_B}(x) = n_B^{-1}\sum_{i=1}^{n_B}\chi[X_i^B \le x],$$

where χ denotes the indicator function. Using these empirical c.d.f.s, perform tests of the formal hypotheses:

$$A(x) = B(x) \qquad \forall x \in Q \subset R \tag{6.7}$$

and

$$A(x) \le B(x) \qquad \forall x \in Q \subset R, \tag{6.8}$$

where the set Q is defined relative to the particular testing situation. The test of (6.7) is conducted using the familiar Kolmogorov–Smirnov (two-sample) test statistic,

$$S_n^1 = \left(\frac{n_A n_B}{n}\right)^{1/2} \sup_{x \in Q \subset R} |\hat{A}_{n_A}(x) - \hat{B}_{n_B}(x)|,$$

where $n = n_A + n_B$. McFadden (1989) noted that the Kolmogorov–Smirnov test could be modified to test the hypothesis of first-order stochastic dominance. The test statistic associated with the hypothesis that B first-order stochastically dominates A is

$$S_n^2 = \left(\frac{n_A n_B}{n}\right)^{1/2} \sup_{x \in Q \subset R} (\hat{A}_{n_A}(x) - \hat{B}_{n_B}(x)).$$

Without relatively strong assumptions on the distributions A and B, such as absolute continuity, the asymptotic distributions of the test statistics are intractable. As an alternative, a number of authors have worked on applying bootstrap and other resampling methods to nonparametric testing problems; two important papers in this literature are Romano (1988, 1989).

We follow Abadie (2002) in using a bootstrap procedure to compute the p-values of the test statistics (6.7) and (6.8) that circumvents the need for strong assumptions on A and B. This is a significant advantage in our application, since, as Abadie notes, the presence of heaping at the minimum wage is not consistent with a continuity assumption. Moreover self-reported (or proxy-reported) wage data, such as those we use in our empirical application, display large numbers of observations heaped at reporting "focal points" (which are typically integers). For all of these reasons the bootstrap methodology (or some other type of resampling procedure) has much to recommend it. The details of the bootstrap procedure that we use can be found in Abadie (2002), as well as a set of relatively weak regularity conditions sufficient to imply consistency.

6.4.2 Tests Utilizing Panel Data

The requirements for testing the third set of implications—those that pertain to individuals working at the same job before and after the minimum wage change who are paid more than the prevailing minimum wage in each period—are of a different nature. The result that was obtained applied to each and every individual who belonged to this set, and therefore was in theory "testable" if we had information on the requisite wage information for only *one* individual. Strictly speaking, no testing procedure is necessary to examine this implication.

In practice, wages are measured with error and there are many determinants of wage rates that are neglected in our modeling framework.

For example, the assumption of fixed wage rates at a given job match (in the absence of minimum wage changes) is clearly counterfactual. Particularly for young workers, such as those in our sample, empirical studies often find that there exists a substantial amount of wage growth for those remaining in the same job. Our strategy of dealing with these issues is admittedly somewhat ad hoc, but (we hope) reasonable. We compare the wage growth of those on the same job (to the extent to which we can perform this conditioning accurately) over years in which the minimum wage changes with the wage growth registered by job stayers over a year-long period that does not include a change in the nominal minimum wage. This amounts to the common difference-in-differences estimator often employed in empirical labor economics; the novel aspect of its use here arises from the fact that a partial equilibrium model has been employed to define which differences are the relevant ones to examine in assessing the welfare impact of a minimum wage change.

We conclude this section with a brief discussion of the general problem of nonstationarity to which we have just alluded. In comparing wage distributions at two points in time, our tests rely critically on the assumption of constancy of the economic environment. When two time points are separated by a substantial amount of time this assumption becomes untenable. There are essentially two avenues available to the analyst. The first is to modify the model so as to allow for limited forms of nonconstancy in the environment. For example, one could posit exogenous shifts in the matching distribution as a function of calendar time or the labor market age of participants. The principle disadvantage of such an approach is generally that it will no longer be possible to form nonparametric tests for the welfare impacts of minimum wage changes. Tests for welfare impacts of minimum wage changes will then only be consistent given the validity of the particular form of nonconstancy introduced into the model and the availability of consistent estimators of any parameters required to characterize the evolution of the environment.

Given our explicit interest in developing robust, nonparametric tests for welfare impacts, we have chosen a second route to minimize the problem of nonconstancy of the environment. Because we use Current Population Survey data in conducting the empirical exercises below, we have access to monthly information on wage distributions. As a result we have the opportunity to look at the impact of the minimum wage change immediately before and immediately after the change, with the observations on the wage distributions being separated only by (approximately) one month. Presumably any substantial changes in the economic environment would be unlikely over such a brief period of time, either at the aggregate or individual level.

6.5 Data and Empirical Results

The data used in the empirical work are drawn from the Current Population Survey, which was described in chapter 2. The first of the two minimum wage changes we examine occurred on October 1, 1996 (when there was an increase from $4.25 to $4.75 per hour), and the second took place on September 1, 1997 (when there was an increase from $4.75 to $5.15 per hour). Using the Outgoing Rotation Group (ORG) subsamples, we are able to compare the wage distributions for the month immediately proceeding the minimum wage change with the month immediately following it. To assess the welfare impact of the earlier minimum wage change, we compare the wage distribution of the September 1996 sample with that of the October 1996 sample (by the sampling design of the CPS these samples are independent in the sense that they do not contain wage observations on the same individuals). To assess the welfare impact of the more recent minimum wage increase that we consider, we compare the August 1997 and September 1997 wage distributions.

As a methodological exercise, we conduct the same tests comparing wage distributions centered on the date of the change in the mandated minimum wage but separated by a longer time interval (approximately five months on either "side" of the date of the minimum wage change). To examine the impact of the 1996 minimum wage change, we compare the monthly wage distributions from May 1996 and February 1997. We compare the monthly wage distributions from April 1997 and January 1998 to examine the impact of the 1997 minimum wage change.

To obtain further evidence on the validity of the tests we conduct, we also apply them to data from a period that spanned *no* change in the nominal minimum wage. The date on which we center the comparisons was October 1, 1998, so that the "one month" comparison involves the wage distributions for September and October 1998, while the "nine-month" comparison involves the wage distributions for May 1998 and February 1999. Since there was no minimum wage change in this period, the model implies that no significant shifts in the wage distributions should be observed.

To conduct the tests that involve comparisons of the wages earned by the same individual at two points in time we utilize information from the March CPS surveys of 1996 to 1998. In particular, we compare the wages of individuals who satisfy the test restrictions (i.e., are employed and paid more than the prevailing minimum wage in each period) in March of year t and March of year $t + 1$ and who work in the same industry-occupation category in both years). In this manner we form three matched samples: March 1996–7, March 1997–8, and March 1998–9. In the first two matched panels, the year long period between observations spans a nominal minimum wage change. The last matched panel does not span a minimum wage change and is essentially used for benchmark purposes.

We focus our attention on labor market participants between the ages of 16 and 24, inclusive. This age group has by far the largest proportion of employed members paid exactly at or within a few cents of the minimum wage, as we saw in chapter 2. We have reasoned that if the minimum wage is to have a substantial impact on the labor market outcomes and welfare of any particular group in the population, it is most likely to be this one.

Before turning to the results, we do want to provide a caveat for the reader to bear in mind when considering the results presented below. As with all event-type studies, we should be concerned with whether the date of the minimum wage change was anticipatable by individuals on the supply and demand side of the market. All minimum wage law changes are proposed and debated prior to enactment, so the date of a legal change is always a questionable marker to use. In the case of the 1997 minimum wage, this is especially true, since that change was included as part of the graduated increase in the federal minimum wage that began with the 1996 installment. In a partial equilibrium model (with no vacancy creation decisions on the part of firms), foreknowledge of future minimum wage changes would have no effect on firm behavior.[3] However, forward-looking individuals on the supply side of the market would alter their participation and job acceptance decisions due to the nonstationarity now present in the environment. For example, say that the value of unemployed search under existing minimum wage is $V_U(m)$ and under the new minimum, once it becomes law, is $V_U(m')$, with $V_U(m') > V_U(m)$. Let the date at which the new law is enacted be t (this is the date at which the impending change becomes known to the population of agents on the supply and demand sides of the market), and let the date of the change in the law be $t' > t$. Then the value of participation will be monotonically increasing over the time interval (t, t'). The unemployment rate will increase over this interval, as new participants enter the unemployment ranks, and will remain above its new steady state level until the effects of the new minimum wage change have "worn off." In the event analysis we conduct, we ignore the anticipation effect and all of the transitional dynamics associated with moving from one institutional environment to another.

6.5.1 Cross-sectional Wage Distribution Results

The empirical results from the cross-sectional comparisons are reported in table 6.1. For the comparisons of the unconditional wage distributions, we conducted tests of equality of the distributions and first-order stochastic dominance (i.e., that the later month's distributions dominates that of the earlier month). When comparing the conditional distributions, those that involve the wage observations in each month that were larger than the greatest of the two minimum wage rates, we compute the same two test statistics. The p-values associated with each test statistic are reported in the table.[4]

The first panel of the table contains information relevant to the evaluation of the minimum wage change that occurred in 1996. From the results reported in the first line, we see that the null hypothesis of equality of the distributions is strongly rejected. This is to be expected, since the distributions are very different (by construction) in their lower tails. In particular, there is no probability mass in the interval $[4.25, 4.75)$ for the October 1996 distribution while there is a substantial proportion of wage observations in that interval in September 1996. We also find strong evidence that the October 1996 wage distribution first-order stochastically dominates the September 1996 wage distribution. This implies that the value of search *could* have increased as a result of the minimum wage change but does not establish that it did.

The second line of table 6.1 reports test results based on the wage distributions for the same two months that are truncated from below at the larger minimum wage value, which in this case is 4.75 (all wages are strictly greater than 4.75). The test of equality indicates whether or not spillover is present. Given the p-value of 0.664, there is no evidence of spillover. The last column reports the test statistic and p-value for the test that the matching distribution is negative exponential. The null is strongly rejected, indicating that the matching distribution is not negative exponential.[5] Taken together, these findings suggest that, based on the cross-sectional wage distributional evidence, there is no evidence that the minimum wage change in 1996 had a significant impact on the value of search. The distributions on which these test statistics are

Table 6.1
Tests of distributional equality, first-order stochastic dominance, and a negative exponential distribution of match values (*p*-values)

Change in m	Months	Samples	n_0	n_1	Test statistics Equality	FOSD	EXP
4.25 to 4.75	9/96 and 10/96	$\{w_0 \geq 4.25, w_1 \geq 4.75\}$	1,575	1,527	3.288 (0.000)	0.070 (0.968)	—
		$\{w_0 > 4.75, w_1 > 4.75\}$	1,345	1,409	0.623 (0.664)	0.205 (0.816)	0.083 (0.000)
	5/96 and 2/97	$\{w_0 \geq 4.25, w_1 \geq 4.75\}$	1,473	1,514	4.044 (0.000)	0.000 (0.994)	—
		$\{w_0 > 4.75, w_1 > 4.75\}$	1,223	1,398	0.647 (0.636)	0.057 (0.976)	0.085 (0.000)
4.75 to 5.15	8/97 and 9/97	$\{w_0 \geq 4.75, w_1 \geq 5.15\}$	1,673	1,409	5.224 (0.000)	0.017 (0.989)	—
		$\{w_0 > 5.15, w_1 > 5.15\}$	1,338	1,280	1.235 (0.062)	1.235 (0.032)	0.071 (0.000)
	4/97 and 1/98	$\{w_0 \geq 4.75, w_1 \geq 5.15\}$	1,450	1,446	6.513 (0.000)	0.074 (0.966)	—
		$\{w_0 > 5.15, w_1 > 5.15\}$	1,087	1,309	1.334 (0.046)	1.334 (0.034)	0.075 (0.000)
No change	9/98 and 10/98	$\{w_0 \geq 5.15, w_1 \geq 5.15\}$	1,577	1,643	0.836 (0.344)	0.171 (0.822)	—
		$\{w_0 > 5.15, w_1 > 5.15\}$	1,479	1,552	0.755 (0.432)	0.341 (0.730)	0.076 (0.000)
	5/98 and 2/99	$\{w_0 \geq 5.15, w_1 \geq 5.15\}$	1,529	1,324	1.574 (0.006)	0.550 (0.434)	—
		$\{w_0 > 5.15, w_1 > 5.15\}$	1,428	1,256	1.286 (0.046)	0.679 (0.288)	0.071 (0.000)

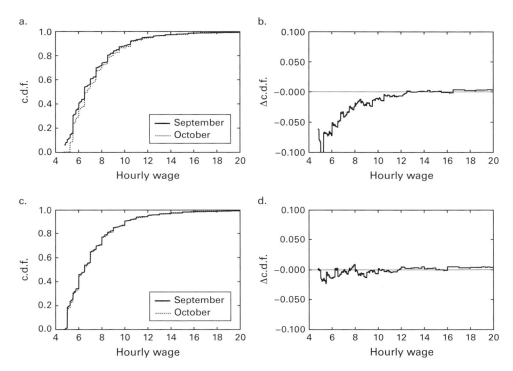

Figure 6.1
(a) Empirical unconditional c.d.f.s, September and October 1996 Current Population Survey data; (b) difference in October and September unconditional c.d.f.s; (c) empirical conditional c.d.f.s, September and October 1996 Current Population Survey data; (d) difference in October and September conditional c.d.f.s

based are presented in figure 6.1. In figure 6.1a and b we see the large differences in the unconditional wage distributions before and after the minimum wage change that account for the overwhelming rejection of the null hypothesis of equality. The lack of difference in the truncated wage distributions (figure 6.1c and d) can be seen from the small differences in these distributions for virtually all $w > 4.75$.

The results in lines 3 and 4 of table 6.1 repeat the exercise above but use months further removed from the date of the minimum wage change (May 1996 and February 1997). Once again, in terms of the unconditional wage distributions, the results are similar to what was observed when September and October 1996 were compared. There is strong evidence that the wage distributions are not equal, and there is strong evidence that the wage distribution in February 1997 first-order stochastically dominates the wage distribution in May 1996. The fact that the p-value is even higher than in line 1 is probably attributable to exogenous impacts such as price increases and productivity growth. The results in line 4 mirror those in line 2. There is no evidence of spillover from the comparison of the truncated wage distributions, and the test of whether this can be attributed to the matching distribution being negative exponential is once again decisively rejected. Based on these results, our (tentative) conclusions remain unchanged: there is no evidence that the minimum wage change of October 1996 significantly affected the value of search.

The middle panel of table 6.1 shows the results of our investigations of the minimum wage change that took place on September 1, 1997. Comparing the unconditional wage distributions of August and September 1997, we see there is there is no evidence of equality and strong evidence for the null hypothesis that the September wage distribution stochastically dominates the one observed in August. The results that pertain to the truncated distributions for the two months (with lower bound 5.15) are presented in the next line. In this case there is some limited evidence for spillover as indicated by the p-value associated with the test for distributional equality, though it is not strong. There is evidence against the null hypothesis that the truncated wage distribution in September first-order stochastically dominates the truncated wage distribution in August. As before, the null that the truncated wage distributions are negative exponential is rejected. Taken altogether, these results contain some qualified support for the notion that the minimum wage change of September 1997 did lead to a change in the value of unemployed search, and that the change could have been positive.

The histograms for the unconditional and conditional wage distributions in August and September 1997 are presented in figure 6.2. In terms of the unconditional wage distributions (figure 6.2a and b), the patterns observed are similar to what we observed in figure 6.1a and b. However, the relationship between the truncated wage distributions for the two months is very different than was the case for the previous regime shift. Figure 6.2d clearly indicates the reason for the rejection of the null hypothesis of stochastic dominance of the September (truncated) wage distribution with respect to the one of August.

When we reexamine the impact of the September 1997 minimum wage change using the April 1997 and January 1998 wage distributions, the results are very similar to what was found using the August and September 1997 wage distributions. In particular, there is a strong indication that the unconditional wage distributions are not equal and that the

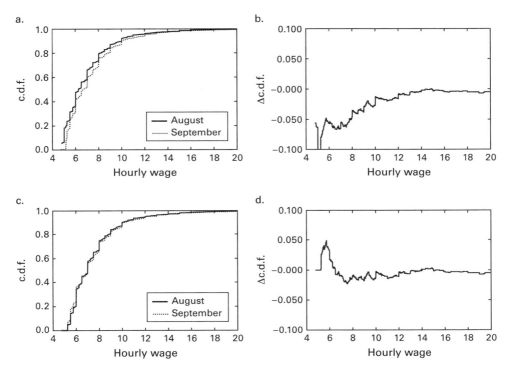

Figure 6.2
(a) Empirical unconditional c.d.f.s, August and September 1997 Current Population Survey data; (b) difference in August and September unconditional c.d.f.s; (c) empirical conditional c.d.f.s, August and September 1997 Current Population Survey data; (d) difference in August and September conditional c.d.f.s

January 1998 distribution first-order stochastically dominates the April 1997 distribution. In terms of the truncated wage distributions, there is evidence of spillover and no indication of stochastic dominance.

The last panel of the table presents test results from the comparison of wage distributions that span no nominal change in the minimum wage. The first line of the panel compares the wage distributions for September and October 1998. Since there is no minimum wage change, if the economic environment is constant the wage distributions should be equal. The p-value of 0.344 indicates that there is no strong evidence that the wage distributions are in fact different. The test for stochastic dominance provides some evidence that the wage distribution for October does stochastically dominate that of September, but we would argue that unless there is a strong indication that the distributions are unequal, the results of such a test should be ignored. The conditional wage distributions, those that involve only wage observations greater than 5.15, indicate that there was no evidence of spillover, which should indeed be the case if the economic environment was constant over this brief period—given no change in the minimum wage. The fact that there is evidence that the matching distribution is not negative exponential leads us to conclude that our test results indicate that there was no significant change in the value of search between the two months, as our model would predict.

This is not the case when we consider the longer interval stretching from May 1998 through February 1999. In this case the tests based on the unconditional distributions indicate that the distributions are not equal, and also that the February 1999 wage distribution first-order stochastically dominates the May 1998 distribution. The tests based on the truncated wage distributions also provide some indication of spillover. We believe that the differences among the results reported in the first two lines and the last two lines of the third panel can be attributed to the length of the measurement period. Comparing two distributions separated by a substantial length of time, even nine months, can lead to spurious findings of welfare changes. To measure the welfare impact of minimum wage changes in a robust manner, it is necessary to utilize wage information from before and after the minimum wage change that is separated by a reasonably small amount of time.

6.5.2 Empirical Analysis Using the Matched CPS Sample

In this section we utilize the matched CPS samples in an attempt to determine something about the welfare effects of the minimum wage changes of September 1996 and October 1997. In describing the CPS data, we noted that it is not possible to be absolutely certain that we have accurately matched individuals from the March surveys of year t and year $t + 1$, though our error rate should be small. More problematic for the utilization of the theoretical results that were derived in section 6.3 is our inability to determine whether the individual is working at the same job in the two periods. This is primarily due to the fact that the CPS does not collect any information on the length of time that individuals have been employed by their current employers. It is not possible to convincingly circumvent this problem, and our solution is admittedly problematic. We will think of individuals as being at the same job in the two periods if the industrial and occupational classification of their job is the same in March of years t and $t + 1$. In determining whether they are the same, we use a relatively crude classification system that distinguishes between about 15 occupational and 20 industrial categories. While we could have utilized three-digit occupation and industry codes, we felt that reporting error, especially given the problem of proxy respondents, would have resulted in too few individuals being classified as "stayers."

To utilize the analytic results from section 6.3, we impose the following restrictions on the matched samples: For the matched sample of March 1996 and March 1997 records, we only include individuals who were paid more than $4.25 in 1996 and $4.75 in 1997. To be included in the matched sample of 1997 and 1998, individuals must earn more than $4.75 in 1997 and more than $5.15 in 1998. Finally, for our "baseline" matched sample of 1998 and 1999, individuals were required to report wages greater than $5.15 in each March survey. After imposing the additional requirement that the individual be employed in the same industry-occupation category in both years, our final samples sizes were 115, 92, and 145 for the 1996–7, 1997–8, and 1998–9 matched panels, respectively. Selected moments of the wage distributions for each panel are presented in table 6.2.

The first thing to note is that the average wage in each of the matched samples that span an increase in the nominal minimum wage increased markedly from the first year of the panel to the second (row 4 of the table). Under our model this could only result from an increase in the value of search attributable to the minimum wage change. There are a number of reasons for us to question this inference, however. First, corollary 15 implies that the mean wage should not have risen by more than $0.50 in the 1996–7 panel or more than $0.40 in the 1997–8 panel. Furthermore for the 1998–9 panel, in which there was no intervening minimum wage increase, there should have been no mean wage change, instead of the large positive increase that was observed.

Second, and related to this last point, is the fact that the mean wage changes registered in the matched samples that spanned a minimum wage increase were actually smaller in absolute value than was the increase observed for the sample in which the wage observations did not span a minimum wage increase (last column of the fourth row). In particular, the average wage changed by $1.18 in the panel with no minimum wage change, as opposed to $0.94 and $1.02 for the panels in which the nominal minimum wage changed. If we consider the panel that spans no minimum wage change as measuring the baseline growth in wages recorded by individuals who stay at the same employer, then there is no evidence that the minimum wage changes of the earlier

Table 6.2
Selected sample moments matched CPS samples, March 1996 to March 1999

	1996–1997	1997–1998	1998–1999
Δm	0.50	0.40	0.00
$\overline{w}_1$	8.016	7.678	7.917
$\overline{w}_2$	8.952	8.692	9.097
$\overline{w}_2 - \overline{w}_1$	0.936	1.015	1.180
$\hat{\sigma}_1$	3.371	3.298	3.561
$\hat{\sigma}_2$	3.939	3.941	4.287
$\hat{\sigma}_{1,2}$	10.065	9.774	8.503
$\hat{\rho}$	0.758	0.752	0.557
$\hat{\sigma}_{w_2-w_1}$	2.596	2.617	3.749
N	115	92	145

years boosted the rate of wage growth through increases in bargaining leverage.

Third, our comparisons of cross-sectional wage distributions have illustrated the problems with assuming constancy of the economic environment over periods of time even as short as nine months. Therefore, aside from the problems of within job wage growth, there is real potential for the environmental parameters to change markedly over a period as long as a year. Given the structure of the CPS, there is no way to obtain a matched sample of individuals (with wage observations) over any shorter period. Other panel data sets could be used for this purpose, though by construction they will not be as representative of the US population as is the CPS.

Putting these caveats aside for the moment, let us briefly consider whether other moments appearing in table 6.2 are roughly consistent with the implications of the model. The strong, and clearly counterfactual, result in corollary 15 implies that the variance of wage changes should be 0 in all of our matched samples. A necessary condition for this to be true would be for the correlation in wages in the two periods to be 1. The correlation between wage observations appears in the third from last row of the table. While the estimated correlation is quite high, at least in the 1996–1997 and 1997–1998 panels, it is clearly not 1. The second from bottom row of the table contains the standard deviation of the wage differences for the three samples. The variance of the wage differences is clearly not equal to zero in any period. Although this strong implication from the model does not hold empirically, there is no doubt that a substantial amount of the variance is attributable to individuals not holding the same job at the two points in time, in addition to garden-variety measurement error in wage reporting.

We have raised a number of issues concerning the inferences it is possible to draw based on the matched CPS samples of individuals whose wages were strictly greater than the minimum wage in each year of the panel and who were employed in the same industry-occupation category. To obtain more valid measures under our model, one would have to access to wage observations on these individuals considerably closer in time than one year. However, we can cautiously advance the interpretation that there is no panel evidence that points to significant welfare gains as a result of changes in the nominal minimum wage in 1996 and 1997.

7   Econometric Issues

7.1   Identification of Choice-Theoretic Search Models

Perhaps the most basic issue treated in applied econometrics exercises is that of identification.[1] Koopmans (1949, p. 132), who originated the term, described the concept as follows:

> In our discussion we have used the phrase "a parameter that can be determined from a sufficient number of observations." We shall now define this concept more sharply, and give it the name *identifiability* of the parameter.

To discuss identification, one needs a model that is characterized in terms of some parameter set Γ, say, a data set, denoted by Z_N, and a class of estimators one is considering, which we will denote by A. The data set is indexed by N, the number of observations, and we will consider the case in which the information in Z_N is a random sample of N draws from the population distribution of labor market outcomes. Elements of the set of possible estimators are just functions of the data Z_N that do not depend on the actual values of the parameters Γ. We will denote a generic element of the set of estimators by a so that an estimate is just $a(Z_N)$. Heuristically speaking, a parameter is identified if there is potential information about its true value that is obtainable from at least some possible data realizations Z_N. On a practical level, we might say that a set of parameters Γ_j is identified if there exists at least one estimator $a_j \in A$ such that

$$\Gamma_j = \plim_{N \to \infty} (a_j(Z_N)).$$

This limited statement attempts to convey the notation that with any given data set Z_N, a parameter may be identified under one set of estimators but not others. By focusing on a subvector of Γ, Γ_j, we want to emphasize that a subset of model parameters may be identifiable while another subset is not. Finally, the fact that we use probability limits here to define identifiability implies that in any finite sample, Z_N, there may not be enough information to obtain an estimate of Γ_j, but as sample size increases there will be almost surely.[2] We are particularly concerned about identification in this book, since the policy experiments we wish to perform require us to have access to "credible" estimates of all of the parameters that characterize the model.

The identification of parameters characterizing an equilibrium search with bargaining model are complex. Fortunately, there is a substantial body of accumulated knowledge regarding the estimation of choice-theoretic (i.e., nonequilibrium) and partial equilibrium search models. The first systematic treatment of identification issues in choice-theoretic search models was conducted by Flinn and Heckman (1982). The authors considered identification in a model similar to our partial equilibrium model, with the exception that the value of α was assumed to be equal to 1.[3] In this case the unknown "primitive" parameters of the model consist of ρ, the instantaneous discount rate, b, the instantaneous utility yield associated with being unemployed, λ, the rate of arrival of job offers, η, the rate of dismissals, and F, the exogenously determined wage offer distribution. Given access to information on (1) accepted wages, (2) the duration of time engaged in search prior to accepting a job, and (3) durations of employment spells, Flinn and Heckman found that all of the parameters could be uniquely identified, with the exception of the parameters ρ and b, under the assumption that $F \in F_R$, where F_R denotes a set of parametric distributions which were termed *recoverable* by Flinn and Heckman.[4] They showed that given that F had the recoverability property, the data were sufficient to consistently estimate either b or ρ given knowledge of the other one.

The Flinn and Heckman (1982) identification analysis was predicated on the assumption that there was no measurement error in the wage data and that the population from which the sample was drawn was homogeneous (i.e., all sample members shared exactly the same labor market environment in terms of the primitive parameters of the model). They recognized that in this case a consistent estimator of the decision rule of the searcher, w^*, was given by the minimum observed wage in the sample, or

$$\hat{w}^* = \min(w_1, \ldots, w_{N_E}),$$

(7.1)

where $(w_1, \ldots, w_{N_E})$ denotes the vector of observed wage rates in the sample and N_E is the number of employed sample members. They formed a "concentrated" maximum likelihood estimator of F, λ, and η that was conditional on the estimated value $\hat{w}^*$. This concentrated likelihood function is developed as follows.

We begin by considering the probability of finding someone in the unemployment state at some randomly selected moment in time. Think of a labor market "cycle" as consisting of a spell of unemployment followed by a spell of employment. If we sample someone during a cycle, what is the probability that they will be in the unemployment part of it? As long as the expected value of spells of unemployment and employment are both well defined, then the average duration of a cycle is $E(t_U + t_E) = E(t_U) + E(t_E)$. The average proportion of time spent in the unemployment state in an average cycle is the long-run, or steady state, probability of finding an agent in the unemployment state at any randomly selected moment in time, or

$$p(U) = \frac{E(t_U)}{E(t_U) + E(t_E)}.$$

Since the durations of spells in both the unemployment and employment states are exponentially distributed, we have

$$E(t_E) = \eta^{-1},$$

$$E(t_U) = [\lambda \tilde{F}(w^*)]^{-1},$$

so that

$$p(U) = \frac{[\lambda \tilde{F}_w(w^*)]^{-1}}{\eta^{-1} + [\lambda \tilde{F}(w^*)]^{-1}}$$

$$= \frac{\eta}{\eta + \lambda \tilde{F}(w^*)}.$$

Knowing that someone is found in the unemployment state at a given moment in time, we need to define the probability distribution associated with duration of the ongoing unemployment spell. We will denote this probability density by $f_U^b(t_U)$, where the "b" superscript refers to the fact that this is the backward recurrence time density.[5] The likelihood that the ongoing unemployment spell has not ended by duration t_u when the individual is sampled is simply the probability that the duration of the unemployment spell is at least t_u, or $\tilde{F}_u(t_u)$. To ensure that the probability density of ongoing unemployment spells is a proper one (i.e., that it integrates to 1) requires that

$$\int_0^\infty f_U^b(x)\,dx = 1$$

$$\Rightarrow f_U^b(t_U) = \frac{\tilde{F}_U(t_U)}{\int_0^\infty \tilde{F}_U(x)\,dx}.$$

It is well known that $\int_0^\infty \tilde{F}_U(x)\,dx = E_U(t_u)$ (when this expectation exists) for positive-valued random variables, so for our application we have

$$f_U^b(t_U) = \frac{\exp\left(-\lambda\tilde{F}(w^*)t_U\right)}{E_U(t)}$$

$$= \frac{\exp\left(-\lambda\tilde{F}(w^*)t_U\right)}{[\lambda\tilde{F}(w^*)]^{-1}}$$

$$= \lambda\tilde{F}(w^*)\exp\left(-\lambda\tilde{F}(w^*)t_U\right),$$

which is simply the population distribution of unemployment spells. This result only holds when the population distribution is of the negative exponential form. Then the likelihood of finding a randomly sampled agent in an ongoing unemployment spell of duration t is

$$L(t_U, U) = f_U^b(t_U)p(U)$$

$$= \lambda\tilde{F}(w^*)\exp\left(-\lambda\tilde{F}(w^*)t_U\right) \times \frac{\eta}{\eta + \lambda\tilde{F}(w^*)}.$$

Now consider the case of employment. The probability of finding an individual in the midst of an employment spell at a given moment in time is simply $p(E) = 1 - p(U)$. We have no spell duration information for people found to be employed at the time of the survey, but we do observe their wage. Assuming that wages are measured without error, the likelihood of finding an individual employed at a moment in time and earning a wage of w is

$$L(w, E) = \frac{f(w)}{\tilde{F}(w^*)} \times \frac{\lambda\tilde{F}(w^*)}{\eta + \lambda\tilde{F}(w^*)}$$

$$= \frac{\lambda f(w)}{\eta + \lambda\tilde{F}(w^*)}.$$

The likelihood for the random sample of N individuals is then

$$L(w_1, \ldots, w_{N_E}; t_1, \ldots, t_{N_U}) = \prod_{i \in S_E} \left[\frac{\lambda f(w)}{\eta + \lambda \tilde{F}(w^*)} \right]$$

$$\times \prod_{i \in S_U} \left[\frac{\eta \lambda \tilde{F}(w^*) \exp\left(-\lambda \tilde{F}(w^*) t_i \right)}{\eta + \lambda \tilde{F}(w^*)} \right],$$

where S_i denotes the set of sample members who are in state i at the time of the survey, for $i = E, U$. Then the log likelihood of the sample is

$$\ln L = -N \ln \left(\eta + \lambda \tilde{F}(w^*) \right) + N \ln \lambda + N_U \ln \left(\tilde{F}(w^*; \mu) \right)$$

$$+ N_U \ln (\eta) + \sum_{i \in S_E} \ln \left(f(w_i) \right) - \lambda \tilde{F}(w^*) \sum_{i \in S_U} t_i. \tag{7.2}$$

The concentrated log likelihood is obtained after we insert the consistent estimate of the reservation wage, or

$$\ln L^c = -N \ln \left(\eta + \lambda \tilde{F}(\hat{w}^*) \right) + N \ln \lambda + N_U \ln \left(\tilde{F}(\hat{w}^*) \right)$$

$$+ N_U \ln (\eta) + \sum_{i \in S_E} \ln \left(f(w_i) \right) - \lambda \tilde{F}(\hat{w}^*) \sum_{i \in S_U} t_i, \tag{7.3}$$

where $\hat{w}^*$ is defined in (7.1). With L^c formally defined, we can now consider a few basic identification issues with regards to this model.

Maximum likelihood estimators derived from the concentrated log likelihood function $\ln L^c$ will be the solutions to the set of first-order conditions

$$\frac{\partial \ln L^c}{\partial \Gamma} = 0,$$

where the parameter vector $\Gamma = (\eta \ \lambda \ \mu)$, and where μ is the vector of parameters that characterize the (recoverable) p.d.f. of wages, f. Note that the first-order condition associated with η is

$$\frac{\partial \ln L^c}{\partial \eta} = 0 \tag{7.4}$$

$$\Rightarrow \quad 0 = -\frac{N}{\eta + \lambda \tilde{F}(\hat{w}^*)} + \frac{N_U}{\eta}$$

$$\Rightarrow \quad \frac{N_U}{N} = \left(\widehat{\frac{\eta}{\eta + \lambda \tilde{F}(\hat{w}^*)}} \right)$$

$$= \widehat{p(U)}.$$

Thus the proportion of sample members who are unemployed at the time of the survey is the maximum likelihood estimator of the steady state probability of finding an individual in the unemployment state. This allows us to "reconcentrate," or further concentrate, the log likelihood function after substituting the maximum likelihood estimator of the steady state probability of unemployment. While performing this further concentration is gratuitous from the perspective of the calculation of maximum likelihood estimates of identified parameters, it is very useful from the point of view of identification analysis.

The reconcentrated log likelihood function has the form

$$\ln L^{cc} = -N_E \ln (\tilde{F}(\hat{w}^*)) + \sum_{i \in S_E} \ln (f(w_i))$$

$$+ N_U \ln (\lambda) + N_U \ln (\tilde{F}(\hat{w}^*)) - \lambda \tilde{F}(\hat{w}^*) \sum_{i \in S_U} t_i,$$

so that the parameters that characterize the reconcentrated log likelihood are only λ and μ. The first-order condition associated with λ is

$$\frac{\partial \ln L^{cc}(\hat{\lambda}, \hat{\mu})}{\partial \lambda} = \frac{N_U}{\hat{\lambda}} - \tilde{F}_w(\hat{w}^*; \hat{\mu}) \sum_{i \in S_U} t_i = 0 \qquad (7.5)$$

$$\Rightarrow \hat{\lambda} = \frac{N_U}{\tilde{F}(\hat{w}^*) \sum_{i \in S_U} t_i}$$

$$= \frac{1}{\bar{t} \tilde{F}_w(\hat{w}^*)},$$

where $\bar{t}$ is the sample mean of the ongoing unemployment spell lengths for the subsample of individuals unemployed at the time of the survey. The first-order condition(s) associated with the parameter(s) μ are

$$\frac{\partial \ln L^{cc}(\hat{\lambda}, \hat{\mu})}{\partial \mu} = 0 = \frac{\partial \tilde{F} \hat{w}^*)}{\partial \mu} \left(\frac{N_U - N_E}{\tilde{F}(\hat{w}^*)} - \lambda \sum_{i \in S_u} t_i \right)$$

$$+ \sum_{i \in S_e} \frac{\partial f(w_i)}{\partial \mu} f(w_i)^{-1}. \qquad (7.6)$$

The maximum likelihood estimators of the parameters λ and μ are determined as the solutions to (7.5) and (7.6), when these solutions exist. However, without further assumptions on the distribution function of wage offers, F, there is no guarantee that the solutions are unique.

Given the maximum likelihood estimates $(\hat{\lambda}, \hat{\mu}, \hat{w}^*)$, the first-order condition given in (7.4) can be used to solve for $\hat{\eta}(\hat{\lambda}, \hat{\mu})$, since

$$0 = -\frac{N}{\hat{\eta} + \hat{\lambda}\tilde{F}_w(\hat{w}^*; \hat{\mu})} + \frac{N_U}{\hat{\eta}}$$

$$\Rightarrow \hat{\eta} = \frac{N_U \hat{\lambda}\tilde{F}_w(\hat{w}^*; \hat{\mu})}{N_E}.$$

Finally, with maximum likelihood estimates of $(\hat{\eta}, \hat{\lambda}, \hat{\mu}, \hat{w}^*)$, we can use the reservation wage function to solve for either b or ρ. Simply replacing unknown parameter values with consistent estimates when available, we have

$$\hat{w}^* = b + \frac{\hat{\lambda}}{\rho + \hat{\eta}} \int_{\hat{w}^*} (w - \hat{w}^*) \, d\hat{F}(w). \tag{7.7}$$

Clearly, knowledge of ρ is enough to uniquely determine b, and vice versa. The key features of the data utilized in model identification were the smallest wage observation in the sample, the mean duration of ongoing search spells, the proportion of the sample engaged in search, and other characteristics of the sample wage distribution (exactly which features of the sample distribution of wages depends on the functional form assumption made regarding F). It was the key dependence of all model parameter estimates on the smallest wage observed in the sample, $\hat{w}^*$, that led to the development of other model specifications and identification strategies that allowed for the possibility of measurement error in observed wages (Wolpin 1987).

7.2 Estimation of the Bargaining Model

Given the data to which we have access, which is a point-in-time sample, the CPS will not be particularly useful for learning much about the vacancy creation process. That is, there will be an equilibrium value of the contact rate, from the perspective of searchers, that is given by $\lambda = q(k)/k$, where $k \equiv \tilde{U}/v$ and $\tilde{U} = Ul$, with U being the proportion unemployed in the labor market and l the proportion of individuals participating in the labor market. While we will be able to provide conditions under which $\tilde{U}$ is estimable from the CPS data, reliable data on vacancies are not available. We will show that given an estimator for λ based on the CPS data, and a consistent estimator for $\tilde{U}$, we will be able to estimate the steady state vacancy rate v if the function q contains no unknown parameters. In this case, estimating v given q or simply estimating λ are equivalent. For this reason the bulk of our identification analysis assumes a fixed value of λ. At the end of this section we consider the estimation of parameters relevant to the vacancy creation process.

We begin our analysis by laying out the information content of the CPS data for purposes of estimating the labor market model developed above. We will see that a major stumbling block to the estimation of such a model is the identification of the bargaining power parameter α. The difficulties of estimating the bargaining power parameter have been appreciated for quite some time. In their discussion of an estimable equilibrium search model, Flinn and Heckman (FH) impose the assumption that the match value (θ here) is split evenly between the firm and worker, but provide little justification for doing so (pp. 142–43). Kooremen and Kapteyn (1990) provide an enlightening discussion and example of the identification of a "sharing" parameter, much like our α, in the context of a cooperative household labor supply model. Eckstein and Wolpin (1995) provide a deeper discussion than FH of the problem of identifying α when using only supply side data, and impose the restriction $\alpha = 0.5$ when estimating their model. The same authors revisit this issue at a later date (Eckstein and Wolpin 1999), and in that research use a clever restriction on the model to obtain an upper bound estimate of the black-white difference in the logarithm of the share parameter (akin to our α). Like FH and Eckstein and Wolpin (1995), they assume that wages are a constant proportion of the match value θ, which is not the case in the model estimated here.

A number of studies using aggregated time series data have obtained estimates of α, as well as of the matching function in some cases. The most comparable to ours is that of Yashiv (2000), in which he estimates the bargaining power parameter and a Cobb–Douglas matching function parameter using aggregate time series data from Israel. Macroeconomic time series studies can potentially avail themselves of information on vacancies, unemployment rates, wage distributions, and firm profitability. The major limitation of these studies is the necessity of relying on a representative agent formulation of the economy, which neglects individual and firm heterogeneity for the most part. This feature is a particular liability when looking at policies with potentially strong distributional impacts, such as the minimum wage.

The recent availability of matched employer–employee data has led to the availability of information on firm performance measures as well as employee characteristics. Cahuc et al. (2006) use French data of this type to estimate a bargaining model, and utilize methods similar to that employed here to identify the bargaining power parameter for different classes of employees. They use a different matching structure in which the match value is given by $\theta = A \times B$, where A is the fixed productivity characteristic value of the worker and B is the productivity characteristic of the firm, and they allow for on-the-job search and contract negotiation as in Postel-Vinay and Robin (2002) and Dey and Flinn (2005). With this matching structure they are able to recover estimates of the distributions of A and B for the firms and workers in their large sample. This specification of match heterogeneity is particularly useful with these types of data, since it is able to generate systematic firm size differences, something that our i.i.d. match heterogeneity distribution cannot. Presumably a minimum wage could be introduced into their model as well, and it would have similar impacts to those produced by the models estimated by Eckstein and Wolpin (1990) and van den Berg and Ridder (1998) in that low-quality firms would drop out of the market, a result beneficial in terms of the equilibrium wage distribution, which comes at the cost of a reduction in contact rates.

We will explore a number of ways in which the model can be estimated using the CPS data available to us (and in one case auxiliary information from other sources), although some of these will be mentioned only in passing. Possible approaches to the underidentification problem include (1) normalization, (2) the use of demand side information, (3) the use of observable heterogeneity in conjunction with exclusion restrictions, and (4) natural experiments. Each approach has its drawbacks, though we will argue that method 2 provides the most "robust" method for model identification if one is willing to make some distributional assumptions. We will present model estimates based on approach 2.

In most empirical implementations of search models an allowance is made for measurement error in the wage data (but not in the duration measures). Allowing for measurement error may be indicated when the sample contains very low wage observations, which without measurement error would imply a perhaps incredibly small reservation wage. When allowing for on-the-job search, which we do in chapter 10, measurement error is required for the model of expected wealth maximization to be consistent with direct job-to-job transitions in which the destination job offers a lower wage than the job which was left.[6]

In the presence of a binding minimum wage, it is not possible to add "classical" measurement error to the model. If the reported wage distribution is assumed to be given by the convolution of the distribution of actual wages and some continuous i.i.d. random variable, then even though the true wage distribution is of the mixed continuous-discrete type, the observed wage distribution will be absolutely continuous. Since this is inconsistent with even the most casual inspection of the data (see table 2.1), classical measurement error cannot be introduced. While one could consider allowing for "contamination" in the data, namely that some unknown proportion τ of wages are measured with classical error while the remainder are not, the estimation of τ would seem not to be possible without further arbitrary assumptions. As a result we assume throughout that all observations are measured exactly. While we have already noted that a large number of observations are "heaped" at focal points, the hope is that the regular pattern of the heaping process will not bias our estimates to any great degree.

The likelihood function based on the CPS data is constructed as follows: Each individual observation can be characterized by the pair of observations (t_i, w_i), $i = 1, \ldots, N$. The variable t_i is the length of the ongoing spell of unemployed search, which is positive if the sample member is unemployed at the time of the survey and is otherwise equal to 0. If the individual is employed, the hourly wage w_i is recorded. If the individual is paid an hourly wage, w_i corresponds to the hourly wage rate they report. If the individual is not paid on an hourly basis, the hourly rate is imputed by dividing the gross weekly wage by the usual hours of work per week. This imputation procedure is standard but is particularly problematic in this application because of the likely undercount of individuals paid exactly the minimum wage that will result. On the positive side, the vast majority of our sample members report an hourly wage rate, so the imputation procedure has to be utilized for less than 20 percent of the sample in any given month.

There are essentially three components of the likelihood function, one for the unemployed, one for the employed paid the minimum wage, and one for those paid more than the minimum. Let us first consider the contribution of a sample member who is unemployed with an ongoing unemployment spell of length t. Given being in the unemployed state, the likelihood of finding someone in an ongoing spell of length t in the steady state is given by $f_U^*(t) \equiv \tilde{F}_U(t)/E(t)$, where $\tilde{F}_U$ is the population survivor function of unemployment durations and $E(t)$ is the population mean duration of unemployment spells. As we showed above, when the population unemployment spell duration distribution is of the negative exponential form, $f_U^*(t)$ is equal to the population density $f_U(t)$.

Thus, given unemployment, the density associated with an on-going spell length of t is

$$f_U(t|U) = \lambda \tilde{G}(m) \exp\left(-\lambda \tilde{G}(m)t\right),$$

where the acceptance match value of m presumes the existence of a binding minimum wage (in the absence of one m is replaced by ρV_U in the expression above). As we have seen,

$$p(U) = \frac{\eta}{\eta + \lambda \tilde{G}(m)},$$

so the joint likelihood of (t, U) is given by

$$f(t, U) = \frac{\eta \lambda \tilde{G}(m) \exp\left(-\lambda \tilde{G}(m)t\right)}{\eta + \lambda \tilde{G}(m)}.$$

Next we consider the likelihood contribution of an individual who is paid the minimum wage m. We will assume that whenever two or more population members are paid the minimum wage m, the minimum wage is binding for their population type. Then conditional on employment the likelihood of being paid m is given by

$$p(w = m|E) = \frac{\tilde{G}(m) - \tilde{G}\left\{[m - (1-\alpha)\rho V_U(m)]/\alpha\right\}}{\tilde{G}(m)}.$$

The likelihood of observing $(w = m, E)$ is

$$p(w = m, E) = \frac{\lambda[\tilde{G}(m) - \tilde{G}\left\{[m - (1-\alpha)\rho V_U(m)]/\alpha\right\}}{\eta + \lambda \tilde{G}(m)}.$$

The contribution of individuals paid more than the minimum wage is determined as follows: To be paid a wage $w > m$, it must be the case that the match value exceeds $(m - (1-\alpha)\rho V_U(m))/\alpha$. Thus the likelihood of being a paid a wage w given employment and $w > m$ is

$$f(w|w > m, E) = \frac{\frac{1}{\alpha}g\left\{[w - (1-\alpha)\rho V_U(m)/\alpha]\right\}}{\tilde{G}\left\{[m - (1-\alpha)\rho V_U(m)/\alpha]\right\}}.$$

Furthermore the probability that a sample member is paid a wage greater than m given that she is employed is

$$p(w > m|E) = \frac{\tilde{G}\left\{[m - (1-\alpha)\rho V_U(m)]/\alpha\right\}}{\tilde{G}(m)},$$

so the likelihood contribution for such an individual is given by

$$f(w, w > m, E) = \frac{\frac{1}{\alpha} g \left\{ [w - (1-\alpha)\rho V_U(m)]/\alpha \right\}}{\tilde{G} \left\{ [m - (1-\alpha)\rho V_U(m)]/\alpha \right\}}$$

$$\times \frac{\tilde{G} \left\{ [m - (1-\alpha)\rho V_U(m)]/\alpha \right\}}{\tilde{G}(m)} \frac{\lambda \tilde{G}(m)}{\eta + \lambda \tilde{G}(m)}$$

$$= \frac{\frac{\lambda}{\alpha} g \left\{ [w - (1-\alpha)\rho V_U(m)]/\alpha \right\}}{\eta + \lambda \tilde{G}(m)}.$$

The log likelihood for the parameters describing the labor market environment of a given population can be written as

$$\ln L = N[\ln(\lambda) - \ln(\eta + \lambda \tilde{G}(m))] + N_U[\ln(\eta) + \tilde{G}(m)]$$

$$- \lambda \tilde{G}(m) \sum_{i \in S_U} t_i + N_M \ln \left(\tilde{G}(m) - \tilde{G} \left(\frac{m - (1-\alpha)\theta^*}{\alpha} \right) \right)$$

$$- N_H \ln(\alpha) + \sum_{i \in S_H} \ln \left(g \left(\frac{w_i - (1-\alpha)\theta^*}{\alpha} \right) \right), \tag{7.8}$$

where N_M is the number of sample members paid the minimum wage, N_H is the number paid more than the minimum wage (and $N_E = N_M + N_H$), S_H is the set of indexes of sample members who are paid more than the minimum wage, and $\theta^* \equiv \rho V_n(m)$ is the "implicit" reservation wage in this population. Recall that G will be assumed to belong to a parametric family, so it can be characterized in terms of a finite-dimensional parameter vector μ. Then the parameters that appear "directly" in the log likelihood are λ, η, μ, α, and θ^*. The value θ^* is not a primitive parameter per se but rather is a scalar that is determined endogenously and is a function of all the parameters of the model, including ρ and b. For purposes of estimation, however, we will treat it as a parameter of the model.[7]

7.3 Model Identification

We now present a discussion of the identification of the model using only CPS data. We begin by considering the case in which there is no binding minimum wage. After describing the identification problems faced in this case we will be in a better position to understand the situation in which a binding minimum wage is present.

Before we begin, let us review the identification results of FH, which are particularly relevant here. They demonstrated that the basic search model with only accepted wage and duration information is fundamentally underidentified, even in the absence of bargaining (i.e., $\alpha = 1$). In particular, they showed that a parametric assumption on G was required, and that only certain distributions with support on a subset of R_+ were identified even under parametric assumptions. In the case we consider here, that of parametric G with support given by R_+, all members of this class of distributions satisfy what they term the "recoverability condition." Thus we need not consider this particular problem further.

They also demonstrated that the parameters (ρ, b) were not individually identified, essentially since they both enter the likelihood function only through the critical value θ^*. Because of this we can treat θ^* as a parameter to be estimated without loss of generality. When all parameter estimates have been obtained, the functional equation that determines θ^* may be used with point estimates of all identified parameters to "back out "the locus of estimates of (ρ, b). This is the procedure followed here. Thus we do not discuss identification of ρ and b explicitly below but instead consider identification of θ^* along with the other true primitive parameters of the model.

7.3.1   No Minimum Wage

We begin by writing the log likelihood function for this problem in a transparent manner:

$$\ln L = N \ln h_U - N \ln D + N_U \ln \eta - h_U \sum_{i \in S_U} t_i$$

$$+ \sum_{i \in S_H} \ln \frac{\frac{1}{\alpha} g \left\{ [w_i - (1-\alpha)\theta^*]/\alpha \right\}}{\tilde{G}(\theta^*)}, \tag{7.9}$$

where $h_U \equiv \lambda \tilde{G}(\theta^*)$ and $D \equiv \eta + h_U$. Just as η is the hazard rate from the employment state, h_U is the hazard rate from the unemployment state; it is defined as the product of the rate of arrival of offers and the probability that an offer will be acceptable. Without auxiliary information to enable the identification of G, it will be impossible to disentangle the two components of h_U.

In discussing identification rigorously, we will need to work with a class of matching distributions. For reasons that will become clear, we will work with distributions with support R_+ that belong to a location-scale family.[8] To be precise, the distribution $G(x; c, d)$ belongs to a location-scale family if and only if

$$G(x; c, d) = G_0 \left(\frac{x - c}{d} \right),$$

where $c \in R$ and $d \in R_+$ are two constants and G_0 is a known function. Assuming that G is continuously differentiable on its support R_+, we have

$$g(x; c, d) = \frac{1}{d} g_0 \left(\frac{x - c}{d} \right)$$

as the probability density function of x. Many commonly used parametric distributions in economics belong to this class.

Given that G belongs to a location-scale family, we can rewrite the last term in (7.9) as follows:

$$\frac{\frac{1}{\alpha} g \left\{ [w_i - (1 - \alpha)\theta^*]/\alpha; c, d \right\}}{\tilde{G}(\theta^*; c, d)} = \frac{\frac{1}{\alpha d} g_0 \left\{ [w_i - (1 - \alpha)\theta^* - \alpha c]/\alpha d \right\}}{\tilde{G}_0 [(\theta^* - c)/d]}.$$

Since $w^* = \theta^*$ when there is no binding minimum wage, we can write

$$w^* = \alpha \theta^* + (1 - \alpha)\theta^*,$$

or

$$\theta^* = \frac{w^* - (1 - \alpha)\theta^*}{\alpha}.$$

Substituting this expression into the denominator, we arrive at

$$\frac{\frac{1}{\alpha d} g_0 \left\{ [w_i - (1 - \alpha)\theta^* - \alpha c]/\alpha d \right\}}{\tilde{G}_0 \{[(w^* - (1 - \alpha)\theta^*)/\alpha - c]/d\}} = \frac{\frac{1}{\alpha d} g_0 \left\{ [w_i - (1 - \alpha)\theta^* - \alpha c]/\alpha d \right\}}{\tilde{G}_0 \left\{ [w^* - (1 - \alpha)\theta^* - \alpha c]/\alpha d \right\}}.$$

This is the p.d.f. of a random variable with a truncated location-scale distribution, with lower truncation point w^*. The "new" location parameter is

$$c' = (1 - \alpha)\theta^* + \alpha c,$$

and the new scale parameter is

$$d' = \alpha d.$$

Since a superconsistent estimator for θ^* ($= w^*$) is available, the two parameters c' and d' will be a function of three unknown parameters: α, c, and d.

Let us begin with the easiest problem, that of estimating the parameters η and h_U. Forming estimators of these two parameters in the bargaining case is identical to the situation that pertained in the case of an exogenous wage offer distribution F. That is, maximum likelihood estimates of these two parameters are given by

$$\hat{h}_U = \frac{N_U}{\sum_{i \in U} t_i}$$

and

$$\hat{\eta} = \frac{N_U^2 / \sum_{i \in U} t_i}{N_E}.$$

Note that the estimators of η and h_U are independent of the specification of G. Of course, the specification of G will be critical in "decomposing" h_U into the products of the terms λ and $\tilde{G}(\theta^*)$.

We now consider the more difficult problem, that of identifying the parameters (c, d, α, θ^*). As in the exogenous wage offer distribution case, a (super)consistent estimator for θ^* is

$$\hat{\theta}^* = \hat{w}^* = \min_{i \in E}\{w_i\}.$$

This estimator converges at rate N. Since all other estimators in our model converge at rate $\sqrt{N}$, we can simply treat $\hat{\theta}^*$ as equal to θ^* when deriving the $\sqrt{N}$ asymptotic sampling distributions for these estimators, as originally noted in FH.

Now we are left with the determination of the three unknown parameters that appear only in the wage distribution associated with the employed sample. For any given specification of G_0, and in fact even when G_0 is treated as unknown, there exist a number of consistent estimators of the location and scale parameters c' and d'. Thus we assume with no loss of generality that consistent estimators of these parameters exist, and denote them by $\widehat{c'}$ and $\widehat{d'}$. With no prior information concerning c, d, or α, no further progress toward identification of the individual parameters can be made. This is the fundamental underidentification problem associated with the asymmetric Nash bargaining model.

Proposition 16 Let G belong to a location-scale family with parameters (c, d). Then a necessary condition for identification of (c, d, α) is that one of the parameters be expressible as a known, invertible function of the other two

Proof See the appendix.

The fact that a restriction on c or d may be sufficient to enable identification of the other parameter characterizing G and the bargaining power parameter α must not be viewed with too much optimism. While the knowledge that $c = 0$ (probably the most common type of restriction that will be imposed in this case) does lead to "theoretical" identification in large samples (as long as G is not negative exponential), the small sample properties of the estimator tend to be poor. This last conclusion comes from conducting Monte Carlo experiments with a variety of scale distributions. If one fixes the scale parameter (d) instead, the performance of an estimator for α tends to be better in reasonably-sized samples. Unfortunately, it is rarely the case that a researcher will feel comfortable fixing the value of a scale parameter a priori. Thus this case is not particularly germane for empirical researchers, and we are left with the impression that under most "reasonable" a priori restrictions on the parameters (c, d), identification of the parameter α will remain tentative at best.

The fundamental reason for the identification problem is not hard to understand intuitively. From payoff data for one side of the market we are attempting to simultaneously determine the total size of the "pie" and the share received by the worker. While strong restrictions on the form of the underlying matching distribution may make α identifiable in theory, these restrictions are probably not believable and even imposing them is likely to produce an estimator with a large (though not infinite) standard error. We next consider whether having CPS information from a labor market with a binding minimum wage alleviates the identification problem to any extent.

7.3.2 Binding Minimum Wage

When there is a binding minimum wage, we can write the log likelihood function most transparently as

$$\ln L = N \ln h_U - N \ln D + N_U \ln \eta - h_U d \sum_{i \in S_U} t_i$$

$$+ N_M \ln \left(1 - \frac{\tilde{G}\left\{[m - (1-\alpha)\theta^*]/\alpha\right\}}{\tilde{G}(m)}\right) \qquad (7.10)$$

$$+ \sum_{i \in S_H} \ln \left(\frac{\frac{1}{\alpha}g\left\{[w_i - (1-\alpha)\theta^*]/\alpha\right\}}{\tilde{G}(m)}\right),$$

where $h_U = \lambda \tilde{G}(m)$. The critical acceptance match value is now known to be equal to m, but we have to estimate the "implicit" critical match value θ^* along with the other primitive parameters of the model. We will consider the identification of the parameters $(\eta, h_U, c, d, \alpha, \theta^*)$.

With respect to the rate parameters η and h_U, no new issues arise. The maximum likelihood estimators for these two parameters are exactly as were given above for the case of no binding m.

Does the mass point at m provide enough additional information to enable identification of α? The answer to this question is no in general, and this is primarily due to the necessity of estimating θ^* simultaneously with the other parameters, something we did not have to do when there was no binding minimum wage. Let us begin by rewriting the terms involving G in their location-scale form. For those paid the minimum wage, the term involving G is written as

$$1 - \frac{\tilde{G}\left\{[m - (1 - \alpha)\theta^*]/\alpha\right\}}{\tilde{G}(m)} = 1 - \frac{\tilde{G}_0[(m - c')/d']}{\tilde{G}_0(m - c/d)},$$

where $c' = (1 - \alpha)\theta^* + \alpha c$ and $d' = \alpha d$. For an individual i who belongs to set H, their log likelihood contribution involving G is written as

$$\ln \frac{g_0(w_i - c')/d'}{\tilde{G}_0[(m - c)/d]}.$$

The fact that (c, d) and (c', d') appear independently in these expressions may bring false optimism. If it were possible to consistently estimate these four terms, then we would be able to consistently estimate α and θ^* since

$$\alpha = \frac{d'}{d},$$

$$\theta^* = \frac{c' - (d'/d)c}{1 - (d'/d)}.$$ (7.11)

Thus all terms are clearly identified given consistent estimates of those four parameters. Unfortunately, it is not possible to consistently estimate c and d from these expressions. These terms only appear in the expression $\tilde{G}_0[(m - c)/d)]$, which is the probability of encountering an acceptable match. Even given knowledge of this probability and the minimum wage m, there are, in general, a continuum of values of (c, d) that can produce the same value of the argument $(m - c)/d$. Thus the pair (c, d) are not uniquely identified. Given this lack of uniqueness, we cannot uniquely determine α and θ^* from (7.11). As was the case in the last subsection, identification may be obtainable if we are willing to impose a priori restrictions on the parameters (c, d). For good reason, most analysts will be hesitant to resort to such devices.

In the empirical results reported in the next chapter, we have for the most part assumed that G is lognormal. This is in keeping with much of the literature in empirical search or even earnings function estimation. The lognormal is not a location-scale distribution and thus the "exact" identification analysis just conducted for that family of distributions does not strictly apply.[9] In practical estimation situations the departures from the truncated location-scale characterization of the empirical distribution of accepted wages are not sufficiently great to enable identification of α.[10] Thus sample information from one side of the market cannot be expected to enable identification of both the total surplus distribution and the sharing rule. This is the larger point to take away from the identification analysis.

7.3.3 Some Additional Identification Devices

In empirical work utilizing a Nash-bargaining structure, it is common to assume symmetric bargaining, namely $\alpha = 0.5$ (e.g., Flinn and Heckman 1982; Eckstein and Wolpin 1993; Del Boca and Flinn 1994). Such a "normalization" is imposed both because of the difficulty of identifying the parameter α, and also due to modeling considerations. In terms of the second point, recall that in our formulation of the behavioral model we assumed that both workers and firms shared a common effective discount rate. If we were to ignore the fact that the searcher has an "outside option" when bargaining with the firm, namely the value of continued search, bargaining over the match surplus could be placed in the framework of a Rubinstein (1982) alternating-offers game. It is well known that in the case of equal discount rates, the solution is equivalent to the symmetric Nash-bargaining solution. Clearly, if α is known, or assumed, then identification of all other parameters (except for ρ and b) follows directly from the analysis of FH.

It is also possible to obtain identification of some parameters by redefining the parameter space with respect to observable characteristics of individuals. From the previous subsection we know that if we sort sample members into a small number of observationally distinguishable classes, identification of the labor market parameters for each class will not be possible. However, if we are willing to restrict the values of certain subsets of the primitive parameters to be constant across at least some of the classes, it will, in general, be possible to obtain identification of the reformulated model. The parameters that will be identified are those that are taken to be constant across at least some groups and those that are considered to be group-specific. Since our original model did not entail any across-group restrictions, this would have to be considered a nonequivalent reparameterization of the original model. It seems difficult to imagine that a researcher could specify a subset of primitive parameters that was common to a number of sub-populations in anything other than an arbitrary manner. We have chosen not to estimate the model under these types of "exclusion restrictions" because we could not find any reasonable ones to impose. We return to a lengthy discussion of these issues in chapter 11.

7.3.4 Use of Demand Side Information to Estimate α

Our analysis of minimum wages takes place in the context of a simple equilibrium model of the labor market. In the end it is not terribly surprising that identification of an equilibrium model using data from outcomes for only one side of the market is a daunting task. In this section we explore identification strategies that utilize both the CPS data and some information readily available from the financial statements of publicly held corporations.

The datum we utilize from the firm side of the market is labor's share of revenue at some "representative" firm j, which we denote by $\pi_W^j(m)$. Now from the model

$$\pi_W^j(m) = \frac{\sum_{i \in E^j} w(\theta_i; m, \rho V_U(m))}{\sum_{i \in E^j} \theta_i},$$

where E^j is the set of employees of firm j at some arbitrary point in time (where it is assumed that $E^j \neq \varnothing$). Dividing both the numerator and denominator by the number of employees at the firm we get the ratio of average wages to average productivity,

$$\pi_W^j(m) = \frac{\overline{w}^j}{\overline{\theta}^j}.$$

If the number of employees at firm j is large enough for the law of large numbers (LLN) to apply, then

$$\pi_W^j(m) \doteq \frac{mp(w = m) + \int_{[m-(1-\alpha)\rho V_U(m)]/\alpha} (\alpha\theta + (1-\alpha)\rho V_U(m))\, dG(\theta)/\tilde{G}(m)}{\int_m \theta\, dG(\theta)/\tilde{G}(m)}.$$

$$(7.12)$$

If there exists no particular firm j with enough employees for the law of large numbers to be applicable, it must be the case that the average wage share of revenues across all firms in the market, $\sum_j \pi_W^j(m)/K$, assumes a value arbitrarily close to the right-hand side of (7.12) in a sufficiently large sample of firms.

We use (7.12) to form an estimator of α jointly with γ, where γ denotes all other model parameters. In particular, we recognize that the wage share of firm revenues is a function of all of the primitive parameters of the model, including α. The idea is to form a concentrated likelihood function in which an estimator for α, written as a function of the parameter vector Γ and an observed value of $\pi_W^j(m)$, is substituted into the log likelihood function. From (7.12) we see that any $\alpha \in (0, 1)$ and $\gamma \in \Gamma$ imply a unique value of the wage share of revenues, which we will now call simply π. Thus

$$\pi = \pi(\alpha; \gamma, m).$$

The function π has the following features (for all m):

$$\lim_{\alpha \to 1} \pi(\alpha; \gamma, m) = 1,$$

$$\lim_{\alpha \to 0} \pi(\alpha; \gamma, m) = \frac{m}{E(\theta | \theta \geq m)} \in (0, 1],$$

and

$$\frac{\partial \pi(\alpha; \gamma, m)}{\partial \alpha} = \frac{\int_{[m-(1-\alpha)\rho V_n(m)]/\alpha} (\theta - \rho V_u(m)) dG(\theta)}{\int_m \theta dG(\theta)} \in (0, 1).$$

Then $\pi(\alpha; \gamma, m) : [0, 1] \to [m/E(\theta | \theta \geq m), 1]$. Furthermore π is monotone in α. Let the observed value of π be denoted by $\tilde{\pi}$. Then for $\tilde{\pi} \in (m/E(\theta | \theta \geq m), 1)$ there exists a unique value $\alpha^*(\tilde{\pi}; \gamma, m)$ such that

$$\tilde{\pi} - \pi(\alpha^*(\tilde{\pi}, \gamma, m); \gamma, m) = 0.$$

Thus the condition required for an interior solution for α to exist is that

$$\tilde{\pi} > \frac{m}{E(\theta | \theta \geq m)}$$

$$\Rightarrow E(\theta | \theta \geq m) > \frac{m}{\tilde{\pi}}.$$

This last condition, which involves $E(\theta | \theta \geq m)$, imposes a restriction on the parameter space Γ, since a subset of the parameters belonging to γ consists of those parameters that characterize the distribution of θ, and a subset of these parameters appears in the conditional expectation function $E(\theta | \theta \geq m)$. We have another condition that the estimated parameters must implicitly satisfy, of course, which is that $\rho V_n(m) < m$. We impose this condition directly by working with the parameterization

$$\tilde{\gamma} \equiv (\rho V_U(m), \lambda, \eta, G).$$

Under a lognormality assumption regarding G, the distribution of θ is completely characterized by the two parameters (μ, σ^2), so that the parameter space for $\tilde{\gamma}$ is given by

$$\tilde{\Gamma}(m) = (-\infty, m) \times R_+^2 \times R \times R_+,$$

since $\mu \in R$ and $\sigma^2 \in R_+$. When we impose the additional condition that $E(\theta | \theta \geq m) > m/\tilde{\pi}$, under the lognormality assumption this implies that

$$\exp(\mu + 0.5\sigma^2) \frac{\tilde{\Phi}(z(m) - \sigma)}{\tilde{\Phi}(z(m))} > \frac{m}{\tilde{\pi}}, \tag{7.13}$$

where $z(m) \equiv (\ln(m) - \mu)/\sigma$.[11] Given values of m and $\tilde{\pi}$, let the set of values of (μ, σ^2) that satisfy (7.13) be denoted by $\Omega(m, \tilde{\pi})$. Last, define the parameter space

$$\Gamma'(m, \tilde{\pi}) = \Gamma(m) \cap \Omega(m, \tilde{\pi}).$$

We form a concentrated likelihood function by substituting our estimator for α into the likelihood (7.8), which gives us

$$\tilde{L}(\tilde{\gamma}; \tilde{\pi}, m) = L(\tilde{\gamma}, \alpha^*(\tilde{\pi}, \tilde{\gamma}, m)).$$

We have the following result:

Proposition 17 Assume that $\tilde{\gamma}^0 \in \text{int}(\Gamma'(m, \tilde{\pi}))$ and $\alpha^0 \in (0, 1)$, where $(\tilde{\gamma}^0, \alpha^0)$ are the true population parameter values. Then the maximum likelihood estimators

$$\hat{\gamma} = \arg \max_{\tilde{\gamma} \in \Gamma'(m, \tilde{\pi})} \ln \tilde{L}(\tilde{\gamma}; m, \tilde{\pi}),$$

$$\hat{\alpha} = \alpha^*(\tilde{\pi}, \hat{\gamma}, m),$$

converge in probability to $\tilde{\gamma}^0$ and α^0, respectively. The asymptotic distribution of $\sqrt{N}(\hat{\gamma} - \tilde{\gamma}^0)$ is normal with mean 0 and covariance matrix $\Sigma_{\hat{\gamma}}$, which is of full rank. The asymptotic distribution of $\sqrt{N}(\hat{\alpha} - \alpha^0)$ is normal with mean 0 and variance $\sigma_{\hat{\alpha}}^2(\Sigma_{\hat{\gamma}})$.

Proof See the appendix.

As we will see below, the use of wage share information from a firm or firms in conjunction with the CPS data allows us to obtain precise and credible estimates of all key model parameters. We do face a problem with this information when we attempt to estimate the model for subpopulations, however. Since we do not have wage and productivity information disaggregated by subpopulation, we are forced to assume that this ratio is the same across all subpopulation members.[12] This is a strong assumption that probably partially accounts for the similarities we observe in the estimates of α across subpopulations.

7.4 Estimation of Demand Side Parameters

In this section we discuss the identification and estimation of demand side parameters, which in the case of this highly stylized model consists of estimating the parameters ψ, the cost of a vacancy, and q, the matching function. We show below that in order to perform policy experiments, we also must have a consistent estimator of the distribution of "outside options," that is, the parameter ζ that indexes the distribution function L. Identification and estimation of the parameters ζ, q, and ψ builds on the consistent estimators of the parameters we have already considered, namely $\lambda, \eta, G, b, \alpha$. We begin the section by discussing identification of these parameters when only cross-sectional CPS information is available. The second subsection contains a discussion of identification when the CPS information from the months spanning the change in minimum wage rates is utilized. In our case, this information is from the September and the October 1996 CPS.

Cross-sectional Information Only   The maximum likelihood estimator developed above, which utilizes cross-sectional CPS information and the labor share of firm revenues, allows us to estimate $\rho V_U(m)$.[13] We have the following result.

Proposition 18 ζ is estimable if ρV_O is continuously distributed with c.d.f. L, ζ is a scalar, $L(x, \zeta)$ is monotone in ζ for all x in the support of R, and a consistent estimate of the labor force participation rate is available.

Proof   Let the consistent estimate of the labor force participation rate be $\hat{l}$. In the population we have

$$l = L(\rho V_U(m); \zeta).$$

Since L is monotone in ζ for all x in the support of L, we can write the inverse function

$$\zeta = L^{-1}(\rho V_U(m), l), \quad \rho V_U(m) \in \text{Supp}(L), \quad l \in (0, 1).$$

Because L^{-1} is a known, continuous function, a consistent estimator of ζ is

$$\hat{\zeta} = R^{-1}(\widehat{\rho V_U(m)}, \hat{l})$$

by the invariance property of maximum likelihood estimators.   ∎

We now move on to consider the estimation of q and ψ. We first consider estimation of the matching function q. We have a consistent estimator of the contact rate from the perspective of searchers on the supply side, which is $\hat{\lambda}$. As was the case above, we assume that q is parametric and is characterized by a finite-dimensional parameter vector ω. Then we have

$$\lambda(Ul, v; \omega) = q\left(\frac{Ul}{v}; \omega\right)\frac{v}{Ul}, \tag{7.14a}$$

where

$$Ul = \frac{\eta l}{\eta + \tilde{G}(r)\lambda(ul, v; \omega)}.$$

Now note that consistent estimates of η, λ, l, U are available from the CPS data augmented with (other CPS) data on the labor market participation rate l. If data on the steady state vacancy rate v are available, then a consistent estimate of ω can be obtained solely by using (7.14a) in the case where ω is scalar.

Knowledge of the function $q(\cdot; \omega)$ is sufficient to enable estimation of the cost of vacancy parameter ψ. Recall that the free entry condition can be written

$$\psi = q(Ul/v; \omega)\tilde{G}(r)J(\rho V_U(m), m, G, \rho, \eta, \alpha), \tag{7.15}$$

where J is the expected value of a filled job. All the arguments in J are directly observable (m), assumed known (ρ), or capable of being consistently estimated from the CPS data augmented with the labor share information. Furthermore, if Ul is estimable, v is observed, and ω known or consistently estimated, than all terms of the expression on the right-hand side of (7.15) can be consistently estimated, thereby directly producing a consistent estimator of ψ.

Unfortunately, information on v cannot be assumed to be (directly) available. Empirical studies of the matching function, particularly those conducted using US data, typically use a vacancy index constructed from help wanted advertising (see Petrongolo and Pissarides 2001 for a survey of these studies). Without information on v, the parameter ω cannot be consistently estimated, and therefore ψ cannot be consistently estimated either. With cross-sectional CPS information and a labor share measure, ψ can only be estimated under the following stringent conditions.

Proposition 19 Augmented cross-sectional CPS information can be used to consistently estimate ψ if and only if the matching function contains no unknown parameters and is monotone in κ.

Proof We only demonstrate sufficiency, for the previous discussion makes necessity clear. Since a consistent estimate of Ul is available, if $q(\cdot;\omega)$ is known, then (7.14a) can be used to recover v given that q is monotone in its sole argument κ (which is monotone in v). Given a consistent estimator of v, and a known ω, all the terms on the right-hand side of (7.15) can be consistently estimated as well as their product. ∎

In summary, using cross-sectional information from the CPS and labor share data, we can recover all the parameters required to perform policy evaluation under the assumption of endogenous contact rates only if we assume that the matching function contains no unknown parameters. This stringent assumption is required due to the absence of credible measures of vacancy rates.

Multiple CPS Cross Sections We next consider identification issues when using the CPS Outgoing Rotation Group samples from two months, $t < t'$, where we assume that a steady state equilibrium (approximately) holds and where the (binding) minimum wages are different. Let the earlier minimum wage be less than the later one (without loss of generality), and denote the minimum wage in period t by m_t. All primitive parameters are assumed to be identical in the two months.

In terms of the matching function, we limit attention to the case where it is Cobb–Douglas, in particular,

$$M(Ul, v; \omega) = (Ul)^\omega v^{1-\omega}, \qquad \omega \in (0, 1),$$

$$\Rightarrow q\left(\frac{Ul}{v};\omega\right) = \left(\frac{Ul}{v}\right)^\omega.$$

Pragmatically speaking, this is not a severe restriction, since M is assumed to be CRS and we know that it will be difficult to precisely estimate more than one parameter characterizing M.

Under the assumption that the cost of a vacancy is a primitive parameter, for an estimator of ω to be permissible requires that it assume a value in the open unit interval. The required condition, stated in terms of a restriction on functions of consistent estimators of model parameters, is as follows.

Condition C Let $\hat{\lambda}_s$, $\hat{J}_s$, and $\widehat{\tilde{G}(m_s)}$ be consistent estimators of the rate of arrival of contacts, the expected value of a filled job, and the probability of drawing a match value greater than the minimum wage, respectively, in the equilibrium associated with minimum wage m_s. Then two estimated equilibria are coherent if

$$\hat{\lambda}_t^{\frac{-\omega}{1-\omega}} \widehat{\tilde{G}(m_t)} \hat{J}_t = \hat{\lambda}_{t'}^{\frac{-\omega}{1-\omega}} \widehat{\tilde{G}(m_{t'})} \hat{J}_{t'}$$

for some $\omega \in (0, 1)$.

Condition C is required if our estimates of the primitive parameters of the model can be used to form an estimator of the Cobb–Douglas parameter ω that lies in the parameter space $(0, 1)$. This condition is a minimal one in the sense that there are other restrictions on parameters implied by the model that are not imposed or checked in forming estimators of the demand side parameters. Model estimates may violate condition C for a variety of reasons. Obviously, even given the correct specification of all other model components (an unlikely event), we could have misspecified the matching function M. Also, while the model structure forces us to consider equilibria not too temporally distant, anticipation of the impending minimum wage change after time t could have led the economy out of a steady state equilibrium at at time t. It also may be the case that the economy would not have reached its new steady state equilibrium at the time of the next measurement, t'. As we will see in the empirical results presented in the following chapter, one of the greatest impediments to the satisfaction of condition C is the small changes in the minimum wage rates and the small proportion of individuals impacted.

Proposition 20 Given access to two equilibrium outcomes, the Cobb–Douglas parameter ω and the vacancy cost parameter ψ are estimable if condition C is satisfied.

Proof See the appendix.

To summarize the results of this section, we have shown that a Cobb–Douglas matching function parameter can be consistently estimated when we have data from two CPS surveys in which data outcomes are generated from steady state equilibrium behavior associated with two values of the minimum wage subject to the satisfaction of condition C. We also showed that the cost of a vacancy can be consistently estimated if estimates of a function of other primitive parameters at the two equilibrium values satisfy a condition that restricts the estimator of the Cobb–Douglas parameter to the unit interval. Although we can never expect the observations in the two CPS surveys to be exactly generated by two distinct steady state equilibria, the hope is that the approximation may be good enough to yield a credible estimate of the matching function parameter.

8   Model Estimates and Tests

The data used in performing the empirical work are described in detail in Chapter 2, along with associated descriptive statistics. The months used in the analysis are September 1996, February and August 1997, and January 1998. As was made clear in the previous chapter, identification of matching function parameters depends on our having access to CPS-ORG data at more than two points in time. For September 1996 we assume that the market was in a steady state equilibrium at the minimum wage $4.25, which was due to expire at the end of the month. When moving to the new steady state equilibrium associated with the minimum wage of $4.75, there will undoubtedly be some transitional dynamics, even under our assumed model structure. To avoid capturing these effects, we will perform the "pooled" estimation exercises using data from five months after the change, when we hope the market has nearly reached its new steady state equilibrium. We cannot allow for even more separation in time between the "before and after" observations since (1) the minimum wage changes once again on September 1, 1997, and (2) the model specification allows for no changes in the price level (the change in the Consumer Price Index between September 1996 and February 1997 was about 1.1 percent).

To examine the sensitivity of our estimates to the particular months chosen, we re-estimate the model when the subsequent minimum wage change occurs at the beginning of September 1997. Unfortunately, the month before the change is August, a period when many students find temporary employment. This phenomenon is particularly at odds with the steady state equilibrium basis of our econometric model. The postchange month used in the pooled estimation exercise is January 1998, which also may exhibit some transitory labor market behavior in conjunction with the holiday period. For these reasons we will not devote as much attention to the estimates generated using these months.

Nevertheless, it is encouraging to note that the estimates of most parameters are stable across these two periods spanning a minimum wage
change.

Estimates of primitive parameters, and particularly the bargaining
power parameter α, were found to be highly sensitive to outliers in the
wage data. As a result we rounded all wage observations greater than
$30 per hour down to $30. This affected only about ten cases in any
given month. For reasons discussed in the previous chapter, it is difficult to add measurement error to the model in order to account for
wage observations less than the minimum wage. For this reason we
truncated all wages (from below) at the legal minimum wage for the
month in question.[1] No other modifications to the duration or wage
information reported by respondents are made.

In the previous chapter we described an estimator that utilized the
same CPS data that has been employed to this point along with one
additional piece of demand side information: the ratio of total wages
paid to firm revenues. It goes without saying that our model is highly
stylized, and that in reality there is no single value of this ratio when
looking across firms in the economy at any point in time. We have opted
to use the value (or a reasonable approximation to it) from one large
US corporation, McDonald's. This firm has been selected for a number
of reasons. First, it is the largest private-sector employer in the United
States, so the law of large numbers results that we relied upon in defining
a consistent estimator of π in the previous chapter should be satisfied.
Second, this firm has a disproportionate number of employees from the
age group in which we are interested, those between the ages of 16 and
24. Moreover a large number of its employees are paid at or near the
minimum wage. Third, McDonald's is one of the few large employers
in this sector that reported sufficiently disaggregated information in its
Consolidated Statement of Income (CSI) to allow computation of the
number in which we are interested.

In obtaining a value for the wage share at McDonald's, we have
used information from the company's 1996 CSI, which covers a period
that includes the survey month of the CPS we are using (September
1996). For purposes of homogeneity we have restricted attention to
revenues and costs associated with restaurants owned by the company
(i.e., we have excluded franchises). We computed our value of "net"
revenue by subtracting "costs of food and packaging" plus "occupancy
and other operating expenses" from "total sales by company-operated
restaurants." The numerator of the ratio is given by "payroll and other

employee benefits." We found the value of this ratio to be 0.576 in 1996. Interestingly the ratio appears to be relatively stable over time. For example, by the same computational method, the ratio equaled 0.568 in 1995 and 0.560 in 1994.

8.1 Parameter Estimates Using Profit Information

Table 8.1 shows estimates of the September 1996 model, with the profit information included. The first column contains the estimates for the entire sample (with those employed at a wage less than 4.25 excluded). The estimated value of λ, 0.309, implies that offers arrive approximately every three months on average.[2] The dismissal rate estimate of 0.031 implies that the average length of a job is about thirty months. We should bear in mind that these estimates apply to young participants, so the relative brevity of a job match is not surprising. The point estimates of the lognormal match distribution parameters μ and σ are 2.301 and 0.528, respectively, and their standard errors of 0.036 and 0.020 indicate that they are precisely estimated. The point estimate of the implicit reservation wage is 3.093 and its estimated standard error is 0.146.

Table 8.1
Model estimates with profit information September 1996

Parameter	All	Males	Females	White non-Hispanic	Black or Hispanic
		Demographic group			
λ	0.309 (0.023)	0.278 (0.027)	0.356 (0.039)	0.328 (0.030)	0.300 (0.040)
η	0.031 (0.003)	0.030 (0.004)	0.034 (0.005)	0.026 (0.003)	0.055 (0.010)
μ	2.301 (0.036)	2.342 (0.044)	2.273 (0.057)	2.331 (0.040)	2.150 (0.092)
σ	0.528 (0.020)	0.554 (0.026)	0.479 (0.028)	0.504 (0.021)	0.627 (0.053)
$\rho V_U(m)$	3.093 (0.146)	3.313 (0.173)	2.798 (0.273)	2.901 (0.202)	3.572 (0.165)
α	0.424 (0.007)	0.427 (0.006)	0.429 (0.013)	0.437 (0.0122)	0.383 (0.106)
N	2,022	1,049	973	1,612	410
$\ln L$	−5,065.676	−2,739.338	−2,582.245	−3,972.758	−1,072.138

Note: Standard errors are in parentheses.

Of most interest to us is the estimate of the bargaining power parameter. The point estimate of α is 0.424 and the estimated standard error
of α is 0.007. With this level of precision it is straightforward to reject
the null hypothesis of symmetric Nash bargaining (or $\alpha = 0.5$). The estimate clearly indicates that this class of worker is at a disadvantage with
respect to extracting match surplus. The use of the profit information
contains a large amount of information regarding the size of the "pie" to
be divided and results in what we consider a reasonable estimate under
our modeling assumptions. It also has allowed us to precisely estimate
the parameter, something that is not feasible if we do not use firm profit
information of some type (even when identification of α is theoretically
possible).

There now exist a few other estimates of the bargaining power parameter obtained using disaggregated data. Cahuc et al. (2006) obtain a
much lower estimate of the bargaining power parameter, as do Dey and
Flinn (2005). The main difference in their modeling approaches from the
one followed here is in the allowance for on-the-job search and a particular assumption regarding the bargaining mechanism. In chapter 10 we
estimate a model with on-the-job search under two different bargaining
assumptions and see that the estimate of bargaining power is strongly
influenced by assumptions regarding whether or not wage contracts
are renegotiable. We discuss these issues at length in chapter 10.

The other columns of table 8.1 demonstrate the relative stability of the
α estimates across demographic groups. As was discussed in section
7.5, this near constancy is largely an artifact of our estimation procedure. Since productivity and wage information is not available by
demographic group in the company's CSI, we have had to assume that
the same ratio applies to all groups. This is the key piece of identifying
information in determining $\hat{\alpha}$, and as a result near constancy of these
estimates is virtually guaranteed.[3]

Even if the group-specific values of $\hat{\alpha}$ are relatively similar, because
of the high degree of precision with which they are estimated there
do exist statistically significant differences between them. For example,
youths who are black or Hispanic are estimated to have a slightly lower
level of bargaining power than others (0.383 vs. 0.437). They also have a
slightly lower estimated value of the mean and standard deviation of
the logarithm of the match value. When we divide the sample along
gender lines, we find that males are estimated to have a slightly higher
degree of bargaining power than females, as well as having higher
values of μ and σ.

Table 8.2
Model estimates with profit information August 1997

Parameter	Demographic group				
	All	Males	Females	White non-Hispanic	Black or Hispanic
λ	0.447 (0.036)	0.397 (0.043)	0.516 (0.063)	0.554 (0.056)	0.341 (0.046)
η	0.034 (0.004)	0.032 (0.005)	0.037 (0.006)	0.033 (0.005)	0.047 (0.008)
μ	2.218 (0.043)	2.318 (0.047)	2.104 (0.078)	2.252 (0.047)	2.167 (0.089)
σ	0.622 (0.024)	0.594 (0.028)	0.646 (0.040)	0.617 (0.026)	0.581 (0.048)
$\rho V_U(m)$	3.944 (0.080)	3.981 (0.116)	3.960 (0.104)	3.857 (0.103)	4.11 (0.136)
α	0.375 (0.006)	0.388 (0.006)	0.355 (0.007)	0.387 (0.005)	0.336 (0.009)
N	2,151	1,112	1,039	1,650	501
$\ln L$	−5,179.436	−2,772.805	−2,379.684	−3,960.016	−1,188.202

Note: Standard errors are in parentheses.

The model estimates in table 8.2 are obtained using the August 1997 data, and they are broadly consistent with those presented in table 8.1. As noted previously, due to the lower aggregate unemployment rate during August 1997, $\hat{\lambda}$ is substantially higher when using this sample. The estimate of $\rho V_U(4.75)$ is significantly greater than the estimate of $\rho V_U(4.25)$, which can be attributed not only to "real" minimum wage impacts but also to inflation. Inflation may also be contributing to the differences in the estimates of the match distribution parameters, particularly σ, in tables 8.1 and 8.2. Estimates of α are substantially lower in August 1997 than in September 1996. This is partially produced by the change in the shape of the estimated match distribution. It may also be due to composition effects, in that the August sample includes more seasonal workers than the September sample, and it may be that this group of workers has less bargaining power than their less seasonal counterparts. We don't want to make too much of this point, since it is at odds with our assumption of a homogeneous population facing fixed primitive parameters. The differences seen across demographic groups in the top panel are broadly mirrored in the estimates obtained using the August 1997 data.

In table 8.3 we use the model to directly determine whether or not the minimum wage increase that occurred at the end of September 1996 was beneficial in the sense of our first welfare measure, the value of unemployed search. In this analysis we only estimate the model for the total sample, and we begin by combining the September 1996 ORG-CPS sample with an analogous one from the February 1997 survey. Given the sample design, these two surveys do not include the same individuals. In combining the surveys, we assigned wages as follows: For individuals who earned less than $4.25 in September 1996, we assigned them a wage of $4.25, the then current minimum. Similarly we assigned all those making less than $4.75 an hour in February 1997 a wage rate of $4.75.

Before turning to the results, we need a word of caution about the interpretation of the estimates. Strictly speaking, the consistency of our estimator in this case depends on the search environment remaining stationary in the wake of the minimum wage change so that all "primitive" parameters assume the same values in September 1996 and February 1997. There are a number of reasons why this assumption may be questionable; we will consider a limited test of it below.

In the absence of endogenous contact rates and a labor market participation decision, no other assumptions are required to obtain valid estimates of primitive parameters and the value of search before and after the minimum wage change as long as the implicit reservation wage after the minimum wage change is no larger than the initial minimum wage rate. In terms of our application, we require $\rho V_U(4.75) < 4.25$. If this is the case, then even under the old minimum wage match values in the interval $[4.25, 4.75)$ are acceptable, since working at the wage associated with such a θ given $m = 4.25$ has a higher value than waiting to search under the new minimum wage. Point estimates from the model indicate that this restriction is not an unreasonable assumption.

By using information from a sample collected four to five months after the minimum wage change, it is hoped that we can ignore transitional dynamics in terms of the unemployment duration distribution. While it is straightforward to adjust the likelihood function for transitional dynamics given exogenous λ and a fixed labor force, this is decidedly not the case under endogenous contact rates and participation decisions. Thus we have chosen a period long enough for us to hope that most transitional dynamics are absent and short enough to hope that price level changes can be ignored.

We estimated the model under three specifications. In specification A, we assume that all primitive parameters remained fixed between

Table 8.3
Model estimates with profit information, September 1996 and February 1997 ($N = 4{,}059$)

Parameter	Specification A	B	C
$\lambda(4.25)$	0.355	0.356	0.353
	(0.018)	(0.018)	(0.022)
$\lambda(4.75)$	—	—	0.404
			(0.022)
η	0.039	0.039	0.039
	(0.003)	(0.003)	(0.003)
μ	2.253	2.244	2.243
	(0.028)	(0.029)	(0.029)
σ	0.575	0.578	0.579
	(0.015)	(0.016)	(0.016)
$\rho V_U(4.25)$	3.415	3.382	3.383
	(0.079)	(0.083)	(0.083)
$\rho V_U(4.75)$	—	3.510	3.511
		(0.096)	(0.096)
α	0.403	0.404	0.404
	(0.003)	(0.003)	(0.003)
$\ln L$	$-10{,}118.373$	$-10{,}117.152$	$-10{,}117.124$
LR test	—	2.442	0.056
p-Value	—	0.118	0.813

Note: Standard errors are in parentheses.

September and February, except for b, and that the rate of contacts between searchers and firms remained fixed. We allow the parameter b to change over time for pragmatic reasons. Because we are imposing constancy in the value of search across the two months, and because the minimum wage changed and all other parameters are fixed, then unless the parameter b changes, these restrictions are consistent given the model structure. Specification B allows the value of search to change between periods but imposes constancy of the contact rate λ. Under specification C, both the contact rate and the value of search are allowed to change after imposition of the new minimum wage.

Comparisons of the estimates under the three specifications reveal few significant differences. Holding the contact rate fixed, the value of search does seem to have increased slightly between September and February, with the likelihood ratio statistic having a p-value of 0.118 under the null of no change. Comparing columns B and C, there is absolutely no indication that the rate of contacts changed over the two

Table 8.4
Model estimates with profit information, August 1997 and January 1998 ($N = 4{,}111$)

Parameter	Specification		
	A	B	C
$\lambda(4.75)$	0.488	0.491	0.506
	(0.028)	(0.029)	(0.035)
$\lambda(5.15)$	—	—	0.476
			(0.033)
η	0.040	0.040	0.040
	(0.003)	(0.003)	(0.003)
μ	2.165	2.157	2.158
	(0.038)	(0.039)	(0.038)
σ	0.670	0.672	0.672
	(0.020)	(0.020)	(0.020)
$\rho V_U(4.75)$	4.056	4.033	4.032
	(0.055)	(0.059)	(0.059)
$\rho V_U(5.15)$	—	4.118	4.116
		(0.072)	(0.071)
α	0.370	0.371	0.371
	(0.005)	(0.006)	(0.005)
$\ln L$	$-10{,}007.255$	$-10{,}006.487$	$-10{,}006.155$
LR test	—	1.536	0.664
p-Value	—	0.215	0.415

months. On the basis of these results we cannot reject the hypothesis that λ is a primitive parameter, in the sense that it was seemingly invariant to *at least this change in the minimum wage.* We will come back to this point below, since assessing the policy impacts of the minimum wage will depend critically on estimates of α and the determination of λ.

We repeated the same exercise for the minimum wage change of September 1, 1997, and present the results in table 8.4. We pooled monthly data from August 1997 and January 1998 in the estimation, and recoded all positive August wages less than \$4.75 to \$4.75 and all positive January wages less than \$5.15 to \$5.15. As mentioned above, results from this exercise are particularly troublesome to interpret due to seasonal employment in August and, to a lesser extent, in January. This is evidenced by the marked drop in the labor market participation rate between August and January, a drop that is not consistent with the small change in the value of search (which determines the participation rate within the model).

Once again, the estimates vary little across specifications. While the point estimate of the implicit reservation wage did increase, the p-value associated with the test statistic is only 0.215. There is no indication that the contact rate λ changed between the two months. Thus the results we obtain are consistent across the two pooled samples. While the value of search seems to have increased to some degree, the change is at best marginally significant. Once again, there is no indication that the parameter λ is endogenous using data that spans the 1997 minimum wage change.

8.2 Estimates of Demand Side Parameters and the Matching Function

We now move on to obtain estimates of the other parameters that characterize the model, namely the flow cost of a vacancy, ψ, the Cobb–Douglas matching parameter (estimable, in principle, when we have access to observations of the steady state equilibrium outcomes under two minimum wages), and parameter(s) characterizing the distribution of outside (of the labor market) values. In forming the estimates of the identifiable primitive parameters, we will begin with those that are estimable using data from a single cross section. In the previous chapter we saw that in this case a one-parameter outside option value distribution can be identified along with the cost of a vacancy, but the matching function M cannot have any unknown parameters. In table 8.5 we utilize the pooled cross-sectional information to consider the estimation of the same parameters, with the addition of the single unknown parameter from the Cobb–Douglas matching function. All the estimation results are contained in table 8.5, including standard errors. As a rule, standard errors are small in relation to the size of the point estimate. Exceptions are the flow vacancy cost across all three specifications, and the estimated match elasticity under the Cobb–Douglas matching function specification. Given the relatively "indirect" manner in which these parameters are estimated, the imprecision of these particular estimates is not surprising. Since the policy experiments reported in chapter 9 are computed using the point estimates of these parameters, one should bear in mind the imprecision in some of these estimates when interpreting those results.

The first column of table 8.5 contains estimates of the parameters ψ and ζ, the latter of which is the parameter of the negative exponential

Table 8.5
Point estimates of remaining parameters

Characteristic	Single CPS samples		Pooled sample
	9/96	8/97	8/97 and 1/98
Vacancy rates			
v_t	0.020	0.030	0.024
	(0.002)	(0.004)	(0.006)
$v_{t'}$	—	—	0.026
			(0.006)
Flow vacancy cost			
ψ	128.960	105.025	2.460
	(13.853)	(12.589)	(1.016)
Match elasticity[a]	0.147	0.333	0.196
	(0.028)	(0.048)	(0.168)
Outside option distribution parameter[b]			
ζ	0.326	0.299	—
	(0.017)	(0.006)	

Note: Standard errors are in parentheses. Standard errors were computed by taking 5,000 draws from the asymptotic normal sampling distribution of the maximum likelihood estimates of parameters describing rates and the distribution G, and using these draws to form estimates of α and all of the quantities reported in the table. The standard errors are the standard deviations of the quantities reported in the table in the sample of 5,000 draws.
[a] This was computed from the relevant matching function for the sample. Using only cross-sectional information, the matching function was $v(1 - \exp(-u/v))$. A CRS Cobb–Douglas matching function was used for the pooled data case so that the elasticity is equal to the Cobb–Douglas parameter associated with the size of the set of unemployed searchers.
[b] The participation rate parameter was not estimated for the pooled data case, since the decline in the participation rate is inconsistent with the increase in the estimate of unemployed search under our assumption of a stable distribution of outside option values.

distribution of out-of-labor-force (OLF) valuations. Since the data used are from the single month of September 1996, a known matching function must be assumed. We use the CRS form

$$M(Ul, v) = v\left(1 - \exp\left(\frac{-Ul}{v}\right)\right).$$ (8.1)

We will compute the vacancy rate v and then the elasticity of the matching function evaluated at the September 1996 equilibrium values of U, l, and v.

The estimated vacancy rate in September was 0.020, which should be compared with the unemployment rate (in the population, which is Ul) of 0.062. The matching function elasticity, with respect to the unemployment rate, is only 0.147. Thus, at these equilibrium levels, the productivity of an additional vacancy, in terms of match creation, was much higher than the productivity of additional unemployed searchers. The estimated flow cost of a vacancy is 128.960, which is a difficult number to interpret per se. Last, the estimated parameter value of the negative exponential distribution of outside values is 0.326, implying that the mean outside value in this population is slightly more than 3.

We repeated the same exercise using the August 1997 data, the main purpose being to assess the variability of the estimates of the primitive parameters over time. The vacancy rate is estimated to be 0.030 in August, 50 percent greater than what was inferred 11 months earlier. This is an outcome variable, of course, so that there is no presumption that it should be constant after a minimum wage change. The flow vacancy cost estimate declines a bit to 105.025. This is supposed to be a primitive parameter, so its value should not change over time. From the large standard error associated with each estimate, and given that they are estimated from independently drawn observations, there is no basis for claiming that the estimates are significantly different across the two minimum wage changes.

The matching function elasticity is found to be substantially higher in August 1997 than in September 1996, increasing from 0.147 to 0.333. It is slightly smaller than the estimated bargaining power parameter obtained using data from that month, whose value was 0.375. These estimates imply that the Hosios condition was approximately satisfied, which has implications for the welfare analysis conducted below. The estimate of the parameter characterizing the distribution of outside values is little changed from the value obtained using the September 1996 data.

We next turn to the estimation of the model parameterizations that were available to us using observations on outcomes associated with two distinct steady state equilibria. We first tried to implement the estimation procedure using the September 1996 and February 1997 pooled data. This was ultimately unsuccessful because the point estimates of the parameters did not satisfy the coherency condition (termed condition C in section 7.6.2). We then attempted estimation using the pooled data from August 1997 and January 1998. In this case condition C was satisfied, and we could obtain estimated values of parameters that were contained in the appropriate parameter space.

The estimated vacancy rates in August 1997 and January 1998 are very similar. Using the pooled information and a different matching function, the vacancy rate for August is estimated to be 0.024 as opposed to 0.030. The largest difference between the estimates of primitive parameters obtained from the single samples and the pooled sample is in the flow cost of a vacancy. That declines to 2.46, which is a huge drop from the single sample estimates of over 100. It should be borne in mind, however, that the estimator of ψ is quite different in the two contexts, that $\hat{\psi}$ is very much a "backed-out" parameter estimate, and that the matching functions are different.

With the pooled data, we were able to estimate a one-parameter matching function. The elasticity of the this function with respect to the search input from the supply side of the market is the Cobb–Douglas parameter ω. We found $\hat{\omega} = 0.196$, which lies between the elasticities computed under the matching function used with the single month data. The similarities in the estimates is moderately reassuring. As was noted above, the estimate of ω is quite imprecise.

We do not report an estimate of the parameter(s) of the distribution of the outside options using the pooled data. Since the estimated value of search increased between August and January, the model implies that the participation rate increased. Instead, it fell by 6 percent. This drop was probably due in large part to students returning to school from seasonal employment. We note that even if the participation rate had increased, a two-parameter distribution of outside options would have been necessary to fit the data, in general. Thus the distributional assumptions made of necessity will depend on the number of months that are pooled, limiting the comparability of estimates across different sampling schemes.

It is of some interest to compare our estimates of the matching function elasticities with those obtained by linear regression estimation using aggregate time series and cross-sectional data on unemployment and vacancy rates. Petrongolo and Pissarides (2001) provide a comprehensive survey of this literature, with empirical results collected in their table 3. Our estimated values of the matching elasticity (with respect to Ul) are at the low end of most of the estimates in the table. They seem to be closer to those obtained when the data used were from local labor markets. For example, Coles and Smith (1996) estimated a Cobb–Douglas matching function using unemployment and vacancy information from local labor markets in England and Wales in 1987, and found a matching elasticity of 0.3.

Our estimates can be expected to differ from those obtained by others for at least two reasons. First, we do not directly use information on vacancies. Although asking a respondent whether or not she is actively searching for work yields only a crude measure of search intensity (and only for those not currently employed), we have a specialized, nationally representative survey (the CPS) that acquires this information from a large group of households on a monthly basis. No such effort is devoted to attaining information on firms' search activities. As a result most studies utilize proxy measures, such as help-wanted advertising, which is of dubious validity. We are able to obtain estimates of the matching function without vacancy information by exploiting the model structure to infer vacancy levels at various points in time. While this circumvents the need for noisy, or even systematically biased, data, the validity of our estimates of v depend critically on the correctness of our model specification. Second, our population of interest is 16- to 24-year-olds, and the matching process may be considerably different for this segment of the labor market. Whether this should result in low estimates of the matching elasticity cannot be investigated within the current framework.

8.3   Model Fit

Our model is constructed using very few parameters. As is true of any model, by definition, it is not a complete characterization of labor market equilibrium in the US economy in the mid- to late-1990s. Clearly, a formal testing of models using explicit statistical criteria to judge their "acceptability" could be somewhat misguided. All models will fail to perform adequately when tested against some data features not explicitly used in forming the estimator of the model parameters; how any particular model fails in an "out-of-sample" testing exercise will depend on which out of sample features are used in the testing exercise, the nature of the estimator, and so on. In this section our modest aim is to explore the degree to which some of the more basic building blocks of the model, such as stationarity, are consistent with the data.

To elaborate on this point a bit further, because it is an important one, consider our assumption that there is no on-the-job search. This is clearly false; ignoring on-the-job search allows us to develop a much more intuitive discussion of the impact of minimum wages on labor market outcomes than would be the case if it were allowed. Aside from the complexity issue, we have chosen to ignore on-the-job search because of the nature of the data available to us. The CPS-ORG data include virtually no employment history information, and certainly do not record job-to-job transitions. By making strong assumptions on the nature of the job-to-job mobility process, it is possible, in general, to estimate a model with on-the-job search and bargaining using only cross-sectional data. But the functional form assumptions made would crucially determine the parameter estimates obtained, and the policy inferences drawn. Our contention is that is best to adapt the model to the data, and to determine parameter estimates as directly related to obvious features of the data as is possible.[4]

Two crucial assumptions behind the analysis are (1) Poisson parameters are constant over time and (2) the matching distribution is lognormal. As we noted in chapter 7, Flinn and Heckman (1982) showed that a parametric assumption for the form of the matching distribution was required for identification of the model. Our model implies that the mapping from the matching distribution to the observed wage distribution should be linear, except for the mass point at the minimum wage rate. The linear relationship implies that the general "shape" of the wage distribution should be the same as that of the parent matching distribution, except at the mass point. So the question regarding the reasonableness of our lognormal matching distribution assumption can be addressed by looking at whether the wage distribution above the minimum looks like it could have been generated by i.i.d. draws from a (truncated) lognormal distribution.

Figure 8.1 contains plots of hourly wage distributions for individuals 16 to 24 years of age in the Outgoing Rotation Groups (ORG) of the Current Population Survey (CPS) in September 1996 and February 1997 (by the sample design of the CPS, these are different individuals). The federal minimum wage was officially changed from $4.25 to $4.75 on September 30, 1996. Thus the data from September are from the month preceding the change those from February 1997 were collected approximately five months after the change. The hourly wage distributions that appear in figure 8.1a and b exhibit a number of common features. In both distributions there are hourly wage rates below the mandated minimum wage, about 5 percent in each month. We have neglected this aspect of the wage distribution, since we do not allow for measurement error and the model assumes compliance with the law. In addition both distributions contain a large amount of probability mass concentrated

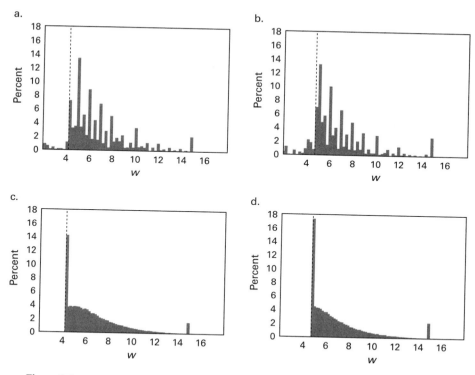

Figure 8.1
(a) Current Population Survey wages, September 1996; (b) Current Population Survey wages, February 1997; (c) simulated wages, September 1996; (d) simulated wages, February 1997

on relatively few points. We have neglected all of these mass points in our econometric specification except for the ones at the two minimum wage values. The relationship between the size of the each mass point (except for that at m) and the probability in the neighborhood immediately surrounding it suggests that integer wage values are serving as focal points with the "true" wage likely to be in the neighborhood of the focal point. This is our rationale for ignoring their existence in our econometric specification.

The plots of the simulated wage distributions generated in figure 8.1c and d are from the estimates of primitive parameters taken from the first column of the top panel of table 8.1. We see that the model predicts slightly more mass at the minimum wage than is observed.[5] For wages above the minimum, the behavioral model smooths out the masses at the focal points, as would a simple kernel estimator, and produces a more

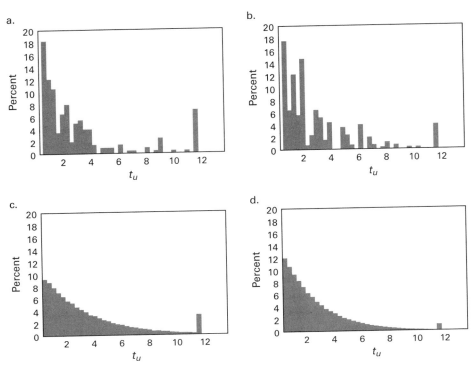

Figure 8.2
(a) Current Population Survey durations, September 1996; (b) Current Population Survey durations, February 1997; (c) simulated durations, September 1996; (d) simulated durations, February 1997

regular looking distribution. In terms of general shape, the distributions seem similar.

We now turn to the investigation of the first assumption, regarding the stationarity of the offer arrival process. Figure 8.2 contains histograms of the durations of ongoing search spells at the time of the interview (the CPS only collects information on the search durations of respondents who report that they are currently looking for a job).[6] The stationary, homogeneous environment we assume implies that the unemployment duration distribution should be negative exponential, as should all point-sampled ongoing spells of unemployed search. In terms of the histograms from the CPS samples, we see a fairly regular pattern of decreasing sample proportions with duration, though there are a number of exceptions that tend to occur at natural focal points.[7] While the shapes of the unemployment spells in the data and from the simulations are not greatly at odds, we went a bit further and conducted some statistical tests for negative exponentiality in the sample distributions. Some tests assumed a parametric alternative (the Weibull distribution) and others a nonparametric one. Without going into detail, all of the tests indicated rejection of negative exponentiality in the September data and marginal rejection of the null in the February data. Given that negative exponentiality would be rejected if there was any heterogeneity in the labor market environment, we view the rather modest statistical rejections that we obtained to not be disturbing enough to cast doubt on the usefulness of the model for carrying out illustrative policy experiments, which are presented in the following chapter.

9 Optimal Minimum Wages

In this chapter we use the estimates of the partial and general equilibrium versions of the model to determine the welfare, employment, and unemployment impacts of the minimum wage. We will begin by plotting the equilibrium steady state distribution of the population across labor market states—namely out of the labor force (OLF), unemployment, and employment—as a function of the minimum wage. The size of the employed population will be equal to the size of the set of firms with filled vacancies. We will also plot the average steady state values associated with each of the three labor market states of OLF, unemployment, employment, and having a filled vacancy. Finally, we will plot the values of the two aggregate welfare measures $TW(m)$ and $PW(m)$, which are differentiated by whether they include the OLF subpopulation.

Let us recall how these various measures are defined. In equilibrium, whether partial or general, there exists a value of search that we denote by $V_U(m)$. We defined an implicit reservation match value by $\theta^*(m) \equiv \rho V_U(m)$. When the minimum wage is not binding, the minimal acceptable match is equal to the $\theta^*(m) = \theta^*(0)$. In the presence of a binding minimum wage, $\theta^*(m)$ serves the role of a shadow value, in the sense the minimum wage makes it unattainable and hence unobservable to the analyst. By the construction of the model, $\theta^*(m) < m$ when m is binding. Individuals on the supply side of the market who have a value of nonparticipation equal to $V_O \geq V_U(m) = \theta^*(m)/\rho$ will not enter the labor market. For a distribution of ρV_O given by L, the proportion of the population out of the labor market is $1 - L(\rho V_U(m)) \equiv \tilde{L}(V_U(m))$. The average value of welfare of individuals in this state is simply given by the conditional expectation $E(V_O|V_O \geq V_U(m))$, or

$$\bar{V}_O(m) = \int_{V_U(m)} V_O \frac{dL(\rho V_O)}{\tilde{L}(\rho V_U(m))}.$$

The rate of arrival of job offers given m is $\lambda(m)$. In partial equilibrium, λ is independent of m. In general equilibrium, λ is a (typically nonmonotonic) function of m. Among job market participants, the steady state unemployment rate is given by

$$p(U|V_O < V_U(m)) = \frac{\eta}{\eta + \lambda(m)\tilde{G}(r(m))},$$

where $r(m) = \max(m, \theta^*(m))$ is the minimal acceptable match value. If we let the steady state proportion of the population in the labor market given a minimum wage of m be denoted by $l(m)$, then the total proportion of the population who will be unemployed in the steady state is simply $p(U|V_O < V_U(m)) \times l(m) = \eta/(\eta + \lambda(m)\tilde{G}(r(m))) \times l(m)$. All individuals who are unemployed have the same value of being in the state, so the average value of being unemployed is the constant $V_U(m)$.

The proportion of the total population in employment in the steady state is

$$p(E|V_O \geq V_U(m)) \times l(m)$$

$$= \frac{\lambda(m)\tilde{G}(r(m))}{\eta + \lambda(m)\tilde{G}(r(m))} \times l(m).$$

The average welfare among the employed is

$$\bar{V}_E(m) = \int \frac{w + \eta V_U(m)}{\rho + \eta} dF(w|m),$$

where $F(w|m)$ is the equilibrium wage distribution given the minimum wage m.

On the firm side, only filled vacancies have positive value. Thus the size of the set of firms with filled vacancies is equal to the size of the set of employed individuals on the supply side of the market. Since all matches greater than $r(m)$ are accepted, we have

$$\bar{V}_F(m) = (\rho + \eta)^{-1} \left\{ \int_{r(m)} \theta \frac{dG(\theta)}{\tilde{G}(r(m))} - \int wdF(w|m) \right\}.$$

The first term inside the braces is the average value of an acceptable match, which is the average revenue to the firm from the match, and the second term is the average wage paid to employed individuals, so the difference is the average (instantaneous) profit from a filled vacancy. Dividing by the "effective" discount rate $\rho + \eta$ converts the instantaneous average profit into a present value.

The results of the policy experiments we conduct depend critically on the assumption made regarding the nature of equilibrium, that is, whether it is best considered partial or general. We first consider the impact of minimum wages on labor market outcomes and welfare under the assumption that *contact rates are invariant with respect to changes in m*. We take the results of this exercise seriously, since the hypothesis testing exercise we conducted in the last chapter led to the conclusion that the contact rate was not significantly changed as the result of a minimum wage increase. Nonetheless, we noted that the test had low power (in a statistical sense) because the minimum wage had been changed by such a small amount. When performing a counterfactual policy analysis that allows minimum wages to assume exceedingly large values in regard to their historical levels, it is difficult to believe that the contact rates will remain constant at any potential minimum wage level. Thus constant contact rates are probably not a bad assumption when contemplating the effects of small changes in the minimum wage relative to an existing level, but it is probably very questionable when considering the impacts of very large changes in m. Unfortunately, since these exercises are hypothetical, we can never be sure of how misleading our implications are under the assumption of the constancy of λ.

Most of our results are presented in graphical form. In figure 9.1, we plot the size of the sets of individuals and firms occupying the various labor market states and the average welfare level in the state as a function of the minimum wage *when λ is held fixed at the estimated value of 0.309*. Figure 9.1a shows the plots of the population sizes in the various states labor market states. Notice that the size of the employed population actually increases by a small amount with increases in the minimum wage up to approximately 8 dollars an hour, after which it begins to decrease relatively rapidly. The size of the OLF population declines as the minimum wage increases up to the point at which the value of unemployed search begins to decrease. The unemployed population grows steadily in the minimum wage. Due to the participation margin, we see that for minimum wage changes through approximately 8 dollars an hour, both unemployment and employment show gains.

Figure 9.1b plots the changes in the average value of occupying each state with changes in m. The average welfare values in the unemployed and employed states are single-peaked in m. The value of m that maximizes the value of the unemployed is \$8.29. The value of

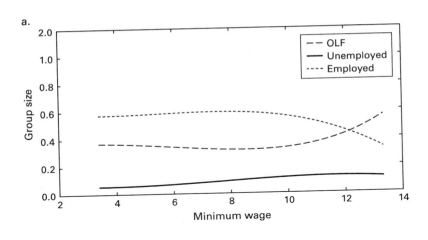

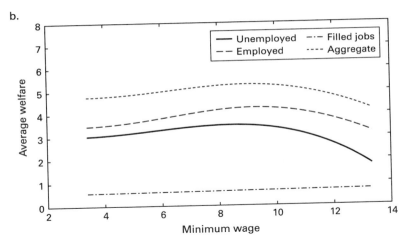

Figure 9.1
Exogenous contact rate: (a) Group size, (b) average welfare

m that maximizes the welfare of labor market participants (the unemployed and the employed) is $8.66. The average welfare of firm owners with filled vacancies is monotonically increasing in m, due to the truncation effect on the distribution of θ and the fact that the threat point of workers, $\rho V_n(m)$, is not rising at a fast enough rate to offset the positive selection impact (on match values) of an increasing m.

The partial equilibrium analysis shows that a doubling of the minimum wage in 1996, led to significant welfare improvements for the population, at least of 16- to 24-year-olds. However, the doubling of the minimum wage leads to a 50 percent increase in unemployment. This result is deserving of additional comment. First, it prompts us to note that policy makers may face significant "side constraints" when choosing a minimum wage level. While it is not a feature of our model, the unemployed may receive transfers from the government, transfers that are financed through taxes on the employed and/or firms. By adding unemployment insurance to the model, high unemployment may have a particularly deleterious effect on social welfare, with a resultant change in the optimal minimum wage. If agents are risk averse, instead of risk neutral as in our model, unemployment could also be evaluated more negatively. On the other hand, allowing for consumption smoothing through the addition of capital markets could substantially alleviate the negative consequences of high unemployment. All this is to say that the particular quantitative result we find for this case is produced by specific features of our model that, if modified, could produce vastly different implications regarding optimal minimum wages.

The second point relates to the use of the unemployment rate as a measure of the success or desirability of a particular minimum wage change. In this partial equilibrium version of the model, a lack of change in the unemployment rate indicates little or no change in the value of unemployed search, employment, or being out of the labor force. We saw how, under our particular model specification, a significant increase in the unemployment rate could be consistent with a significant gain in welfare for the supply side of the market (or could be consistent with a large welfare loss). This is another example to back our persistent claim that minimum wage effects can only be evaluated within a relatively complete model of the labor market.

We now repeat the counterfactual policy exercise for the case where contact rates are determined in equilibrium using the matching function framework. The results are presented in figure 9.2. The conclusions we draw are strikingly different. In figure 9.2a we see that the size of the employed population declines rapidly in the minimum wage, as do the total numbers of employed and unemployed individuals. The decrease in the number of employed individuals is already notable for an m of $5. From figure 9.2b we see that the average welfare of employed individuals increases in the minimum wage up to $3.33, at which point it begins to decrease in m. The average welfare of firms is monotonically increasing in m; this is the case due to the constant erosion in the worker's threat point as m increases, in combination with the truncation effect. When we form the aggregate (labor market) welfare measure,

a.

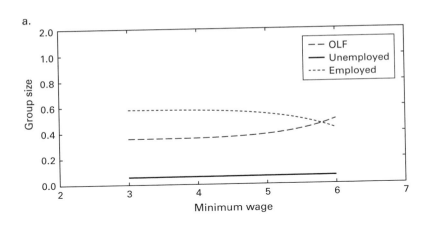

b.

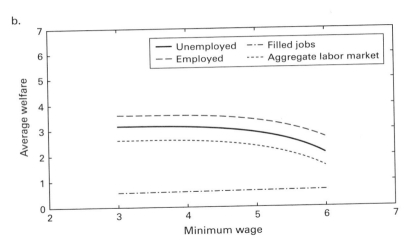

Figure 9.2
Endogenous contact rate: (a) Group size, (b) average welfare

the end result is a single-peaked function of m that has its maximum at $3.36.

We urged caution in the interpretation of the results of the partial equilibrium policy experiment, and we do here as well. First, there is the matter of the empirical evidence presented in the previous chapter. Although the power of the test may be low, we could not reject the partial equilibrium model's implications for contact rates given the range of observed minimum wage variability. Second, although we

Table 9.1
Policy experiments based on estimates from September 1996 CPS-ORG data

Outcome	Baseline	Optimal m given	
		Fixed λ	Endogenous λ
m	4.25	8.66	3.36
		(+1.038)	(−.209)
OLF proportion	0.365	0.318	0.358
		(−0.129)	(−0.019)
Unemployment rate	0.096	0.142	0.092
		(+0.479)	(−.042)
Aggregate labor market welfare	613.974	762.408	624.509
		(+.242)	(+0.017)

Note: Proportionate change with respect to baseline.

have formally closed the model so as to make contact rates endogenous, the matching function is pretty much a black box. Even given that the matching function may be a reasonable approach to general equilibrium modeling in the nondirected search context, the functional form chosen for $M(U, v)$ will generally have significant impacts on the policy experiment results. Unfortunately, although we can plausibly argue that we have a reasonable idea of the value of the argument U, we do not believe that the same can be said regarding the vacancy rate, v. Our identification analysis in chapter 7 made clear that without direct observation of v, this value can only be determined under extremely strong assumptions on M. Since knowledge of both v and M is necessary to estimate other demand side parameters, assumptions regarding M are ultimately untestable. This makes the interpretation of the policy experiments especially delicate.

The results of the policy experiment are summarized in table 9.1. Column 1 contains the baseline values in the reference month of September 1996. Under our model, whether or not with endogenous contact rates, the aggregate labor market welfare measure was 613.974. Column 2 contains the results from the model in which λ is fixed. As was noted above, the aggregate labor market welfare-maximizing value of m is $8.66 in this case, which is slightly more than double the baseline value. At this value of m there is significantly more participation in the labor market by individuals on the supply side, with the OLF rate decreasing 13 percent from its baseline value. There is a marked increase in the unemployment rate of labor market participants, on the order of

Chapter 9

48 percent. Nonetheless, aggregate labor market welfare increases by 24.2 percent.

Under endogenous contact rates (the last column of the table), the optimal minimum wage is 20 percent less than the baseline value. At this value of m, the market participation rate is slightly greater than at the baseline, and the unemployment rate among participants decreases by about 5 percent. Aggregate labor market welfare is less than 2 percent greater than in the baseline. Thus this large decrease in the minimum wage translates into relatively small effects on outcomes and welfare under this model.

The exogenous (with respect to m) contact rate specification produces a very large "optimal" minimum wage by US historical standards, and the endogenous contact rate specification produces a very small one. Can these two predictions be considered "bounds" in any reasonable sense? It may seem reasonable to suppose that contact rates will vary with sufficiently large increases in the minimum wage, but of course the same can be said about the dismissal rate, bargaining power, and virtually all of the "primitive" parameters that characterize the market. Given the small changes in the minimum wage that were observed, and the relatively small number of matches that were directly impacted by changes in the minimum wages observed in the data, identification of changes in parameters of an econometric model (be it "structural" or not) with respect to changes in the minimum wage is extremely difficult. Our formal econometric tests for a change in the contact rate for searching individuals did not lead us to conclude the contact rate was endogenous *with respect to this small policy intervention*. This does not mean that it is valid to conclude that the contact rate, or other rate and distributional parameters, would be unaffected by a sufficiently large change in the minimum wage. In particular, at the "optimal" minimum wage rate of $8.66, it may well be the case that the contact rate will be different than the estimated value of λ for September 1996. However, given the range of policy choices in the data, we have no way to assess the accuracy of model predictions for such high minimum wage rates.

The policy analysis in this chapter was conducted under the counterfactual assumption that there was no on-the-job search, and the reader may well question whether a policy analysis based on a model that ignores this important characteristic of labor market careers in the United States should be given any credibility whatsoever. In the next chapter we address this well-founded concern. Even with slightly different bargaining assumptions, another data set, and a different estimator, we find some of the same qualitative features of the policy analysis conducted with that richer model. While in partial equilibrium, substantial increases in minimum wage rates lead to gains in social welfare, this is not the case when contact rates are endogenized. Thus this general finding appears somewhat robust with respect to significant changes in the structure of the labor market model.

10   On-the-Job Search

10.1   Introduction

All of our analysis to this point has focused on the situation where an individual must be unemployed to be considered for a job, an assumption that is, particularly in regard to the US labor market, highly counterfactual. In this chapter we extend our basic model to include on-the-job (OTJ) search. On the face of it, the change is extremely straightforward. We think of unemployed searchers encountering potential job matches at a constant rate λ_U when they are labor market participants (this rate was simply referred to as λ above when we didn't allow for search on the job). It is natural to think that employed individuals also encounter new job opportunities at some rate λ_E, not necessarily equal to λ_U. We now consider the case in which $\lambda_E > 0$.

If the wage offer distribution is taken as exogenous, given by $F(w)$, say, then the addition of OTJ search is reasonably simple. In the exogenous wage offer distribution case, we can denote the employment state of the individual by w, her current wage rate, where we set $w = 0$ when she is unemployed. When she is employed at some wage $w > 0$, two distinct events can occur at each moment in time (because time is treated as continuous, the likelihood that both events occur simultaneously is 0). As in the case where $\lambda_E = 0$, her job may be "exogenously" terminated, in which case she is sent back to the unemployment state and begins a new unemployed search spell. With $\lambda_E > 0$, she may also be contacted by another firm. It is assumed that in this case the alternative wage offer, w', is observed immediately. The common assumption that is made, which we will employ as well, is that there are no direct costs associated with changing employers. If jobs differ along only one dimension, the rate of remuneration, then any job that pays a wage higher than the individual's current wage rate w will be strictly preferred by the individual, and will result in a job change. Then the "reservation wage" for an employed individual currently receiving a wage w is given by $w^*(w) = w$, and the individual will change jobs at the moment she receives a competing job offer if and only if $w' > w^*(w) = w$.[1]

In the case of OTJ search in a stationary environment, the rate at which the individual leaves the employment state due to a job loss is, as before, η. The rate at which she leaves her current job for another is

$$h_E(w) = \lambda_E \tilde{F}(w),$$

where $\tilde{F} \equiv 1 - F$, the survivor function. With a fixed wage offer distribution, it immediately follows that

$$\frac{\partial h_E(w)}{\partial w} = -\lambda_E f(w) < 0,$$

so the rate of "voluntary" departures from a job is a decreasing function of the current wage rate. The fact that at most one of these events can occur in any moment of employment at a job paying a wage of w implies that the total rate of leaving the job paying a wage of w is given by

$$h_T(w) = \eta + h_E(w).$$

By adding OTJ search to the standard "partial-partial" equilibrium[2] model of search, we are able to generate a number of empirical predictions that are supported by the evidence, at least to some degree. A few of the most important implications are the following:

1. Individuals with higher wages tend to have longer tenures at their job. Since the mean duration of a job spell is simply $h_T(w)^{-1}$, and since $\partial h_T(w)/\partial w < 0$, the claim follows.

2. Wages always increase when there is a job-to-job transition. Since the reservation wage for a voluntary job movement from a job paying a wage of w is simply w, it follows tautologically that the new job must pay a wage w' that is strictly greater than w. Note that this claim is not true if there is an intervening unemployment spell between the two jobs. In that case we know that $w \geq w^*(0)$, the reservation wage in the unemployment state, and $w' \geq w^*(0)$, but there is a strictly positive probability that $w' \leq w$.

3. The rate of transition from a job paying a wage of w into unemployment is independent of w. This result follows from the strong assumption that η, the rate of job destruction, is independent of the wage rate paid at the job.

The first two model implications are generally consistent with empirical observation. Jobs with lower wages usually last shorter periods of time than do jobs paying higher wages. Because the timing of arrivals of events is random, this implication only holds "on average." In particular, there are jobs paying very high wages that may be destroyed in a matter of weeks, while a lower paying job may last years. There is positive probability associated with each of these events, so model implications involving rates of change only hold on average.

Regarding the second implication, in the majority of job-to-job transitions, wages are found to increase, though there is a substantial proportion of such transitions associated with wage decreases. For example, in Flinn (2002a) it was found that wages increased in 71.1 percent of the job-to-job transitions of young US males.[3] There are many reasons that individuals change jobs, so the fact that not all job-to-job changes are associated with immediate wage increases is not surprising. For example, in the papers by Dey and Flinn (2005, 2008) in which jobs are characterized by wages and whether they provide health insurance, the utility associated with a given job is a function of two characteristics, and while all job-to-job transitions are utility-increasing, they need not be wage-increasing.

A more direct, but less economically interesting, explanation for such observations is the existence of substantial degrees of measurement error in wage observations. In a well-known, albeit imperfect, validation study of wage and earnings reporting information using the Panel Study of Income Dynamics (PSID) instrument, Bound et al. (1994) find evidence of substantial reporting error in these variables and measure the validity of responses under a classical measurement error assumption.[4] Other indications of the existence of substantial amounts of measurement error in wage reports can be gleaned from the cursory inspection of hourly wage reports collected in the Outgoing Rotation Group samples from the Current Population Survey. As documented for a few particular months in the late 1990s for groups of very young labor market participants, there is evidence of a substantial amount of "heaping" of observations on integer values of and the statutory minimum wage. Without knowing the actual pay rate of these individuals, we cannot be certain that this heaping results from systematic misreports, though this seems very likely.

The third implication is the most empirically questionable. It is often found that the rate of transition from a job paying a wage of w into unemployment is a decreasing function of w. Why haven't researchers

modified the model in the seemingly straightforward way of allow-
ing job offers to consist of the pair (w, η), where η is the rate of losing
the job due to termination? If it is assumed that η is a nonincreasing
deterministic function of w, then the model will produce a result consist
with empirical observation by construction. Moreover, as long as $\eta(w)$
is a deterministic function, employed individuals at a job $(w, \eta(w))$ will
accept all jobs with wage $w' \geq w$, as was the case when η was constant
in the population.[5] Such a simple generalization continues to produce
implication 2 above, so no wage decreases associated with a job-to-job
transition are implied. In order to produce a nonequilibrium model consistent with both η and w nonindependent and some wage decreases in
job-to-job transitions, it is sufficient to allow the function to be stochastic, so that it is possible to draw offers from some joint distribution of
(w, η) such that $w' > w$, $\eta' > \eta$, and $V_e(w', \eta') > V_e(w, \eta)$.

   While such a "fix up" solves the problem of counterfactual empirical implications, it comes at the cost of introducing an arbitrarily
specified bivariate distribution for (w, η) into the model, with no theoretical underpinnings for the form of the function or the dependence
between the dependent variables. The Dey and Flinn (2005) analysis
mentioned above develops an estimable model that does generate a
fairly complicated relationship between w and η that is produced within
an equilibrium model of Nash bargaining between workers and firms. In
their model, which attempts to explain the relationship between wages
and employer-provided health insurance coverage, a worker-firm pair
has the possibility of covering the match with health insurance, which
involves paying a premium, that reduces the likelihood of the termination of the match due to a negative health shock. In equilibrium,
higher match values are covered by health insurance, which yields a
positive association between wages, and the employer-provided health
insurance coverage, which generates the negative association between
wages and the likelihood of exit into unemployment that is observed
in the data.

10.2   Model Specifications

In this section we use two behavioral specifications to examine minimum wage effects in the presence of OTJ search. The structure of the
models described is essentially identical to that which we have been
using up to this point. In partial or general equilibrium frameworks
there are difficult, though interesting, issues to consider regarding the

behavior of firms "bidding" for the services of an individual at a point in time. The two model specifications we consider differ in how they treat the interactions between competing firms in this circumstance.

The differences and similarities of the two approaches are simple to describe. Say that a firm currently employs a worker who has a certain productivity θ (at the firm) and is paid a wage w. The employee meets another potential employer, and the (potential) productivity at that job is immediately revealed to be θ'. In both of the bargaining settings we consider, efficient mobility decisions are made. That is, the employee will change firms if and only if $\theta' > \theta$. The models differ solely in the nature of the wage determination process.

We devote most of our attention to the most theoretically interesting and difficult case, one that allows direct wage competition between two firms. This setup has been used by Postel-Vinay and Robin (2002), Dey and Flinn (2005), and Cahuc et al. (2006). Firms, competing for the same individual's services at a moment in time, are assumed to engage in a Bertrand competition for the employee, with the firm associated with the worst productivity level dropping out of the auction at the point where the match does not generate positive surplus for the firm. If, for example, the individual's productivity at the new potential employer exceeds that at his current firm, so that $\theta' > \theta$, it is assumed that the current firm makes a (doomed) effort to retain her services by making higher and higher wage offers until it drops out of the bidding at a wage offer $\tilde{w} = \theta$. In this case the employee moves to the new firm, and the outside option used to set her wage is the value of being employed at the "losing" firm at a wage equal to $\tilde{w} = \theta$ (i.e., when she receives all of the surplus of employment match).

The other situation that can arise under renegotiation is when the employee's productivity at the new firm is less than or equal to her current productivity, but greater than her current wage, or $w < \theta' \leq \theta$. Although the employee will not leave the current firm, given the model's property of efficient mobility, she will use the threat of leaving to increase her current wage w. In this case the potential employer bids for the individual's services until it reaches the point $\tilde{w} = \theta'$, at which point the potential employer drops out of the auction. The renegotiated wage at the current employer uses the value of being employed at the match value θ' with a wage equal to $\tilde{w} = \theta'$ as the outside option.

Our second bargaining scenario considers the case where each labor market participant's outside option value is equal to the value of unemployed search, independent of their current labor market state. Of course, this is the option value for those searching in the unemployment state at the time they encounter a potential employer. The second bargaining scenario posits that the value of unemployed search serves as the outside option even for employed searchers. This may be due to the fact that employed individuals are not able to credibly convey their current employment conditions (including wage or wage offer) to a new potential employer, while at the same time not being able to credibly reveal wage offers from potential employers to their current employers.

An alternative justification is one of lack of commitment. If offers must be rejected or accepted at the instant when they are tendered, then a worker loses her outside option the moment after it is received. When the option is lost, the only relevant one becomes quitting into the unemployment state, the value at which is always $V_U(m)$. Thus wage payments will always be determined using this outside option. Knowing this, a worker may insist that the firm transfer a lump sum amount to them to obtain their services at the moment when they have two employment options. To the extent that this is not recorded as a wage payment, this will have no effect on the wage process. Since all mobility is efficient in any case, such payments will have no impact on the mobility process. Thus the empirical wage-mobility process should be consistent with model assumptions even in the presence of unobservable (to us) one-time payments associated with the receipt of an offer by an employed individual.[6]

If we are to take the policy implications of these models seriously, the distinction between the two cases is potentially important. As we will see, the different specifications generate quite different estimates of primitive parameters, and sometimes radically diverse policy prescriptions regarding the minimum wage level. We will begin our discussion with the theoretically most interesting specification of two firm interactions, the one that generates contract renegotiations.

10.2.1 The Model with Renegotiation

As was true in previous chapters, offers are assumed to arrive to unemployed searchers at the constant rate λ_U, although now offers also arrive to employed individuals at the constant rate $\lambda_E > 0$. There exists a matching distribution, G, though in this chapter we will assume that θ is discrete, primarily for computational purposes. The set of values that θ can take is given by $\Omega_\theta = \{\theta_j\}_{j=1}^L$, where $0 < \theta_1 < \cdots < \theta_L < \infty$.

An employment spell begins when an unemployed searcher accepts a wage $w(\theta, U)$, where U denotes that the outside option is continued search in the unemployment state and θ is the match value associated with the job that was accepted. The acceptance set of matches from the unemployment state is given by $A(m)$, with $\theta^A(m)$ being the minimal θ value in $A(m)$.[7]

We denote the current labor market state of an employed individual by (θ, w) and any potential new state by (θ', w'). Consider the case of a currently employed individual with wage w and match value $\theta \in A(m)$ who meets a new potential employer at which the match value is θ'. Assume that the potential match value will only be reported to the current employer if the employee has an incentive to do so. One situation in which this will be the case is when $\theta' > \theta$. When this occurs, assume that a bargaining process for the individual's services begins between the current and potential employers and stops when one of the firms' surplus reaches zero, as in Bertrand competition. The loser of the competition will be the current employer when $\theta' > \theta$. Let the maximal value of match θ to the worker be given by $Q(\theta)$. Then the objective function for the Nash bargaining problem when $\theta' > \theta$ is

$$S(\theta', w', \theta) = \{V_E(\theta', w', \theta) - Q(\theta)\}^\alpha \times \{V_F(\theta', w', \theta) - 0\}^{1-\alpha},$$

where $V_F(\theta', w', \theta)$ denotes the new firm's value of the match. Note that, as before, the expected value of a vacancy, which is the firm's payoff in case the vacancy is not filled, is zero.

In the renegotiation case, the firm's value of the current employment contract is defined as follows. Over an infinitesimally small period of time ε, the firm earns a profit of $(\theta - w)\varepsilon$, which is discounted back to the present with the "infinitesimal" discount factor $(1 + \rho\varepsilon)^{-1}$. With "approximate probability" $\eta\varepsilon$, the match is exogenously terminated, and the firm earns no profit. With approximate probability $\lambda_E\varepsilon$, the worker receives a job offer from an alternative firm. If she reports this offer to her current firm, her wage will be renegotiated.[8] With approximate probability $(1 - \lambda_E\varepsilon - \eta\varepsilon)$, the worker does not receive another job offer and is not exogenously dismissed over the period ε. In this case the status quo is maintained. The term $o(\varepsilon)$ represents all other states that can occur over the period ε that involve two or more events, and which has the property that $\lim_{\varepsilon \to 0} (o(\varepsilon)/\varepsilon) = 0$. We denote the value to the firm as

$$V_F(\theta', w', \theta) = (1 + \rho\varepsilon)^{-1}\{(\theta' - w')\varepsilon + (\eta\varepsilon \times 0)$$

$$+ \left(\lambda_E\varepsilon \sum_{\tilde\theta \in B(\theta,\theta')} V_F(\theta', w(\theta', \tilde\theta), \tilde\theta)p(\tilde\theta)\right)$$

$$+ \left(\lambda_E\varepsilon P(\tilde\theta \le \theta) \times V_F(\theta', w', \theta)\right) + (\lambda_E\varepsilon P(\tilde\theta > \theta') \times 0)$$

$$+ \left((1 - \lambda_E\varepsilon - \eta\varepsilon) \times V_F(\theta', w', \theta)\right) + o(\varepsilon)\},$$

where $V_F(\theta', w(\theta', \tilde\theta), \tilde\theta)$ represents the equilibrium value to a firm of the productive match θ' when the worker's next best option has a match $\tilde\theta$, and where a value $\theta_j \in B(\theta', \theta)$ if and only if $\theta_j \le \theta'$ and $\theta_j > \theta$.

The interpretation of the arguments involving λ_E is as follows: given a dominant and dominated match value pair (θ', θ), we can partition Ω_θ into three sets. Since efficient mobility is an implication of our model structure, any new draw of a match value at a prospective employer that is greater than the match value at the current employer, θ', results in an immediate departure. This event implies a value to the firm of 0 under our assumption on its outside option (since it goes back to the state of having an unfilled vacancy). Moreover, if the employee meets a prospective employer at which her productivity is equal to θ', then she will be indifferent regarding which offer to accept because both offer a contract giving her all of the rents.[9] Independent of whether she stays, the firm will receive a value of 0 in this case as well. By our definition of the set B, we have assumed that she stays in such a case.

The set $B(\theta', \theta)$ contains all of those values that result in a renegotiation of the contract (w) at the current firm and that do not result in a departure. Since the total surplus associated with a match value is strictly increasing in the match value, the amount of surplus the individual can appropriate from θ' is strictly increasing in the value of the outside option. If the current outside option is θ, then any outside option greater than θ and less than θ' will result in a renegotiation. The value of the job to the firm at that point in time will be $V_F(\theta', w(\theta', \tilde\theta), \tilde\theta)$, where $w(\theta', \tilde\theta)$ will be the new wage paid and $\theta < \tilde\theta \le \theta'$. Finally, all potential matches less than or equal to the current outside option will not be reported to the firm, since the value of the outside option associated with these values is no greater than the current one. When such an offer arrives, the value of the firm's problem does not change. After rearranging terms and taking limits as $\varepsilon \to 0$, we have

$$V_F(\theta',w',\theta) = \left(\rho + \eta + \lambda_E P(\tilde{\theta} > \theta)\right)^{-1}$$

$$\times \left\{\theta - w + \lambda_E \sum_{\tilde{\theta} \in B(\theta,\theta')} V_F(\theta', w(\theta',\tilde{\theta}), \tilde{\theta})p(\tilde{\theta})\right\}.$$

The worker's value of being employed is defined similarly. The value of the worker's problem is given by

$$V_E(\theta',w',\theta) = \left(\rho + \eta + \lambda_E P(\tilde{\theta} > \theta)\right)^{-1} \times \left\{ w + \eta V_U \;(m) \right.$$

$$+ \lambda_E \left[\sum_{\tilde{\theta} \in B(\theta,\theta')} V_E(\theta', w(\theta',\tilde{\theta}), \tilde{\theta})p(\tilde{\theta}) \right.$$

$$\left. \left. + \sum_{\tilde{\theta} \in C(\theta')} V_E(\tilde{\theta}, w(\tilde{\theta},\theta'), \theta')p(\tilde{\theta}) \right] \right\},$$

where $V_E(\theta', w(\theta',\theta), \theta)$ is the equilibrium value of employment to a worker with match value θ' when her next best option has a match value of θ and the set $C(\theta')$ is the set of all $\theta_j \in \Omega_\theta$ such that $\theta_j > \theta'$. As we saw in the case of the firm, when an employee encounters a firm with a new match value $\tilde{\theta}$ that is lower than her current match θ but belongs to the set $B(\theta',\theta)$, her new value of employment at the current firm becomes $V_E(\theta', w(\theta',\tilde{\theta}), \tilde{\theta})$. Instead, when the match value at the newly contacted firm is greater than the current match value θ', the employee will change employers, and the new value of employment is given by $V_E(\tilde{\theta}, w(\tilde{\theta},\theta'), \theta')$. Thus the match value at the current firm becomes the relevant outside option of the worker that is faced by the new firm. Finally, when the match value at the prospective new employer is less than the current dominated match value θ, the new contact is not reported to the current firm since it would not improve the terms of the current contract. Because of this selective reporting, the value of employment contracts must be monotonically increasing within a job with at a particular firm. As originally noted by Postel-Vinay and Robin (2002), wage declines can be observed when moving directly between firms, though the value of the employment match must always be increasing.

With a new match value of $\theta' > \theta$, the surplus attained by the individual at the new match value with respect to the value she could attain at the old match value after extracting all the surplus associated with it is

$V_E(\theta', w(\theta', \theta), \theta) - Q(\theta)$,

where $Q(\theta) \equiv V_E(\theta, w(\theta, \theta), \theta)$ is the value of employment to the employee if she receives the total surplus of the match θ. In this case the wage function has the property that $\theta = w(\theta, \theta)$. Then

$$Q(\theta) = \left(\rho + \eta + \lambda_E P(\tilde{\theta} > \theta) \right)^{-1}$$

$$\times \left\{ \theta + \eta V_U(m) + \lambda_E \sum_{\tilde{\theta} \in C(\theta)} V_E(\tilde{\theta}, w(\tilde{\theta}, \theta), \theta) p(\tilde{\theta}) \right\}.$$

The model is closed after specifying the value of nonemployment, $V_U(m)$. We will learn more about the manner in which minimum wages impact job acceptance, the unemployment rate, and the equilibrium wage offer function in detail below. As was shown above, there is a minimal acceptable match value from the unemployment state denoted by $\theta^A(m)$, such that for all $\theta_j \geq \theta^A(m)$ the match is accepted. We define the set of acceptable match values out of the unemployment state by $D(\theta^A(m))$. We note that for the firm to earn nonnegative flow profits, it is necessary that $\theta^A(m) \geq m$.

The searcher's value of being unemployed is defined as

$$V_U(m) = \left(\rho + \lambda_U P(\tilde{\theta} \geq \theta^A(m)) \right)^{-1}$$

$$\times \left\{ b + \lambda_U \sum_{\tilde{\theta} \in D(\theta^A(m))} V_E(\tilde{\theta}, w(\tilde{\theta}, U), U) p(\tilde{\theta}) \right\},$$

where the outside option is that associated with remaining in the unemployment state U.

The equilibrium wage function, $w(\theta', \theta)$, is defined as follows: When an employed agent with an (acceptable) outside option θ meets a dominating match θ', the Nash-bargained wage is given by

$$w(\theta', \theta) = \arg\max_{w \geq m} S(\theta', w, \theta).$$

When an unemployed agent meets a new potential employer, the solution to the Nash-bargaining problem is given by

$$w(\theta, U) = \arg\max_{w \geq m} S_U(\theta, w, U),$$

where $S_U(\theta, w, U) = \{V_E(\theta, w, U) - V_U(m)\}^\alpha \times \{V_F(\theta, w, U)\}^{1-\alpha}$.

Table 10.1
Equilibrium wage matrix

Dominated value	Dominant value				
	θ_j	θ_{j+1}	...	θ_{L-1}	θ_L
θ_L					θ_L
θ_{L-1}				θ_{L-1}	$w(\theta_L, \theta_{L-1})$
$\vdots$				$\vdots$	$\vdots$
θ_{j+1}		θ_{j+1}	...	$w(\theta_{L-1}, \theta_{j+1})$	$w(\theta_L, \theta_{j+1})$
θ_j	θ_j	$w(\theta_{j+1}, \theta_j)$	...	$w(\theta_{L-1}, \theta_j)$	$w(\theta_L, \theta_j)$
U	$w(\theta_j, U)$	$w(\theta_{j+1}, U)$	...	$w(\theta_{L-1}, U)$	$w(\theta_L, U)$

The equilibrium wage function is defined by the matrix given in table 10.1. The value θ_j is the minimal acceptable match value from the set Ω_θ defined above, which was denoted as $\theta^A(m)$. The wage function is not defined for values of $\theta_j < \theta^A(m)$. Moreover the bargaining mechanism always produces efficient mobility, meaning that the current match value (i.e., the "dominant" one) is always at least as large as the "dominated" match value, which generates the outside option value in the Bertrand competition between firms.

An important feature of the Bertrand competition for workers given the discreteness of θ is that when the dominated value is equal to the dominant value, a positive-probability event, the worker captures all of the rents from the match. This means that the wage rate in this case is equal to the match value, simplifying the computation of the equilibrium wage function.

The equilibrium wage function computation is conducted in the following recursive manner: We begin by assuming that the only acceptable match value to an unemployed searcher is θ_L, which is the largest match in the set Ω_θ, so that $\theta^A(m) = \theta_L$. We begin with a guess of the value of unemployment generated by a decision rule that specifies only the highest match value is acceptable, which we will denote by $\tilde{V}_U(\theta_L)$.[10] In terms of an employment spell, the state (θ_L, θ_L) is an absorbing state, since no further job mobility can take place from that state during the current employment spell. The only way such a spell can end is through exogenous termination, which occurs at the constant rate η. The individual's value of being in such a spell (given the value of unemployment V_U) is

$$\tilde{V}_E(\theta_L, \theta_L, \theta_L) = \frac{\theta_L + \eta V_U(\theta_L)}{\rho + \eta}, \tag{10.1}$$

where the second argument in $\tilde{V}_E$ is the wage rate associated with the state (θ_L, θ_L), which is equal to θ_L. The firm's value is 0.

An unemployed searcher only accepts a match of θ_L, the probability of which is $p(\theta_L)$. When the unemployed searcher accepts the one employment contract available to her, it has the associated value

$$\tilde{V}_E(\theta_L, w, U) = \frac{w + \lambda_E p(\theta_L) \tilde{V}_E(\theta_L, \theta_L, \theta_L) + \eta \tilde{V}_U(\theta_L)}{\rho + \lambda_E p(\theta_L) + \eta},$$

while the value to the firm is

$$\tilde{V}_F(\theta_L, w, U) = \frac{\theta_L - w}{\rho + \lambda_E p(\theta_L) + \eta}.$$

The wage associated with this state is

$$\tilde{w}(\theta_L, U) = \arg\max_w (\tilde{V}_E(\theta_L, w, U) - \tilde{V}_U(\theta_L))^\alpha \tilde{V}_F(\theta_L, w, U)^{1-\alpha}.$$

The (new) implied value of unemployed search is then

$$\tilde{V}'_U(\theta_L) = \frac{b + \lambda_U p(\theta_L) \tilde{V}_E(\theta_L, \tilde{w}(\theta_L, U), U)}{\rho + \lambda_U p(\theta_L)}.$$

If $V'_U(\theta_L)$ is sufficiently "close" to the initial guess $V_U(\theta_L)$, then we say that the value of search when only θ_L is acceptable is given by $V_U(\theta_L) = \tilde{V}'_U(\theta_L)$. If not, we replace $V_U(\theta_L)$ with $\tilde{V}'_n(\theta_L)$, and repeat the process. We continue the iterations until convergence. [11]

A similar technique is used for the cases in which we set $\theta^A = \theta_j$ $j = 1, \ldots, L - 1$, for all j for which $\theta_j \geq m$. Each different "potential" critical value implies a unique wage distribution associated with it and a value of unemployed search given by $V^*_U(\theta_j)$. The optimal acceptance match chosen by the individual is the one that produces that highest value of searching in the unemployment state, namely

$$\theta^A(m) = \theta_j \Leftrightarrow V^*_U(\theta_j) = \max\{V^*_U(\theta_k)\}_{k=1}^L.$$

The equilibrium wage matrix is the one associated with that value of $\theta^A(m)$. If, for example, $L = 10$ and $\theta^A(m) = \theta_4$, then the (lower triangular) wage matrix is 8×7.

This is the algorithmic approach used to compute the wage matrix in table 10.1. Changes in primitive parameters will, of course, sometimes change the critical acceptance match $\theta^A(m)$, but not always because of the discreteness of the distribution. This property will be observed in some of the examples that we present below. While the discrete distribution assumption does have some negative aspects, computation of the equilibrium wages/values is simplified and some of the impacts of minimum wages on labor market outcomes and welfare are somewhat more transparent.

10.2.2   The Model without Renegotiation

The model without renegotiation is considerably simpler to describe. As we learned in the introduction to this section, the outside option in this case is always equal to the value of unemployed search, $V_U(m)$. There is efficient mobility, which means that the match value at a new firm in a job-to-job transition is strictly greater than the match value at the firm the individual is leaving. This implies that all job-to-job transitions are associated with an increase in an individual's wage. Since there is no renegotiation, the wage at a given firm is constant over the duration of employment at that firm.[12]

We now characterize the mobility-wage process in the no renegotiation case. The value of employment at an acceptable match value θ_i is given by

$$V_E(\theta_i) = \frac{w(\theta_i) + \eta V_U + \lambda_E \sum_{j>i} p_j V_E(\theta_j)}{\rho + \eta + \lambda_E p_i^+},$$

where $p_i^+ \equiv \sum_{j>i} p_j$. Given our assumption regarding the outside option in the bargaining problem, the value of the wage associated with acceptable match value θ_i is determined as

$$w(\theta_i) = \arg\max_{w \geq m} \left(\frac{w + \eta V_U + \lambda_E \sum_{j>i} p_j V_E(\theta_j)}{\rho + \eta + \lambda_E p_i^+} - V_U \right)^\alpha$$

$$\times \left(\frac{\theta_i - w}{\rho + \eta + \lambda_E p_i^+} \right)^{1-\alpha}$$

$$= \arg\max_{w \geq m} \left(w - (\rho + \lambda_E p_i^+) V_U(m) + \lambda_e \sum_{j>i} p_j V_E(\theta_j) \right)^\alpha \qquad (10.2)$$

$$\times (\theta_i - w)^{1-\alpha}$$

$$= \max \left\{ m, \alpha \theta_i + (1-\alpha) \left[(\rho + \lambda_e p_i^+) V_U(m) - \lambda_e \sum_{j>i} p_j V_E(\theta_j) \right] \right\}.$$

The wage-setting rule is a simple extension of that associated with the bargaining problem in the absence of on-the-job search (i.e., $\lambda_E = 0$).

It is straightforward to show that the wage function is monotonically nondecreasing in the match value in this case, that is,

$$w(\theta_i) \leq w(\theta_{i+1}) \leq \cdots \leq w(\theta_L),$$

where $\theta^A(m) = \theta_i$. The weak inequalities follow from the fact that a binding minimum wage will, in general, produce multiple acceptable match values at which the minimum wage is binding. If θ_H was the smallest acceptable match value with an associated wage rate greater than m, then $w(\theta_H) < w(\theta_{H+1}) < \cdots < w(\theta_L)$, so the wage sequence will be strictly increasing over this set of acceptable matches. The monotonicity in the wage function in the no-renegotiation case will have important implications in determining the optimal minimum wage rate. In the renegotiation case, monotonicity of the wage in the current match value depends on the values of the primitive parameters. In this case, it does not.

The solution of the model is completed by determining the minimal acceptable match value from the unemployment state. This is accomplished by computing the value of search for each of the possible acceptance sets, differentiated by the lowest match value included in the set. When the minimum wage is less than all match values, there are L possible values of θ^A. When there is a minimum wage m that is greater than some subset of possible match draws, the search for the value θ^A is restricted to the subset of Θ_θ with values of θ greater than or equal to m. Let the value of search be given by $\tilde{V}_U(\theta_i)$, when θ_i is the minimal acceptable value. Then $V_U = \max\{\tilde{V}_U(\theta_i)\}_{i:\ \theta_i \geq m}$ and $\theta^A = \theta_j$ is the associated minimal acceptable match value when the arg max of the right-hand side is equal to j.

10.2.3 Examples
To fix ideas, we present some examples of the equilibrium wage function computations. We set the parameters of the search environment at $\alpha = 0.25, \lambda_U = 0.2, \lambda_E = 0.05, \eta = 0.01, \rho = 0.01$, and $b = -5$. We assume that the match distribution has six mass points, with

θ Values	$p(\theta)$
5	0.1
8	0.2
11	0.25
14	0.2
17	0.15
20	0.1

Table 10.2
Wage matrix, $m = 0$

Dominated θ value	Dominant θ value					
	5	8	11	14	17	20
20						20
17					17.00	17.35
14				14.00	13.84	14.19
11			11.00	10.27	10.11	10.46
8		8.00	6.70	5.96	5.80	6.15
5	5.00	3.32	2.02	1.80	1.12	1.47
U	4.78	3.10	1.79	1.06	0.90	1.25

We begin by considering the case where there is no minimum wage. For these values of the parameters, we find that all match values in Ω_θ are acceptable when a unemployed searcher meets a firm, namely $\theta^A(0) = 5$. The equilibrium wage distribution is given in table 10.2. The most striking feature of this wage matrix may be the degree of nonmonotonicity in the wages observed when the outside option is U, $\theta = 5$, or $\theta = 8$. For individuals coming out of unemployment, the highest wage offer observed is the one associated with the lowest acceptable match value, $\theta = 5$. Although the value of the employment contract is strictly increasing in the match value found by the unemployed searcher, wages are not. In fact, were it not for the wage associated with the highest match value, exactly the opposite would be true. A similar pattern is observed in every row of the matrix that contains more than three entries.

The low wages associated with the high match values, holding constant the dominated value, are the employee's payment for the future bargaining advantages that the match conveys during the employment spell. Under this set of parameters, the rate of meeting other employers, 0.05, is quite high relative to the rate of exogenous termination of the job (and employment) spell, 0.01. Combined with the relatively low discount rate of 0.01, the wage "compensation" for the future bargaining advantage is high. Obviously, when there is no OTJ search, a high match value delivers no future bargaining advantage, and there are no "compensating differentials" observed in the wage function. As an illustration, we determine the equilibrium wage rates for the same parameter values used to generate table 10.2, except that we set $\lambda_E = 0$. The wage function in this case is as shown in table 10.3.

Table 10.3
Wage matrix, $\lambda_c = 0$

	Dominant θ value					
Dominated θ value	5	8	11	14	17	20
U		7.60	8.35	9.10	9.85	10.60

Without renegotiation, the match value of 5 that was previously acceptable is no longer so. The wages are much higher coming out of the unemployment state, since there is no bargaining advantage component of remuneration. Most important, for our purposes, the wage function is monotonically increasing in θ because wages are the only way to transfer match surplus to the worker and the outside option is the same, $V_U(0)$, at all jobs.

We now return to the example wage function in table 10.2 to discuss implications of the model regarding patterns of wage changes over an employment spell. Given the arrival of a "reportable" competing match value, two things can occur. If the new match arrival is larger than the current dominated match value and less than or equal to the current match value associated with the job, there is no job mobility, but there is renegotiation of the wage contract. Since the only "negotiable" element of the employment contract is the wage, this is increased. Thus, while the worker remains at the same firm, all wage changes are positive.

In the second case, where the new match value exceeds the value of the current match, there is job mobility and contract negotiation. The old dominant match value becomes the new dominated match value and generates the outside option value. Although both the dominant and dominated match value increase with a job-to-job move, the wage rate need not. Once again, this is because part of the employee's share of the surplus is generated by the OTJ bargaining option, and this option value may increase to such an extent in the job-to-job move that a wage reduction is required to satisfy the surplus division rule.

We turn to considering the impact of binding minimum wages in the model specification that allows contract renegotiation. In the model without OTJ search, minimum wages can only be binding in one particular manner, which is by constraining the choice set of the worker and the firm. In that case, a binding minimum wage always produced an acceptance match value, θ^A in our notation, that is greater than what we refer to as the "implicit" acceptable match value. In other words,

Table 10.4
Wage matrix, $m = 1.5$

Dominated θ value	Dominant θ value					
	5	8	11	14	17	20
20						20
17					17.00	17.35
14				14.00	13.84	14.19
11			11.00	10.27	10.11	10.46
8		8.00	6.70	5.96	5.80	6.15
5	5.00	3.40	2.10	1.50	1.50	1.55
U	4.82	3.32	2.02	1.50	1.50	1.50

workers would have accepted lower matches than m, but were constrained not to by minimum wage law. In that setting, the minimum wage essentially serves as a coordination device that enables workers with little bargaining power to achieve more of the surplus produced by the match. The cost of this gain was a lower probability of finding an acceptable match.

The minimum wage potentially plays an altogether different role in the presence of OTJ search under renegotiation. We illustrate the role of the minimum wage when it is set at (relatively) low and high values. All the parameters describing the labor market environment remain the same. In the first example, the minimum wage is set at \$1.50. Since all match values are acceptable when $m = 0$, and since the the minimum match value is 5, clearly all matches are still in the choice set of the bargaining worker-firm pair, by which we mean that the firm can earn nonzero flow profits when paying m for all $\theta \in \Omega_\theta$. Solving the model, we find that the equilibrium wage matrix is given in table 10.4.

The first important thing to note about this example is that the acceptance match value has remained the same at $\theta^A(1.5) = 5$. All matches that were previously accepted in equilibrium still are.[13] However, the minimum wage constraint on the bargaining process has changed the bargained outcomes for most of the wages associated with dominated values of $\theta = 5$ and U. The impact has come through the improvement in the wage distribution that resulted from not allowing the firm to be fully compensated for its contribution to the future bargaining power of the individual during the current employment spell. Where the minimum wage is binding, the implication is that the individual is receiving more than her "fair" share of the surplus, which in our example is set at 0.25. This is a benefit to the supply side of the market, particularly

Table 10.5
Wage matrix, $m = 13$

Dominated θ value	Dominant θ value		
	14	17	20
20			20
17		17.00	17.35
14	14.00	13.84	14.19
U	13.00	13.00	13.00

those in unemployment and who have found employment at the minimal acceptable match value. Firms still earn positive profits whenever they employ an individual who has a dominated match value less than the value of the current match, and minimum wages cannot affect the wage payment when $\theta' = \theta$.

Finally, consider the case where, even under renegotiation, the minimum wage is set at such a high level that otherwise acceptable job matches are deleted from the worker-firm choice set. In this example, we set $m = 13$. The wage function becomes as shown in table 10.5.

In comparison with the relevant rows and columns of table 10.4, the new, extremely high, value of the minimum wage has no discernible impact on the wages negotiated during OTJ search. The new minimum wage has a large impact on the wage offers to currently unemployed workers, though the probability of getting an acceptable offer has substantially decreased.

10.3   Endogenous Contact Rates

10.3.1   Specification of the Matching Function with OTJ Search

We now extend the model to a very simple general equilibrium setting where contact rates between searchers on both sides of the market are determined endogenously. We use the matching function structure, once again, to accomplish this task. Most applications of the matching model assume away OTJ search. A natural way to attempt to incorporate OTJ search into the matching framework, suggested in Petrongolo and Pissarides (2001), for instance, is to define collective search effort as

$$S = U + \tau E,$$

where τ denotes the relative search effectiveness of employed searchers, which we might presume to be less than 1. We can then define a meeting function

$$M = m(S, V),$$

which gives the total amount of meetings between firms and an intensity-weighted measure of searchers. In this case the rate of meetings between firms and unemployed searchers is given by

$$\lambda_U = \frac{m(S, V)}{S},$$

while the meeting rate between employed searchers and firms is given by

$$\lambda_E = \tau \frac{m(S, V)}{S}.$$

The ratio of contact rates for employed and unemployed searchers is[14]

$$\frac{\lambda_E}{\lambda_U} = \tau.$$

FM used a directed search formulation of the problem, in which it was assumed that a firm creating a vacancy chooses between a vacancy directed toward unemployed searchers or employed searchers. Each type of vacancy is associated with a different flow cost to the firm. For example, in attempting to find unemployed searchers, the firm might place advertisements in newspapers or on the Internet, whereas a firm looking for recruits already employed might target their competitors. These types of search activities can be expected to have different costs and success rates in terms of initial contacts. Moreover, given a successful recruitment effort, it is clear that the expected payoffs can differ greatly. A firm contacting an unemployed searcher will have a successful recruitment effort as long as the match draw is greater than or equal to $\theta^A(m)$. The outside option used in the wage bargaining process is $V_U(m)$ in this case. Conversely, a firm searching among individuals who are already employed at a job with associated match value $\theta_j \in A(m)$ will have a lower probability of a successful recruitment effort, since only a draw of $\theta' > \theta_j$ will ultimately lead to positive profits for the firm. In addition, under the model with wage renegotiation, the successfully recruited individual will have an outside option $Q(\theta_j) \geq V_U(m)$, so a firm making a successful match with an employed individual will earn lower profits, on average. The advantage a firm searching among employed individuals has is that there are usually many more of them than there are unemployed searchers in steady state equilibrium.

Let the number of matches in the "unemployed" search market be given by

$$M^U = M^U(U, K_U),$$

and the number of matches in the employed search market by

$$M^E = M^E(E, K_E).$$

For the purpose of implementation, we assume that each market-specific matching function is Cobb–Douglas, with

$$M^U = U^{\omega_U} K_U^{(1-\omega_U)},$$

$$M^E = E^{\omega_E} K_E^{(1-\omega_E)},$$

where $\omega_j \in (0, 1)$, $j = U, E$.

Firms may create vacancies in either type of search market, so the expected values of vacancies in the two markets are equal in equilibrium. Let the flow cost associated with a vacancy in market be ψ_j, $j = U, E$. Then the expected value of holding a vacancy in the unemployed search market, V_{K_U} is expressed as

$$\rho V_{K_U} = -\psi_U + \frac{M^U(U, K_U)}{K_U}$$
$$\times \sum_{\tilde{\theta} \in A(m)} p(\tilde{\theta})[V_F(\tilde{\theta}, w(\tilde{\theta}, U), U) - V_{K_U}],$$

while the expected value of a holding a vacancy in the employed agent search market satisfies

$$\rho V_{K_E} = -\psi_E + \frac{M^E(E, K_E)}{K_E}$$
$$\times \sum_{\tilde{\theta} \in A(m)} p_{SS}(\tilde{\theta}) \sum_{\theta' > \tilde{\theta}} p(\theta')[V_F(\theta', w(\theta', \tilde{\theta}), \tilde{\theta}) - V_{K_E}],$$

where $p_{SS}(\cdot)$ is the steady state distribution of match values across jobs. Imposing the FEC on each market, we have

$$\psi_U = \frac{M^U(U, K_U)}{K_U} \sum_{\tilde{\theta} \in A(m)} p(\tilde{\theta}) V_F(\tilde{\theta}, w(\tilde{\theta}, U), U), \tag{10.3}$$

$$\psi_E = \frac{M^E(E, K_E)}{K_E} \sum_{\tilde{\theta} \in A(m)} p_{SS}(\tilde{\theta}) \sum_{\theta' > \tilde{\theta}} p(\theta') V_F(\theta', w(\theta', \tilde{\theta}), \tilde{\theta}). \tag{10.4}$$

10.3.2 Labor Market Participation Decisions

In FM, the participation decision framework described in section 3.5 is generalized to allow for changing participation rates with age. This extension is primarily necessitated by estimation issues that are discussed more fully in the next section and in FM. We provide a brief outline of the participation model for purposes of completeness. The model allows for participation decisions to be a function of the individual's age, though in a very mechanical manner. A more complete treatment would allow for individuals to trade off participation in the labor market with the accumulation of human capital associated with school attendance, but that extension is the subject of our ongoing research.

We write the value of being out of the labor force as

$$V_O(\xi, a) = \frac{\xi + r(a)}{\rho},$$

where ξ is a continuous random variable which is independently and identically distributed in the population with c.d.f. F and $r(a)$ is a weakly decreasing function of the individual's (potential labor market) age, a. The draw ξ is taken to represent an individual's constant flow value of being out of the labor force, while $r(a)$ is the (common to all agents) flow value of being out of the labor force as a function of their potential labor market age. Dividing by ρ gives the function V_O a present value interpretation.

Since the (flow) value of occupying the out of the labor force state is nonincreasing in the age of the individual, and since the value of the unemployment state is constant, labor force participation is an absorbing state.

An individual of potential labor market age a will be in the labor market if

$$V_O(\xi, a) \leq V_U(m)$$

$$\Rightarrow \xi < \rho V_U(m) - r(a),$$

so the participation probability of an individual of age a under minimum wage regime m is

$$\pi(a, m) = F(\rho V_U(m) - r(a)).$$

Given that the function r is nonincreasing in a, the participation rate is nondecreasing in a. It is also immediately obvious that increases in the value of search induced by a change in the minimum wage will result in increases in the participation rate at all ages.

The participation decision adds the distribution function F and the function r to the set of model parameters. After selecting parametric forms for these functions, the participation decision can be integrated into the model, and estimates of the parameters characterizing F and r can be obtained given the satisfaction of certain identification conditions.

10.4   Estimation Issues

We will explore a few issues that arise in estimating the OTJ search model of search and bargaining that were not present in the model without OTJ search, whose estimation we considered in detail in chapter 7. Readers interested in pursuing these issues further are referred to FM for additional discussion.

Without OTJ search, all employment spells contain only one job spell, by definition. With OTJ search, employment spells may consist of a large number of jobs; the distribution of job spells per employment spell will primarily depend on the rate parameters characterizing the model, as well as the matching distribution G. In addition, without OTJ search, the steady state distribution of wages is achieved immediately, since it is simply the truncated (from below, at the reservation wage w^*) population wage offer distribution. Instead, in the model with OTJ search, the steady state wage distribution is only attained after a cohort of labor market entrants have been in the labor market a sufficiently long period of time.[15] For these reasons a stock sample-based estimator like the one described in section 7.2 cannot be used without significant adjustments, modifications that allow the distribution of observed sample characteristics to systematically differ from the analogous steady state distribution. To accomplish this, FM utilize a different type of estimator (method of simulated moments, or MSM), and add information on transitions between labor market states over a one-year period to get a sense of the mobility process between jobs within and between employment spells.

The data used to estimate the model contain information on households and individuals within them from the 1996 panel of the Survey of Income and Program Participation (SIPP). A main objective of the SIPP is to provide accurate and comprehensive information about the principal determinants of the income of individual households in the United States. The SIPP collects monthly information on individual's labor market activity, including earnings, average hours worked, and whether the individual changed jobs during the month, which makes it an attractive data set with which to study employment dynamics of job seekers and workers.

Although the size of the SIPP's target sample is large, our sample size has been greatly reduced through the imposition of several restrictions. FM only include individuals aged 16 to 30 who did not participate in the armed services or in any welfare program (e.g., TANF, Food Stamps, WIC) during the sample period. In addition to these general selection criteria, we imposed a restriction that is particular to estimating a stationary on-the-job search model with minimum wages. The minimum wage changed from $4.75 to $5.15 on September 1, 1997, and remained at $5.15 for the remainder of the SIPP survey period. Even though the SIPP interviews individuals every four months for up to twelve times from 1996 to 2000, we used data only from February 1998 to February 2000 in order to allow adequate time for the labor market to adjust to the policy change and to avoid minimum wage changes within the survey period. A drawback of defining a sample window close to the end of the panel, however, is that discontinuities in respondents' employment histories become increasingly present as individuals approach the end of the survey period. Because our econometric specification relies heavily on identifying transitions between labor market states, it is essential that individuals have complete labor market histories. After excluding individuals with incomplete histories, our final sample consisted of 3048 individuals.

FM use a moment-based estimation procedure to estimate the model. The set of sample moments is estimated using cross-sectional data from February 1998 and February 1999, as well as data that describes individuals' labor market careers between these two points in time. The cross-sectional moments include the proportion of the sample that is unemployed, the mean and standard deviation of wages, and the proportion of workers who earn the minimum wage. Other moments describe employment transitions and wage changes between the two points in time, and include the proportion of individuals employed in February 1998 who lose their job before February 1999, and the mean wage change among workers who have a job-to-job transition during the year.

Table 10.6 contains descriptive statistics generated from the data. In February 1998, 4.3 percent of the sample was unemployed. Among

Table 10.6
Descriptive statistics: Individuals aged 16 to 30 years

	February 1998		February 1999
Proportion unemployed	0.043		0.030
Mean wage	$9.47		$10.39
Standard deviation of wages	$4.67		$5.09
Proportion of minimum wage earners	0.033		0.018
Proportion earning wage greater than $20	0.043		0.053
Proportion employed in February 1998 that exit into unemployment within 12 months		0.064	
Proportion employed in February 1998 with at least one job change within 12 months		0.291	
Mean wage at initial job among individuals employed in February 1998 who have job-to-job transition before February 1999		$8.43	
Mean wage change among individuals employed in February 1998 who have job-to-job transition before February 1999		$0.90	
Standard deviation of wage change among individuals employed in February 1998 who have job-to-job transition before February 1999		$4.33	
Mean wage at first job for those unemployed in February 1998 who become employed within 12 months		$8.48	
Standard deviation of wages at first job for those unemployed in February 1998 who become employed within 12 months		$4.43	

employed workers, the mean and standard deviation of wages were $9.47 and $4.67, with 3.3 percent of workers earning the minimum wage. Our moment-based estimation strategy allows us to include workers in the sample with wages below the minimum wage, although they comprise a very small proportion of the sample.[16]

Turning to measures of employment and wage dynamics, we see that 29 percent of workers in the sample who were employed in February 1998 transitioned directly to another job before February 1999 (i.e., had no intervening spell of unemployment). This indicates that a model that assumes $\lambda_E = 0$ may be seriously misspecified. The mean wage in February 1998 for these workers is $8.43, about one dollar less than the mean wage of the full sample. While the mean change in wages across jobs for these workers of $0.90 is fairly small, the distribution of changes is considerably dispersed (the standard deviation of the change is $4.32). The size of the mean wage change is due partially to the existence of wage decreases across consecutive jobs, as 32.2 percent of employed workers accept new jobs with lower wages. However, the nature of the wage-bargaining process between individuals and firms in the model that includes renegotiation does not imply that wages have to be at least as large at the destination job as at the current job in order for the individual to leave his current job. Workers may leave their current jobs to accept new, lower wage jobs if the option value of renegotiation is large enough.

The transition rate from employment to unemployment is also included in the set of moments that measure employment dynamics. The percentage of individuals in the sample who are employed in February 1998 and who exit into unemployment before February 1999 is 6.4 percent. The group of individuals who make this transition consist of both those who "voluntarily" leave their job and those who are "involuntarily" dismissed. Among those individuals who make the opposite transition, from unemployment to employment, the mean wage at the first job is $8.48. This is about one dollar less than the mean of the cross-sectional wage distribution in February 1998 for the full sample. The distribution of initial wages for the individuals making this transition is also slightly less dispersed than is observed in the cross-sectional distribution.

As one can see from a comparison of the February 1998 and 1999 statistics, it does not appear that a steady state assumption is appropriate. If this group of individuals were in the steady state phase of their labor market careers, we should observe no systematic differences in labor market outcomes across the two years, which obviously is not the case. By allowing individuals to enter the labor market at different ages, we can capture most of these systematic changes in the sample distributions in a simple way. For example, the fact that fewer sample members are in jobs paying the minimum wage in 1999 can be attributed to the fact that they have had an additional year to locate better jobs. How much improvement in this statistic we would expect to see depends on the age distribution of the sample at the initial sampling date (February 1998) and the parameters that describe the labor market environment. The same kind of argument can be made with respect to differences in the mean wage level, the proportion unemployed, and so on.

The MSM estimator worked well in practice in terms of delivering precise estimates of primitive parameters characterizing the supply side of the market after imposing standard parametric assumptions on many of the unknown functions. For example, the matching distribution G was restricted to be a discrete approximation to a lognormal distribution. The estimator also managed to produce reasonable values for the bargaining power parameter α under all of the model specifications that were estimated.[17]

In terms of the demand side of the model, the unknown parameters characterizing the employed and unemployed search markets are the flow cost of holding a vacancy, ψ_U and ψ_E, and the two parameters characterizing the constant returns to scale Cobb–Douglas matching technologies in the two search markets, ω_U and ω_E. If the stock of vacancies in each market was observable, then these parameters would all be identified, in theory. Without our observing the vacancy rates, however, we can identify only one set of parameters and assume the other set to be known. Since there is a wide range of estimates of matching function parameters (see Petrongolo and Pissarides 2001), we simply set $\omega_U = \omega_E = 0.5$. By this assumption, it is possible to ("conditionally") consistently estimate ψ_U and ψ_E.

Much of our attention in the estimation phase of the analysis concerns the sensitivity of estimates of primitive parameters and policy implications to the assumption made regarding the presence or absence of renegotiation. In terms of setting up a kind of "horse race" between the two assumptions, it is important to note that the primitive parameters are exactly the same in the two behavioral specifications. The difference between them is in the (implicit) specification of the mapping from the selected sample characteristics into the point estimates. Formally, we let the sample characteristics used to define the MSM estimator be denoted by X. Let the vector of primitive parameters characterizing the supply side of the market be given by φ, and let the value of the simulated sample characteristics under behavioral specification z be given by $\tilde{X}_z(\varphi)$, where $z = 1$ denotes the case of renegotiation and $z = 2$ denotes the case of no renegotiation. The positive-definite weighting matrix, A, is computed by resampling the data. Then the estimate of the primitive parameters under behavioral specification z is given by

$$\hat{\varphi}_z = \arg\min_{\varphi} (X - \tilde{X}_z(\varphi))' A (X - \tilde{X}_z(\varphi)), \qquad z = 1, 2.$$

Associated with the estimated $\hat{\varphi}_z$ is the value of the distance function evaluated at $\hat{\varphi}_z$, denoted by $D_z \geq 0$, $z = 1, 2$.

Given the estimates of the primitive parameters of the model that characterize the supply side of the market, we can conduct a bootstrap-based test between the renegotiation and no-renegotiation specifications of the model. The idea behind the test is the following. Given the actual data and the weighting matrix A, we found what seems to be a large difference in D_1 and D_2. In order to assess the "significance" of the difference, we resampled the original data set 50 times,[18] recomputed the weighting matrix A each time, and then reestimated the model with the resampled data characteristics vector and weighting matrix under both bargaining assumptions. More formally, we can define

$$D_z^r = \min_{\varphi} (X^r - \tilde{X}_z(\varphi))'A^r(X^r - \tilde{X}_z(\varphi)),$$

where r denotes the bootstrap replication, $r = 1, \ldots, 50$. We then define the difference

$$\Delta D^r \equiv D_1^r - D_2^r$$

and look at the distribution of the (50) values of ΔD^r. If fewer than two of the values are negative, we could conclude that there was strong support for the no renegotiation assumption, based on the data characteristics we included in defining the estimator and given all the other usual caveats that apply.

10.5 Estimation Results

Table 10.7 gives the estimates from the models, both with and without renegotiation. As the estimates in the first column indicate, without renegotiation the average time between contacts for unemployed searchers is $(0.505)^{-1}$, slightly less than 2 months. Once a job offer is received, the acceptance probability is $\tilde{G}(m) = 0.49$, resulting in a mean unemployment duration of $(\lambda_U \tilde{G}(m))^{-1} = 4.1$ months. An employed individual receives an alternative job offer from a competing firm approximately every $(0.309)^{-1} = 3.24$ months. Given an offer, the probability that the worker accepts it and changes employers depends on his or her current match value. The estimated exogenous dissolution rate of jobs is 0.013, implying that workers are exogenously terminated from their jobs every $(0.013)^{-1} = 6.4$ years, on average.

The estimates for the model with renegotiation in the second column of table 10.7 indicate that the average time between contacts for unemployed searchers is $(0.505)^{-1}$, which is identical to the estimate in

Table 10.7
Model estimates

	Without renegotiation	With renegotiation
m	5.15	5.15
λ_U	0.505 (0.006)	0.505 (0.055)
λ_e	0.309 (0.004)	0.156 (0.005)
η	0.013 (0.001)	0.010 (0.001)
μ_θ	1.615 (0.048)	2.621 (0.058)
σ_θ	0.846 (0.026)	0.175 (0.059)
α	0.380 (0.010)	0.320 (0.012)
Distance function value	743.77	1,216.34

Note: Instantaneous value of search, b, set equal to -2 in both estimations.

the model without renegotiation. For all other parameters the estimates differ, sometimes noticeably, across the two bargaining specifications. When a job offer is received by an unemployed searcher, the probability that individual accepts it is $\tilde{G}(m) = 0.99$. Thus the estimated length of an unemployment spell is $(\lambda_U \tilde{G}(m))^{-1} = 2$ months, about half the time implied by the model without renegotiation. Once employed, an individual receives an alternative job offer from a competing firm every $(0.152)^{-1} = 6.4$ months, approximately half as frequently as in the model without renegotiation. This is expected, since in order to generate the same amount of wage dispersion as in a model without renegotiation, offers must arrive less frequently. The estimated exogenous dissolution rate of jobs is 0.010, which implies that workers are exogenously terminated from their jobs every 8.3 years, on average.

In the model with renegotiation, the average $\ln \theta$ draw in the population is 2.621 with a standard deviation of 0.175 (the implied mean and standard deviation of the match draw θ in levels are 7.19 and 7.35). Without renegotiation, these values are 1.615 and 0.846 (with the mean and standard deviation of the match draw θ in levels being 13.96 and 2.46). The differences in the estimates of these parameters across models stem from differences in the estimates of the bargaining power parameter. The estimate of the bargaining power parameter for workers is

0.32 when renegotiation is allowed and is 0.38 when workers are not allowed to renegotiate. The lower bargaining power in the model with renegotiation causes the same set of observed wages to be mapped to a match distribution that is centered to the right of the match distribution in the model without renegotiation. This was apparent in the different transition rates out of unemployment implied by the two models given the same job offer arrival probability—the larger mean and smaller standard deviation of the match distribution in the model with renegotiation leaves almost no mass of the distribution near the minimum wage, leading all unemployed searchers to accept any job offer they receive.

Figure 10.1a and b plots the wage functions against workers' current match value. Figure 10.1a depicts the case where workers are not allowed to renegotiate their wage at their current job. The wage function is increasing in the current match value, as expected. Figure 10.1b depicts the case where workers are allowed to renegotiate their wage at their current job. Each wage function plotted in this figure corresponds to a different outside option. The wage functions corresponding to the outside options of unemployment, U, and the minimal acceptable match value, θ_9, are nonmonotone.[19] Workers coming out of unemployment, for example, accept lower initial wages at jobs with higher match values as payment for future bargaining advantages. The wage function loses this feature as the outside option increases. Outside options of at least θ_{14}, for example, produce a wage function that is increasing in the dominant match value.

The demand side parameter estimates are shown in table 10.8. Setting the Cobb–Douglas parameter equal to 0.5 in the model without renegotiation results in vacancy rates for unemployed and employed searchers of 0.009 and 0.092 and corresponding flow costs of a vacancy of $92.45 and $54.26, respectively. The vacancy rates are considerably smaller in the model with renegotiation, equal to 0.004 for vacancies for unemployed searchers and 0.024 for vacancies for employer workers. The corresponding flow costs are larger for vacancies for the unemployed than in the model without renegotiation, $137.85, but smaller for vacancies for employed searchers in the model with renegotiation, $30.75.

We now consider the distribution of the (50) values of ΔD^r, which are used to construct a relatively informal bootstrap-based horse race between the two bargaining specifications. At the bottom of table 10.7 we see that the value of the distance function associated with the no

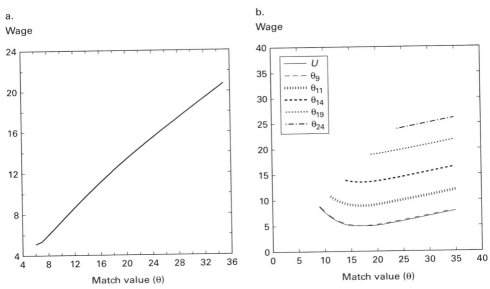

Figure 10.1
Wage function and workers' current match value: (a) For workers not allowed to renegotiate their wage at their current job, the wage function is increasing in the current match
value. (b) For workers allowed to renegotiate their wage at their current jobs, each wage
function corresponds to a different outside option. The wage functions corresponding to
the outside options of unemployment U and the minimal acceptable match value θ_9 are
nonmonotone. Workers coming out of unemployment, for example, accept lower initial
wages at jobs with higher match values as payment for future bargaining advantages. The
wage function loses this feature as the outside option increases.

Table 10.8
Point estimates of demand side parameters

	Without renegotiation	With renegotiation
Vacancy rate		
Unemployed	0.009	0.004
Employed	0.092	0.024
Flow vacancy cost		
Unemployed	$92.45	$137.85
Employed	$54.26	$30.75

renegotiation case is sufficiently less than the value associated with the renegotiation case, which gives a large value of $\Delta D = D_1 - D_2 = 472.57$. Our bootstrap procedure produced 50 new values of this difference, one for each replication. Over the 50 replications, the average value of ΔD^r was 468.93, with the minimum value being 417.08 and the maximum value being 544.66. While the number of replications is fairly small, there is no indication that performing more replications would alter the finding that within our modeling structure, the no renegotiation bargaining protocol is significantly more consistent with the data features that are used to define our estimator.

10.6 Optimal Minimum Wages with OTJ Search

In attempting to tease policy implications from such a stylized modeling framework, it is essential to get some idea of the sensitivity of implications regarding the "optimal" minimum wage to variations in behavioral assumptions. FM computed optimal minimum wages, assuming (1) renegotiation or no renegotiation and (2) general or partial equilibrium. This gives us four environments to consider.

The structure of the social welfare function is identical to the one that we considered previously in section 4.2.1, and applied in the no-OTJ search case in chapter 9, with equal weights applied to all agents on both sides of the market. As was the case before, we think of groups of agents comprised of OLF individuals, unemployed individuals, employed individuals, and firms with filled vacancies. The only difference from the no-OTJ search case is that the expected value of being in the employment state is a more complex expression. This has no practical significance, however, since in both the no-OTJ and OTJ cases, the expected value of being employed is computed using simulation methods.

Table 10.9 shows the results of the policy experiments for the four model specifications considered. In comparing the results across specifications, it is important to bear in mind that each of the four experiments are run using the specification-specific parameter estimates. The results cannot be used to say how the choice of equilibrium framework and renegotiation possibilities impact the choice of an optimal minimum wage for a given set of parameter values. While such a comparison may of some interest, in our view it is not the appropriate way to compare policy implications across regimes.

Consistent with the results obtained in chapter 9, in three of the four regimes we find the social welfare-maximizing minimum wage to be

Table 10.9
Policy experiments under OTJ search

Equilibrium type	PE	PE	GE	GE
Renegotiation?	No	Yes	No	Yes
Characteristics				
m^*	$12.05	$14.05	$4.70	$13.30
Baseline U	0.051	0.022	0.051	0.022
"Optimal" U	0.140	0.042	0.046	0.035
Welfare change (%)	1.70	3.50	0.5	22.4

substantially greater than the federally mandated minimum wage of $5.15 that was in effect during the sample period. Under the partial equilibrium specification, we see that the minimum wage has a much less beneficial effect in the case without renegotiation. While a binding minimum wage does improve aggregate welfare, the maximizing level is at $12.05 an hour. When we allow for renegotiation between workers and firms, the situation changes, and the optimal minimum wage in terms of maximizing social welfare is $14.05. This is mainly because adverse employment effects are absent in the model with renegotiation until we get to very high levels of the minimum wage.

The optimal minimum wages in both models are dramatically higher than the baseline value of $5.15. Average aggregate labor market welfare is maximized at these values, despite the associated rise in the unemployment rate. In the model without renegotiation, the unemployment rate increases from 5.1 to 14.0 percent when the minimum wage is set to maximize aggregate labor market welfare ($m = 12.05$). When renegotiation is allowed, the increase in the minimum wage leads to an increase in the unemployment rate from 2.2 percent to 4.2 percent.

Allowing the contact rates to be determined endogenously leads to a dramatic decrease in the optimal minimum wage in the model without renegotiation and a small decrease in the model with renegotiation. A minimum wage of $4.70 maximizes the social welfare function when workers are not allowed to renegotiate on the job. Since this minimum wage is lower than the statutory minimum wage, the unemployment rate in this case actually decreases with respect to the steady state unemployment rate associated with the baseline model. For the model with renegotiation, the optimal minimum wage is in the neighborhood of what was observed in the partial equilibrium case.

Which set of policy experiment results should be given the most cred- ibility? Under our model structure and the MSM estimator employed, there was fairly strong empirical evidence in favor of the no rene- gotiation specification. Other things equal, the general equilibrium version of the model should be preferred when assessing policy impacts that involve "large" potential changes in the policy instrument. Taken together, these considerations lead us to conclude that in the model with OTJ search, there is no strong evidence to support the view that substantial increases in the minimum wage would lead to significant improvements in aggregate welfare. Then again, as was the case in chapter 9, there is no strong evidence that lowering or eliminating the minimum wages in effect during the relevant sample periods would have significantly increased the average welfare level in the economy.

11 Heterogeneity

In the models discussed to this point, we have for the most part neglected "observable" heterogeneity within the population. By assuming that all agents inhabit the same labor market, the only source of heterogeneity we allowed was that generated by the timing and values of draws from the fixed productivity distribution G. In particular, we did not consider permanent differences among individuals in observed or unobserved characteristics, which are focal points in most empirical analyses of the impacts of minimum wages on employment outcomes. While there are some sound pragmatic reasons for imposing this strong homogeneity assumption, it is undoubtedly true that model estimates and inferences can change dramatically depending on the manner in which heterogeneity is or is not included in the specification of the model. In this chapter we explore the reasons for being concerned about the possible presence of heterogeneity in the population, as it relates both to model misspecification issues, our ability to fit data, and the validity of policy inferences generated on the basis of our theoretical and empirical analyses. Following this discussion, we turn to practical issues regarding the incorporation of heterogeneity in search-based models of the type considered here. As we will attempt to make clear, while the presence of observed and unobserved heterogeneity is virtually undisputable in any empirical social science application, how to introduce it into a particular modeling framework is anything but clear. If heterogeneity is added to an empirical specification in a thoughtless manner, estimates and inferences may be no better than those from models that ignore heterogeneity altogether.

11.1 Introducing Heterogeneity into the Basic Search Model

To fix ideas, we provide an overview of the problem of introducing heterogeneity into equilibrium search-based models of the labor market by considering the basic search with bargaining in partial equilibrium model (i.e., exogenously determined contact rates). In this model, where search only occurs in the unemployment state, the rate of job finding is λ, the rate of job separations is η, the discount rate is ρ, the flow utility value in the unemployment state is b, the match value distribution is given by G, and the bargaining power of the employee is given by α. The only decision the labor market participant faces is whether to accept a wage offer generated by a draw from the match distribution G. In chapter 3 we showed that when the searcher's objective is expected wealth maximization, wage offers are independent draws from the fixed distribution G, and the individual is infinitely lived,[1] when there is no binding minimum wage, then the searcher's decision could be characterized in terms of the simple rule

Accept if $\theta \geq \theta^*$,

Reject if $\theta < \theta^*$,

where

$$\theta^* = b + \frac{\lambda\alpha}{\rho+\eta} \int_{\theta*} (\theta - \theta^*)dG(w).$$

This implicit equation yields a unique solution for θ^*, which we denote by $\theta^*(\Xi)$, with $\Xi = (\rho\,\lambda\,\eta\,b\,G\,\alpha)$, to emphasize its dependence on *all* the parameters characterizing the economic environment. With no binding match value, we know that the reservation wage is equal to the reservation match value, or $w^*(\Xi) = \theta^*(\Xi)$.

The basic model is characterized in terms of six parameters, one of which is a function (G), and in principle, it is conceivable that there may exist population heterogeneity in any or all of these parameters. To make our discussion more concrete, we begin by considering the case where all parameters are homogeneous in the population with the exception of the matching distribution, G. From a large number of empirical analyses, we know that less educated members of the labor force are more likely to be found in minimum wage jobs. While this could be due to differences in bargaining power, α, as well as in differences in G, for example, for the moment we will consider there to be two groups in the population, otherwise similar, except that a member of group j draws match values from G_j upon encountering a potential employment opportunity. In the case of no binding minimum wage, the reservation match value to individuals of type j is given by

$$\theta_j^* = b + \frac{\alpha\lambda}{\rho+\eta} \int_{\theta_j^*} (\theta - \theta_j^*)dG_j(\theta), \qquad j = 1, 2.$$

We will assume that the type 2 matching distribution exceeds the type 1 matching distribution in the first-order stochastic dominance sense, that is,

$$G_2(x) \le G_1(x) \qquad \text{for all } x > 0,$$

$$G_2(x) < G_1(x) \qquad \text{for some } x \in (0, \infty).$$

This implies that

$$\theta_1^* < \theta_2^*.$$

In terms of the impact of this (potentially) observable heterogeneity on observable outcomes in the labor market, it is immediately apparent that the steady state unemployment rates will differ for the two groups, as will the accepted wage distributions. The hazard rate associated with exits from the unemployment state for group j is

$$h_U^j = \lambda\tilde{G}_j(\theta_j^*), \qquad j = 1, 2.$$

Without further restrictions on the match distributions, we cannot order the hazard rates for the two subpopulations. While $\tilde{G}_1(x) \le \tilde{G}_2(x)$ under our assumption regarding stochastic dominance, the reservation match values are ordered so that $\theta_1^* < \theta_2^*$, which implies that

$$h_U^1 \mathrel{\substack{\le \\ >}} h_U^2.$$

The accepted wage offer cumulative distribution function for group j is given by

$$G_j(w|w \ge \theta_j^*) = \frac{G_j\{[w - (1-\alpha)\theta_j^*]/\alpha\} - G_j(\theta_j^*)}{\tilde{G}_j(\theta_j^*)}, \qquad w \ge w_j^* \equiv \theta_j^*. \quad (11.1)$$

If the support of each distribution is the positive real line, as we will assume in the example below, then the region of overlap between the accepted wage distributions of the two groups is $[\theta_2^*, \infty)$, while wages on the interval $[\theta_1^*, \theta_2^*)$ only are observed for the members of group 1.

Although it is clear that the accepted wage distribution of group 1 cannot first-order stochastically dominate the accepted wage distribution of group 2, it is not possible to show that the accepted wage distribution of the second group first-order stochastically dominates that of group 1, at least without further restrictions on the parameter space.

Example 21   We illustrate the impact of population heterogeneity in G by a simple example. We set λ to 0.35, η equal to 0.01, ρ equal to 0.0042, b equal to -20, and α equal to 0.4. The two distributions of match values are both lognormal, with

$$\ln \theta \sim \begin{cases} N(1.2, 0.36) & \text{in subpopulation 1,} \\ N(1.4, 0.36) & \text{in subpopulation 2,} \end{cases}$$

with π, the proportion of the population of type 1, equal to 0.7.

The reservation match values in the subpopulations 1 and 2 are 3.461 and 5.574, respectively. The hazard rates out of the unemployment state in the two groups are given by

$$h_U^1 = \lambda \tilde{G}_1(\theta_1^*) = 0.165,$$

$$h_U^2 = \lambda \tilde{G}_2(\theta_2^*) = 0.104.$$

The accepted wage offer distributions have different supports since $\theta_1^* \neq \theta_2^*$. Figure 11.1a shows a plot of the accepted wage density for subpopulation 1, and figure 11.1b shows a plot of the analogous density for sub-population 2. Given that the entire population is composed of 70 percent of type 1 individuals and 30 percent of type 2, we have computed the population accepted wage density as

$$f(w) = f_1(w)\pi + f_2(w)(1 - \pi), \qquad w \geq \min(\theta_1^*, \theta_2^*),$$

which is presented in figure 11.1c.

We see from figure 11.1c that "mixing" two truncated lognormal distributions, where the truncation points are the respective reservation match values, results in a mixed distribution of a quite noticeably different shape than each of the constituent truncated lognormal distributions.[2] In the canonical model of unemployed search in a stationary continuous time environment, the distribution of unemployment spell lengths is negative exponential with hazard $h_U = \lambda \tilde{G}(\theta^*)$. Within the two subpopulations the operation of the labor market, and the distribution of labor market outcomes, is exactly as before. However, in terms of the population distribution of unemployment spell durations,

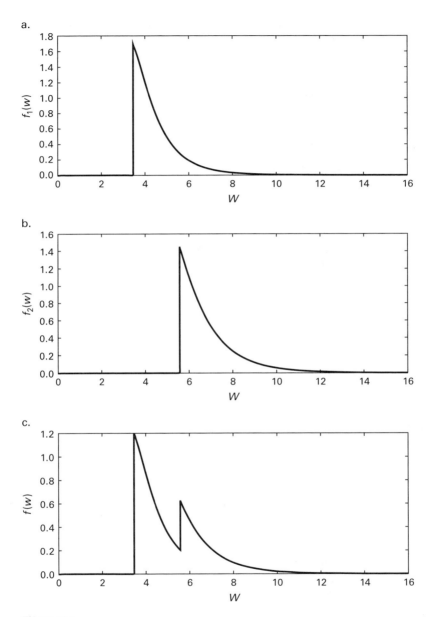

Figure 11.1
Wage density: (a) Type 1, (b) type 2, (c) population wage density

things are quite different. We can analyze the changes by computing the population distribution of unemployment spells as

$$f_U(t) = f_U^1(t)\pi + f_U^2(t)(1 - \pi),$$

which can be written as

$$f_U(t) = h_U^1 \exp(-h_U^1 t)\pi + h_U^2 \exp(-h_U^2 t)(1 - \pi).$$

The population c.d.f. is

$$
\begin{aligned}
F_U(t) &= F_U^1(t)\pi + F_U^2(t)(1 - \pi) \\
&= (1 - \exp(-h_U^1 t))\pi + (1 - \exp(-h_U^2 t))(1 - \pi) \\
&= 1 - \exp(-h_U^1 t)\pi - \exp(-h_U^2 t)(1 - \pi).
\end{aligned}
$$

As a result the hazard function associated with the population distribution of unemployment spells is

$$
\begin{aligned}
h_U(t) &= \frac{f_U(t)}{\bar{F}_U(t)} \\
&= \frac{h_U^1 \exp(-h_U^1 t)\pi + h_U^2 \exp(-h_U^2 t)(1 - \pi)}{\exp(-h_U^1 t)\pi + \exp(-h_U^2 t)(1 - \pi)}.
\end{aligned}
$$

After some algebra we can express the derivative of the population hazard with respect to t by

$$h_U'(t) = -\frac{\pi(1 - \pi)(h_U^1 - h_U^2)^2 \exp(-(h_U^1 + h_U^2)t)}{\exp(-h_U^1 t)\pi + \exp(-h_U^2 t)(1 - \pi)}.$$

This derivative is strictly negative for all $t \geq 0$ except when (1) $\pi = 1$ or $\pi = 0$ and/or (2) $h_U^1 = h_U^2$. In either case we say that the distribution of types in the population is degenerate, which simply means that there is no variance in the "type" distribution in the population—a rather convoluted way to say that the population is homogeneous. Whenever there is population heterogeneity of any type, the hazard function will exhibit negative duration dependence everywhere on R_+.[3] This is a very powerful result, and we will we devote more attention to what it does and does not imply. Barlow and Proschan (1981) present an analysis of the properties of "mixed" hazard functions, and our example is a special case of their general result. They considered general conditional hazard functions $h(t|\omega)$, where ω denotes a type. Let the distribution of types be given by $K(\omega)$, and assume that the conditional hazard functions are differentiable with respect to t. In the general case, the marginal hazard function is given by

$$h(t) = \frac{\int f(t|\omega)dK(\omega)}{\int_t^\infty \int f(u|\omega)dK(\omega)du} \tag{11.2}$$

$$= \frac{\int h(t|\omega)\exp\left(-h(t|\omega)t\right)dK(\omega)}{\int \exp\left(-h(t|\omega)\right)dK(\omega)}. \tag{11.3}$$

These authors showed that, assuming that K is not degenerate:

1. If $h'(t|\omega) \leq 0$ for all t and ω, then $h'(t) < 0$ for all t.
2. If $h'(t|\omega) \geq 0$ for all t and ω, then $h'(t) \gtrless 0$.

In other words, the class of conditional hazard functions that are *nonincreasing everywhere* on the domain of the function (R_+) is *closed* under the operation of mixing. This means that the the marginal, or empirical, hazard function defined by (11.2) inherits the nonincreasing property of the conditional hazards. However, when the conditional hazards are not nonincreasing everywhere, the derivative of the marginal hazard rate cannot be unambiguously signed. Thus the class of nondecreasing hazards is not closed under the operation of mixing.

An important point to remember is that the negative duration dependence property of the marginal hazard function produced by mixing type-specific constant hazard rates is independent of the form of the mixing distribution, K. Negative duration dependence is produced as long as the variance in types, σ_ω^2, is strictly positive. In particular, this implication is independent of the exact form of K. In our example, K was discrete with two mass points, but the same result applies when K is absolutely continuous. Both produce negative duration dependence everywhere on R_+.

The negative duration dependence in the marginal hazard is produced entirely through a *composition* effect. In our example, where both conditional hazard functions are constant, we can write the marginal hazard as

$$h_U(t) = h_U^1 \pi(t) + h_U^2(1 - \pi(t)),$$

where $\pi(t)$ is the proportion of the total population of unemployed with an ongoing spell of length t who belong to subpopulation 1. In terms of individuals beginning a search spell (i.e., with $t = 0$), the proportion of those from subpopulation 1 is just $\pi(0) = \pi$, since the selection process has not as yet begun. The proportion of type 1 individuals remaining unemployed at duration t is greater (less) than π when h_U^1 is less (greater) than h_U^2, for $t > 0$. In our example the type 1 individuals have a lower escape rate from the unemployment state than do the type 2 individuals. This implies that

$$\pi'(t) > 0, \qquad t \geq 0,$$

$$\lim_{t \to \infty} \pi(t) = 1,$$

$$\Rightarrow \lim_{t \to \infty} h_U(t) = h_U^1.$$

In other words, the marginal hazard rate always lies in the interval $[h_U^1, h_U^2]$, is decreasing in the duration of the unemployment spell, and in the limit converges to the lowest hazard rate of the the two groups (h_U^1 in this example).

The important point to note is that variation in one or more primitive parameters, in this particular case, the match distribution, produces different distributions of outcomes for the various subpopulations. The manner and extent to which the distributions of outcomes differ depends on the sources and extent of the heterogeneity. For example, if the source of the heterogeneity had been in terms of the flow value of unemployment, b, with $b_1 > b_2$, with population members homogenous in all other dimensions (including match distributions), then we would have $\theta_1^* > \theta_2^*$, with

$$h_U^1 = \lambda \tilde{G}(\theta_1^*) < \lambda \tilde{G}(\theta_2^*) = h_U^2, \tag{11.4}$$

and the accepted wage distributions would display a first-order stochastic dominance relationship, with

$$G(w|\theta_1^*, \theta \geq \theta_1^*) \succ_{FOSD} G(w|\theta_2^*, w \geq \theta_2^*). \tag{11.5}$$

We would have generated these same qualitative implications if all heterogeneity had been captured solely in terms of the discount rate, ρ, as well. In particular, if $\rho_1 < \rho_2$, and all other parameters are the same, then $\theta_1^* > \theta_2^*$, and (11.4) and (11.5) follow. Instead, if the heterogeneity had been in the rate of arrival of offers only, with $0 < \lambda_1 < \lambda_2$, then $\theta_1^* < \theta_2^*$, and

$$h_U^1 = \lambda_1 \tilde{G}(\theta_1^*) \lesseqgtr \lambda_2 \tilde{G}(\theta_1^*) = h_U^2.$$

The ambiguity can be resolved if restrictions are placed on the wage offer distribution, involving log concavity or closely related properties.[4] The accepted wage distribution can be unambiguously ranked in terms of stochastic dominance as in (11.5).

As we have seen, the implications associated with allowing heterogeneity in a single primitive parameter depend, in general, on which parameter is considered to be heterogeneous. Obviously, if more than one parameter is heterogenous, then neither the offer arrival rates nor the accepted wage distributions typically can be unambiguously ordered. Introducing heterogeneity into the model by allowing a selected subset of the parameters included in Ξ to be nonhomogeneous necessitates choosing which ones are to be regarded as homogeneous in the population. This is an extremely arbitrary process, and for that reason many analysts estimating these kind of models tend to allow either none of the parameters to be heterogeneous or to allow all of them to be heterogeneous. Since we believe that there are strong arguments that can made in favor of allowing all parameters to be heterogeneous, at least if there exists sufficient identifying information in the data, this is the approach we will mainly be considering in the remainder of this chapter.

11.2   Detecting Heterogeneity

While one might imagine that heterogeneity is ubiquitous in all empirical social science applications, it is important to be able to tell when, in the context of the stationary search framework, it seems necessary to introduce it into the modeling framework and when it is not. Introducing heterogeneity into a model when it is not appropriate can possibly result in loss of efficiency in estimation, inconsistent parameter estimates, and misleading policy inferences.

One rather omnibus test for the presence of unobserved heterogeneity in the context of the type of model we have been discussing can be constructed by building on the results of Barlow and Proschan (1981) discussed above. In chapter 3 we explained why the stationary search framework is heavily utilized in both applied theoretical and empirical analysis of the labor market; namely, because it is tractable. Nonstationary models typically include a variety of time-varying state variables, and the model must be solved for each possible path of the state variables, resulting in what is referred to as the curse of dimensionality. In our application, instead, we need not condition on the length of time the agent has occupied a given labor market state or, even more demandingly, her entire labor market history, in order to characterize her decisions at any point in time. The only states that matter in decision-making were her current state of OLF (which is an absorbing state), unemployment, or the state of being employed at a given wage.[5]

The strong Markov assumption places tight restrictions on the data-generating process (DGP) that may be counterindicated by the data. The principal restriction is that conditional on all relevant state variables, the distribution of the duration of state occupancy is negative exponential, which means that the hazard rate associated with the state is constant. For example, in all the model specifications discussed in the book, the hazard rate associated with the unemployment state is given by

$$h_U = \lambda_U \tilde{G}(\max(\theta^*, m)),$$

where θ^* is the reservation match value with no binding minimum wage and m is the statutory minimum wage rate. The important point here is that the exit rate is independent of the duration of the unemployment spell, and is the same for all members of the population.

There are a number of tests of the constant hazard assumption, some that take place in a parametric setting and some that are nonparametric. As usual, parametric tests typically are more powerful if the parametric assumptions assumed are correct, whereas nonparametric tests have less power than their "correctly specified" parametric analogs but are robust with respect to certain types of misspecification of the parametric functional form. We will discuss testing issues primarily in a parametric setting, but we will refer to some nonparametric alternatives later in this section.

A parametric specification of the hazard function entails imposing a particular functional form assumption on the dependence between the hazard rate and the spell duration, for example,

$$h_U(t; \kappa),$$

where κ is a finite-dimensional parameter vector. It is important that the parametric function be flexible enough so that

$$\frac{\partial h_U(t; \kappa)}{\partial t} > 0 \quad \text{for some } t \in R_+ \text{ for a measurable set of } \kappa \in \Omega_\kappa,$$

$$\frac{\partial h_U(t; \kappa)}{\partial t} < 0 \quad \text{for some } t \in R_+ \text{ for a measurable set of } \kappa \in \Omega_\kappa,$$

where Ω_κ is the parameter space of κ under this functional form specification.

To further fix ideas, in implementing the test, we will consider a particular function form assumption, the Weibull, a distribution that nests the negative exponential as a special case.[6] The Weibull distribution has a p.d.f. given by

$$f_U(t;c,d) = cdt^{d-1}\exp(-ct^d)\chi[t \geq 0], \qquad c > 0, \, d > 0,$$

where $\chi[v]$ is the indicator function that takes the value 1 if v is true and the value 0 if v is false. The hazard function associated with the Weibull is given by

$$h_U(t;c,d) = cdt^{d-1}.$$

It is obviously the case that the negative exponential distribution corresponds to the Weibull when $d = 1$. Given information on the duration of unemployment spells, we can form a maximum likelihood estimator for $\kappa = (c,d)'$, $\hat{\kappa}$. A log likelihood ratio statistic, for example, can easily be computed to test the null hypothesis: $H_0 : d = 1$ at any prespecified level of significance.

If we cannot reject the null hypothesis of a constant hazard (under the Weibull specification), then we will say that the unemployment duration distribution is consistent with the assumption of a stationary labor market environment with agents using stationary policy functions, *and with the additional assumption that all agents inhabit the same labor market environment and use the same decision rules.* There is no indication of heterogeneity in this case, conditional on the stationary labor market/policy rules assumption.

Say instead that the data are not consistent with the null hypothesis, once again under the Weibull assumption. Our conclusion regarding the appropriate model specification now depends on our point estimate of d. Duration dependence under the Weibull assumption is given by

$$\frac{\partial h_U(t;\kappa)}{\partial t} = cd(d-1)t^{d-2},$$

which clearly is negative when $d < 1$ and is positive when $d > 1$. If $\hat{d}$ is significantly less than 1, then there exists negative duration dependence, and this finding is consistent with our model specification in the sense that negative duration dependence exists everywhere on R_+, and, from the results of Barlow and Proschan, this is consistent with "mixed" negative exponential distributions. Thus this finding could be interpreted to imply that the model is stationary but the agents inhabit different stationary environments. Such a finding indicates that it would be advisable to introduce either observable or unobservable time-invariant heterogeneity into the model.

What if instead we find that $\hat{d}$ is significantly greater than 1? This is a more problematic result, since positive duration dependence is not consistent with mixed constant hazards. This implies that the entire structure of the behavioral model is suspect. We will say a bit more about this situation below.

Whatever the results of our estimation and testing in this example, we may be concerned about the validity of the Weibull assumption within which the exercise was conducted. We briefly mention two other approaches that generalize the testing environment.

The first approach is to proceed with parametric estimation of the hazard function, but to considerably relax some of the restrictive features of the Weibull functional form. For example, Flinn and Heckman (1983) estimate a parametric hazard that contains a polynomial in duration. While their functional form specification is considerably more general, consider the case

$$h(t;\kappa) = \exp\left(\kappa_0 + \kappa_1 t + \kappa_2 t^2 + \ldots + \kappa_p t^p\right),$$

where p is the order of the polynomial. The test of a constant hazard is now $H_0 : \kappa_1 = \kappa_2 = \ldots = \kappa_p = 0$. This is in some sense a more general test of the constant hazard hypothesis, since we have not restricted the hazard function to be a (particular) monotone function of duration. Other approximations to the hazard function could be used as well, though the polynomial approximation seems a natural basis to use.

The second generalized testing environment utilizes test statistics that are not based on a parametric specification of the hazard. As described in Lawless (2003), there exist nonparametric tests for the constancy of the hazard function when the hazard is restricted to be monotone in duration and when nonmonotonicity is allowed. In either case, a non-rejection of the null hypothesis is consistent with the lack of heterogeneity in our stationary environment, while an indication of a decreasing hazard is evidence of the presence of heterogeneity. As before, increasing hazards are inconsistent with the fundamental modeling assumption of one or more stationary environments.

Durations of time spent in job and employment spells can also be used to look for evidence of heterogeneity. For example, in all of the models considered above, both those with and without OTJ search, the distribution of employment spell durations follows a negative exponential distribution (with parameter η) under the model.[7] We can utilize the same types of hypothesis testing procedures using employment spell information to look for evidence of heterogeneity and model misspecification. Once again, under the stationarity assumption, a constant hazard rate out of employment spells (into the state of unemployment, by definition) implies that all labor market participants share the same value of η. A finding of a decreasing hazard everywhere on R_+ implies that η is heterogeneous in the population. A finding of positive duration dependence, however, over any subinterval of R_+ implies that the model is misspecified.

To use information from the duration of job spells to examine the issue of heterogeneity raises a few more subtle issues. Under the model with OTJ search, the hazard out of a job spell is equal to $h_J(\theta) = \lambda_E \tilde{G}(\theta) + \eta$. Since there is heterogeneity in the accepted θ distribution, we expect that the (marginal) hazard rate out of job spells should exhibit negative duration dependence. This composition effect arises due to the fact that longer job spells tend to have higher match values, thus making departure less likely. In this case the marginal hazard function should exhibit negative duration dependence. If not, this is evidence of model misspecification.[8]

To this point we have emphasized the use of duration data in looking for evidence of heterogeneity and model misspecification. Of course, virtually all estimable search models rely heavily on wage information, so it is natural to ask whether this information is useful for detecting heterogeneity in population parameters. The answer is largely negative, primarily because wage distributions are generated by the heterogeneity (in match values) that is an integral part of the model specification. If heterogeneity in matching distributions was present, a marginal accepted wage distribution may be a mixture of heterogeneous accepted wage distributions, with a dose of measurement error thrown in to further complicate matters. This makes the task of detecting heterogeneity in observed wage distributions impossible without imposing, a priori, functional form assumptions on the conditional matching distributions, and, if present, the distribution of measurement error in wages.

We can illustrate this point by looking, once again, at figure 11.1. If we were so fortunate as to have access to wage data with no measurement error, the marginal distribution of wages could be interpreted as (1) being generated from a mixture of two underlying single-peaked matching functions or (2) one multi-peaked matching distribution (the case of no heterogeneity). If we were to impose the restriction that all conditional matching distributions be unimodal, which the search framework does not require, then we could interpret the bimodal observed distribution as indicating that there are at least two subpopulations.[9]

We conclude this section with the following cautionary note: the finding that duration distributions have constant hazards does not alone demonstrate that the homogeneous stationary search environment is "correct." In experimental work, Brown et al. (2009) found that students put in a stationary, continuous time search environment tended to reduce their reservation wage as a function of the duration of the search spell. In this case the search environment was set up to be stationary, and the subjects knew the characteristics of the search environment in which they found themselves. After modifying the nature of the search environment in several ways, the authors concluded that subjects were merely getting bored.

In order to capture this "boredom effect," it is enough to modify the flow value of utility in the unemployed search state to make it a decreasing function of time, that is, $b'(t) < 0$. If all other characteristics of the environment remain constant, this modification results in a decreasing reservation wage function, or $w^{*'}(t) < 0$, and this results in positive duration dependence in the conditional (on the particular search environment parameters) hazard function. When the authors compute the marginal hazard function, they find a relatively constant hazard rate. In this case, mixing duration distributions that exhibit positive duration dependence produces a marginal hazard function with no pronounced nonconstancy of the hazard. While the tests we have suggested in this section provide some useful information regarding the existence of heterogeneity and the appropriateness of the stationary search framework, they provide an admittedly incomplete picture of the search process at the individual level.

11.3 Observed Heterogeneity

The distinction between unobserved and observed heterogeneity is less obvious than it may appear. Typically we think that observed differences in individuals, such as demographic characteristics, educational attainment, family background, which are available in many labor force surveys, constitute observed heterogeneity, while all other unmeasured characteristics represent unobserved heterogeneity. Although this is tautologically the case, the important issue in terms of model estimation is the mapping between observed characteristics and subpopulation groups.

In terms of population heterogeneity, we will think of there being $J \geq 2$ subpopulations when there are a finite number of types. In some cases we allow there to be a continuum of subpopulations, but this is not so common in most attempts to estimate parameters of behavioral models.

It is important to bear in mind that when we speak of "heterogeneity," we are not referring to match heterogeneity, which we sometimes allow to be continuously distributed in the population and sometimes not (e.g., in chapter 10). A matching distribution is only one of the parameters characterizing a particular subpopulation. If there are a continuum of subpopulations, then there are a continuum of matching distributions as well. In most of this chapter we will be considering the case where there are a finite number of subpopulations, indexed by j, $j = 1, \ldots, J$, with each subpopulation characterized by a distinct vector of parameters Ξ_j. To say that there are J distinct subpopulations is to say that

$$\Xi_j \neq \Xi_{j'}, \qquad j = 1, \ldots, J, j' = 1, \ldots, J, \, j \neq j',$$

$$\Omega_\Xi = \{\Xi_1, \ldots, \Xi_J\}.$$

That is, there is a set Ω_Ξ that contains all of the distinct parameter vectors characterizing the J subpopulations.

Let a particular population member i be characterized by an observable vector X_i. Then there is what is called *perfect sample separation information* when

$$\Xi = s(X_i), \qquad \Xi \in \Omega_\Xi,$$

where s is a known function. That is, by observing the vector X_i, we can assign the individual to a given subpopulation (or sublabor market) characterized by one of the parameter vectors belonging to the set Ω_Ξ.

Example 22 If we believe that labor markets are solely segmented by gender, and if gender is one of the characteristics included in the observed vector X, then we assign individual i to a labor market 1 (female) if i is female and to labor market 2 (male) if i is male. The implicit assumption is that all individuals of the same gender belong to the same labor market.

Under the assumption of perfect sample information, estimation can often proceed in a straightforward manner. For example, the maximum likelihood estimator described in chapter 7 can be applied to observationally distinguishable subpopulations. To estimate the model with no restrictions on the parameters across subpopulations, one simply partitions the sample into the various subgroups and then estimates the model separately for each subsample.[10] Given that the data included in the estimator are available for all subpopulations, the maximum likelihood estimator, for example, of Ω_Ξ is given by

$$\ln L(\Xi_1, \ldots, \Xi_J | \{Y_i, X_i\}_{i=1}^N) = \sum_{j=1}^{J} \sum_{i | X_i \in S_j} \ln L(\Xi_j | Y_i), \qquad (11.6)$$

where Y_i are the endogenous outcomes observed for sample member i and X_i are her observable characteristics.

While it is our belief that in most cases restricting certain primitive parameters to be the same across subpopulations, while allowing others to differ, should be avoided due to its arbitrariness, pragmatic concerns regarding identification may lead one to impose such restrictions. Such restrictions of homogeneity can be directly imposed on (11.6),

$$\hat{\Omega}_\Xi = \arg \max \ln L(\Xi_1, \ldots, \Xi_J | \{Y_i, X_i\}_{i=1}^N),$$

where whatever restrictions on parameters across subpopulations exist are imposed in the definition of the set Ω_Ξ.

Adding to our discussion of the previous section, we can consider how the existence of perfect sample separation information can be used to "test for" the existence of subpopulations. Consider the example given above, where the analyst suspects that males and females occupy distinct labor markets, with no restrictions in (estimable) parameters across them. In each case there are 6 parameters (including the matching distribution) to estimate per subpopulation (gender), so that the full specification includes 12 parameters. Under the null hypothesis that both genders belong to the same market, $\Xi_1 = \Xi_2$. If we were employing a maximum likelihood estimator, then we could utilize a likelihood ratio test to examine the the conformity of the null with the data. Alternatively, likelihood ratio tests could be conducted when the null hypothesis placed restrictions on subsets of the primitive parameters. For example, one could imagine allowing the rate parameters, λ_U and η, as well as ρ, to be identical in the two markets, but for b (which is essentially a preference parameter), G, and α to differ across genders. Since our position is that it is difficult to imagine a priori restrictions holding on only subsets of primitive parameters, in our view these types of tests may be less useful in detecting heterogeneity in observables due to the non–theory-based nature of the restrictions.[11]

11.4   Unobserved Heterogeneity

We use the term "unobserved heterogeneity" advisedly, since we do not want to imply that observable characteristics of individuals are not important elements of the analysis in this case. A more appropriate way to characterize this situation is one of *imperfect sample separation information*. In the extreme case in which no observable characteristics of individuals are available, or at least there exists no available information useful for predicting an individual's subpopulation type, we have a situation of "pure" unobserved heterogeneity.

We continue to assume that there are a finite number of types in the population, $j = 1, \ldots, J$. The only difference with respect to the situation of perfect sample separation information is that the assignment function $s(X_i)$ is stochastic. In this case the assignment function is a probability distribution that maps the characteristic vector X_i into a probability distribution over types. (When there exists perfect sample separation information, these probability distributions are degenerate, and each characteristic vector maps into a given type with probability one.) To explicitly indicate that s is now a probability distribution, we will use the notation $P_j(X)$ to represent the probability that an individual with characteristics X belongs to subpopulation j. Naturally $P_j(X) \geq 0, j = 1, \ldots, J$, and $\sum_{j=1}^{J} P_j(X) = 1$.

By adding imperfect sample separation to the model, we have enlarged the parameter space to include not only the vectors of primitive parameters associated with type, Ω_Ξ, but also the functions P_j, $j = 1, \ldots, J$. These probability functions are not "primitives" of the model; they should instead be thought of as a form of measurement error. It is standard practice to parameterize these functions as parsimoniously as possibly. A typical choice is to assume a multinomial logit structure. Say that the dimensionality of X is $(K \times 1)$. Then let

$$P_j(X) = \frac{\exp(X'\gamma_j)}{\sum_{l=1}^{J} \exp(X'\gamma_l)}, \qquad j = 1, \ldots, J.$$

A normalization is required, so let the vector $\gamma_1 = \mathbf{0}$. This parameterization adds $(J - 1) \times K$ parameters to be estimated, which is one reason J, the number of unobserved types, and K, the dimensionality of X, are kept small in virtually all applications.

When the characteristic vector X is defined, its dimensionality in all applications with imperfect sample separation information is at least one, since X always includes the value 1 in its first row, which serves to define a generalized intercept term. In this way, we can nest the situation of "pure" unobserved heterogeneity in the above specification. When no measured characteristics of X that differ across sample members appear in the conditional probability functions $P_j(X)$, the multinomial logit specification becomes

$$P_j = \begin{cases} \dfrac{1}{1+\sum_{l=2}^{J} \exp{(\gamma_l)}}, & j = 1, \\[2ex] \dfrac{\exp{(\gamma_j)}}{1+\sum_{l=2}^{J} \exp{(\gamma_l)}}, & j = 2, \ldots, J. \end{cases}$$

This is the most basic specification involving unobserved heterogeneity, and adds only $J-1$ "nonbehavioral" parameters to the estimation task.

It is conceptually straightforward to extend the estimation problem to incorporate imperfect sample separation information, though practical problems of identification may arise when using small samples and assuming a large number of subpopulations. There is a practical problem with knowing how many subpopulations exist, of course, but we defer the discussion of that issue for the moment. Say that we have settled on a number of subpopulation types equal to J, and for each individual in our sample observe the vector (Y_i, X_i). If we employ the same type of maximum likelihood estimator as in the perfect sample separation case, the revised log likelihood function is

$$\ln L(\Xi_1, \ldots, \Xi_J, \{\gamma_j\}_{j=2}^{J} | \{Y_i, X_i\}_{i=1}^{N})$$

$$= \sum_{i|} \ln \left(\sum_{j=1}^{J} L(\Xi_j | Y_i) P_j(X_i; \gamma_2, \ldots, \gamma_J) \right),$$

where we have added the $\{\gamma_j\}_{j=2}^{J}$ to the P_j functions to emphasize the manner in which these parameters enter the log likelihood function. The maximum likelihood estimator of the behavioral and measurement error parameters is then

$$\{\hat{\Omega}_\Xi, \{\hat{\gamma}_j\}_{j=2}^{J}\} = \arg\max \ln L(\Xi_1, \ldots, \Xi_J, \{\gamma_j\}_{j=2}^{J} | \{Y_i, X_i\}_{i=1}^{N}).$$

We conclude this section with a discussion of the advantages and disadvantages of this approach to incorporating observed heterogeneity into the analysis. Perhaps the most important advantage is that it keeps the dimensionality of the behavioral problem tractable from the perspective of numerical analysis. By assuming that there are J different environments, where J is typically small, there exist only J sets of behavioral rules that need to be computed. For example, in our partial equilibrium models without OTJ search, there was only one policy variable that needed to be determined for each market, which was the reservation match used by unemployed searchers. Given that a market was characterized by the vector of parameters Ξ, there exists a unique value of the reservation match value, $\theta^*(\Xi_j)$ in market j (assuming that θ is continuously distributed in each market). If $J = 4$, for example, then we need only solve for four critical match values.

A second advantage is the enhanced ability to fit observed patterns in the data not consistent with a population homogeneity assumption. By allowing a fairly general form of mixing, observed accepted wage distributions, for example, can be better matched when $J > 1$ than when $J = 1$. As we learned in section 11.2, mixing allows us to generate decreasing duration dependence in unemployment and employment spell hazard functions, which often times are more consistent with observed patterns than is the constant hazard implication implied when $J = 1$.

The primary disadvantage of the approach is the lack of guidance regarding the number of submarkets to specify. As was just stated, allowing J to grow will increase the ability of the model to fit data, but this must be balanced against problems of interpretation and the standard statistical issue of overfitting. In some sense, the setup is reminiscent of factor analysis, where the observed characteristics "load" on the unobserved factors (i.e., markets) according to the functions $\{P_j(X)\}_{j=1}^{J}$. Because the market parameter vectors, Ξ_j, are only probabilistically associated with observable types, they must be labeled, after the fact, in a somewhat arbitrary fashion. In the gender-based example, we might set $J = 2$, and find that in one market unemployment spells last longer on average, wages are lower on average, and so forth, and call this the "bad" market. If X only consisted of a gender indicator, it is likely that we would find that women are more likely to belong to the bad market. But this begs the question of what this "bad market" really is. Since men also belong to it, it is not defined solely in terms of gender, so what occupational or industrial characteristics does it have? The problem of interpretation of markets is amplified as J grows, just as is the case in traditional factor analysis applications.

Model specification in the imperfect sample separation case involves setting both the number of markets, J, and the contents of X. Analysis usually proceeds after fixing a vector X, and some reasonably standard, but not uncontroversial, hypothesis testing techniques are used to determine the number of submarkets. Typically testing "up" is done. In this case one first estimates the homogeneous model ($J = 1$). Then the model is estimated after adding one additional market, and a test statistic is computed that determines whether the more disaggregated model, in this case with $J = 2$, fits the data "significantly" better. If $J = 1$ is rejected in favor of $J = 2$, the process is repeated comparing the model fits for $J = 2$ versus $J = 3$, and it proceeds in this manner for ever higher numbers of markets. When the less disaggregated model is not rejected, the exercise stops.

Since the sequential nature of the testing is not taken into account when setting the size of each of the tests, this mode of testing is not consistent. A more fundamental objection can be made regarding the stepwise procedure underlying the test. While $J = 2$ may not fit significantly better than $J = 1$, $J = 3$ may. Proceeding stepwise in this manner would lead to a bad decision in terms of the number of submarkets in such cases.

The conclusion regarding this method for incorporating observed heterogeneity into behavioral models is that it is the most promising one available. Its main short-coming is the introduction of parameters, the γ_j vectors in our example, that are not part of the behavioral specification. When considering the impacts of a policy change within a population, it is probably necessary to consider these parameters as primitive, since they are not part of the model. However, one cannot rule out the possibility that a policy may change the type distribution, making counterfactual policy evaluation results potentially misleading.

11.5   An Extended Example

To illustrate some of the issues that have been discussed in this chapter, we provide a brief empirical analysis that adds both observed and unobserved heterogeneity to the basic search and bargaining model that has been used throughout. In this example we utilize more recent CPS data, whose analysis may be of some interest alone, given the dramatic decline in the health of the labor market observed recently and the recent nominal minimum wage increases that have occurred from 2007 through 2009.

The data with which we work are taken from the October 2009 Current Population Survey. As before, we have restricted the age of sample members to be in the interval 16 to 24 years, inclusive. Moreover we have inflation-adjusted all of the monetary quantities that appear in the model, which are the hourly wages of those sample members employed at the time of the survey and the minimum wage, so that the 2009 magnitudes are expressed in 1996 dollars. While the federal minimum wage has recently been raised to $7.25, its 1996 value is $5.30. This is only slightly higher than the 1997 federal minimum wage of $5.15. As we saw in chapter 1, over the last forty years nominal minimum wage changes only have served to offset some of the erosion in purchasing power from the time of the previous nominal minimum wage hike.

Before beginning the analysis, it is worthwhile to point out the enormous changes in labor market outcomes from 1996 to 2009 for the group of labor market participants we study. In September 1996, the unemployment rate in the estimation sample we utilized was 9.7 percent, and in October 2009, for a sample selected in an identical manner, the unemployment rate had climbed to 17.7 percent. The proportion of the sample paid exactly the minimum wage also changed significantly. In September 1996, the proportion of the sample paid the minimum wage was equal to 5.3 percent, and in October 2009, that proportion stood at 8 percent.[12]

We begin by estimating the homogeneous model using the October 2009 data. The homogeneous model implies that all agents, no matter what their observable and unobservable characteristics, inhabit the same labor market. The only heterogeneity in the market is the ex post heterogeneity associated with match draws from the (nondegenerate) distribution G. The labor market is characterized in terms of the parameters ρ, the discount rate, λ, the rate of arrival of offers to unemployed searchers, η, the rate of job destruction, μ and σ, the parameters characterizing the lognormal distribution of match values, b, the flow value of utility in the unemployed state, and α, the generalized Nash-bargaining power parameter. In this illustrative exercise we merely estimate the value of unemployed search directly and do not take the extra step of "backing out" the flow value of utility b. Following our earlier discussion of identification of this model, we fix the discount rate at 0.004 (denominated in months). We also estimate the Nash-bargaining power parameter using the iterative technique described in chapter 7, and using the same employee share of revenues that we used with the 1996 to 1997 data.[13]

The homogeneous population model estimates are reported in the first column of table 11.1. The rate of arrival of job offer estimate of 0.443 implies that a searcher-firm contact occurs about every 9 weeks. On average, jobs last slightly more than 2 years. Estimates of the lognormal match distribution parameters are fairly different than those obtained using the CPS data from 1996. The estimates imply that the mean of the match distribution in 1996 was 11.477, and that the match distribution mean declined precipitously to 7.951 in 2009. The distribution became considerably more dispersed in 2009, with the standard distribution of the match distribution increasing from 6.508 in 1996 to 9.367 in 2009.

Table 11.1
Estimation with no and only observed heterogeneity

Parameter	Population		
	All	Females	Males
λ	0.443	0.584	0.355
	(0.056)	(0.133)	(0.050)
η	0.047	0.041	0.054
	(0.004)	(0.065)	(0.006)
μ	1.638	1.439	1.825
	(0.132)	(0.240)	(0.142)
σ	0.933	0.990	0.874
	(0.053)	(0.088)	(0.064)
$\rho V_N(m)$	4.943	4.893	5.008
	(0.025)	(0.036)	(0.032)
α	0.293	0.287	0.300
	(0.006)	(.008)	(0.008)
$\ln L$	$-7,960.452$	$-3,936.282$	$-4,007.666$
N	1837	936	901

Source: CPS data, October 2009.
Note: Asymptotic standard errors in parentheses.

These changes are to be expected given the oft-noted decline in real wages and increases in wage dispersion over the last several decades.

In addition to changes in the match distribution, we see that workers did considerably worse in staking claims to match-specific rents, with the Nash-bargaining power parameter falling from 0.424 in 1996 to 0.293 in 2009. This is a potentially interesting way to think about shifts in the wage distribution over time. Since the matching distribution is meant to represent productive values across workers and jobs, the general shift in the match distribution can be thought of as representing real productivity declines. Even if bargaining power had remained the same, these shifts would be expected from the changes in the wage distributions observed over the last twenty years. The estimated bargaining power declines have tended to amplify these negative productivity impacts on wages.

We now introduce observed heterogeneity into the model. In this example we simply subdivide the sample into males and females, and reestimate the model for both subsamples, as in chapter 8. Before discussing the results, it is important to consider the rationale behind incorporating observed heterogeneity in this manner.

None of the parameters characterizing the model have been restricted to be the same across the two populations, with the exception of the discount rate, ρ, the value of which was assumed and not estimated. It seems natural to allow the matching distribution G to vary across the populations, given the well-documented differences in the occupational distributions of men and women, educational specializations, and so forth. Given any difference in the labor market environments by gender, one is compelled to allow the value of unemployed search to differ for males and females.

The more substantive restrictions involve the rate parameters, λ and η. Since η has not been endogenized in any of the models considered in this monograph, there is no compelling reason to restrict it to be homogeneous in the two populations. As we discuss in the following section, the matching function approach to endogenizing the rate of arrival of offers makes assumptions that require all agents within the same labor market to receive offers at the same rate. In the case of random search, the contact rates between males and firms will be identical to the contact rate between females and firms, so that $\lambda_F = \lambda_M$. If the labor markets are partitioned instead, so that firms can direct their search toward male or female workers, and the equilibrium expected values of an employee differ by gender, the equilibrium contact rates will differ by gender as well. In this case we expect $\lambda_F \neq \lambda_M$. In an illustrative exercise such as we are conducting here, the safe way to proceed is to not restrict the contact rates to be identical.[14]

As we see in columns 2 and 3 of table 11.1, the point estimates of λ_F and λ_M indicate that females receive offers at a substantially higher rate than males, though the large estimated standard error associated with $\hat{\lambda}_F$ implies that the null hypothesis of $\lambda_F = \lambda_M$ cannot be rejected at conventional significance levels. Males tend to have their jobs terminate at higher rates than females; the point estimates of η_F and η_M imply that the average length of the females' jobs is 24.4 months, while the corresponding figure for males is 18.5 months.

There are large differences in the estimates of the parameters characterizing G_F and G_M, the gender-specific matching distribution. The implied means of θ are 7.950 for females and 11.477 for males, whereas the standard deviation of θ is 9.367 for females and 6.508 for males. Thus the female distribution exhibits more positive skew than the male distribution, but the female distribution exhibits considerably more concentration on low values of θ than does the male. We find that the bargaining power (α) of males and females is not significantly different.

However, males do enjoy a significantly higher value of unemployed search. While a number of individual parameter estimates are not significantly different for males and females, an overall test of equality is handily rejected.[15] Although the difference in log likelihood values is statistically significant, the improvement is from -7960.452 for the homogeneous model to -7943.948 for the heterogeneous one.

Instead of assuming that all heterogeneity is perfectly observable, we now allow types to be unobservable. There is an important estimation detail to consider in terms of this application. In the case of observable heterogeneity, we could inspect the wage distribution of each type and determine whether the minimum wage was binding or not, simply by noting whether all wage observations associated with a given type were greater in value than the minimum wage. If there was more than one wage observation equal to the minimum wage, we concluded that the minimum wage was binding and used the appropriate likelihood function specification for that case. In our gender-based example we concluded that the minimum wage was binding for each gender, and used the same specification of the log likelihood function for each.

In the example below, we assume that the population is divided into two types, with separate sets of parameters characterizing the labor market for each, with the exception of the bargaining power parameter α. Since we don't know any sample member's type, we cannot check, a priori, whether the minimum wage is binding for each type or only for one.[16] The log likelihood function is given by

$$
\ln L = \sum_{i \in \{w_i = 0\}} \ln \left\{ \sum_{j=1}^{2} P_U(j) \lambda_j \tilde{G}_j(r_j) \exp\left(-\lambda_j \tilde{G}_j(r_j) t_i \right) \pi_j(X_i) \right\}
$$

$$
+ \sum_{i \in \{w_i = m\}} \ln \left\{ \sum_{j=1}^{2} \chi[\rho V_N^j(m) < m](1 - P_U(j)) \right.
$$

$$
\left. \left(\frac{\tilde{G}_j(m) - \tilde{G}_j\{[m - (1-\alpha)\rho V_N^j(m)]/\alpha\}}{\tilde{G}_j(m)} \right) \pi_j(X_i) \right\}
$$

$$
+ \sum_{i \in \{w_i > m\}} \ln \left\{ \sum_{j=1}^{2} \chi[w_i > m](1 - P_U(j)) \right.
$$

$$
\left. \left(\frac{g_j\{[w_i - (1-\alpha)\rho V_N^j(m)]/\alpha\}}{\tilde{G}_j(r_j)} \right) \pi_j(X_i) \right\},
$$

where $r_j = \max{(m, \rho V_j^N(m))}$,

$$P_U(j) = \frac{\eta_j}{\eta_j + \lambda_j \tilde{G}(r_j)},$$

and $\pi_j(X_i)$ is the probability that an individual with observed characteristics X_i, a $1 \times K$ vector, is a (unobserved) type j. In particular, we assume that

$$\pi_1(X_i) = \frac{\exp{(X_i \beta)}}{1 + \exp{(X_i \beta)}},$$

where β is an unknown $K \times 1$ vector of coefficients.

In practice, we estimated the model twice, once imposing the restriction that both types were bound by the minimum wage, and the other time imposing the condition that only type 1 individuals faced a binding minimum wage. When estimating under the restriction that both types are bound by the minimum wage, we restrict $\rho V_N^j(m) < m, j = 1, 2$. When estimating under the restriction that only the first type is bound by the minimum wage, the constraints are $\rho V_N^1(m) < m$ and $\rho V_N^2(m) > m$. We then compared log likelihood values across the two restricted log likelihood functions, and took our estimates from the one with the highest log likelihood value.

We estimated two specifications of the model, which only differ in terms of the observable characteristics X_i that are used in the type-probability function. In the first specification, X_i only includes a constant term, so that $\pi_1(1) = \exp{(\beta_1)}/(1 + \exp{(\beta_1)})$. In this case we simply report an estimate of $\hat{\pi}_1$, along with an estimate of the associated asymptotic standard error (derived using the delta method). In the second specification, X_i includes a constant term, the number of years of schooling completed by the sample member, and three indicator variables associated with the characteristics female, black, and hispanic.

We found that under both specifications of $\pi_1(X)$, the restricted log likelihood function associated with the case in which both types faced a binding minimum wage constraint produced the highest log likelihood value. We also found that the point estimate of the common value of α, while reasonable, had an extremely large estimated asymptotic standard error, indicating that the parameter was tenuously identified in the model with unobserved heterogeneity. To improve the performance of the estimators of the model with unobserved heterogeneity in this example, we set the value of α to 0.5 in both subpopulations.

Table 11.2
Estimation with unobserved heterogeneity

Parameter	No-covariate types		Covariate types	
	1	2	1	2
λ	0.399	0.183	0.279	0.264
	(0.121)	(0.042)	(0.043)	(0.063)
η	0.050	0.067	0.061	0.026
	(0.019)	(0.056)	(0.008)	(0.008)
μ	2.281	1.912	1.923	2.428
	(0.240)	(0.031)	(0.093)	(0.095)
σ	0.183	0.233	0.377	0.526
	(0.042)	(0.052)	(0.043)	(0.039)

Source: CPS data, October 2009.
Note: Asymptotic standard errors are in parentheses.

Table 11.2 contains the estimates under the two specifications of $\pi_1(X)$. The first two columns contain the estimates of the specification in which no individual covariates are present. The estimate of the probability that an individual is type 1 is about 0.7. Type 1 individuals inhabit a labor market in which contacts between searchers and firms are more common and where jobs last longer on average. Type 1 individuals seem to have a better match distribution than do those of the other type; the mean match values are 9.952 and 6.955, and the standard deviations of θ are 1.837 and 1.6452 for types 1 and 2, respectively.

There are large differences in the point estimates of $V_N^1(m)$ and $V_N^2(m)$. There are two things to note about the estimates of these values. First, the estimate of $V_N^1(m)$ is quite inprecise; in fact the difference between the estimates is not significant at the 0.05 level. Second, the estimate of $V_N^2(m)$ implies that virtually no type 2 are paid the minimum wage. As noted above, the 2009 minimum wage expressed in 1996 dollars was slightly less than 5.30. The maximum likelihood estimate of $V_N^2(m)$ is essentially equal to this amount.

When covariates are added to the conditional "type" probability function, model estimates improve markedly in terms of precision. The estimates of this specification appear in columns 3 and 4 of table 11.2. The point estimates of the rate of arrival of contacts are now very similar, and much more precisely estimated. There are substantially larger differences in the expected length of a job, with jobs for type 2 individuals lasting, on average, over twice as long as those obtained by type 1 individuals. The job matching distribution for type 2 individuals seems far superior to the one from which type 1 individuals draw. The mean match values are 7.345 and 13.018 and the standard deviations are 2.871 and 7.350 for types 1 and 2, respectively. Even though the labor market of the type 2 individuals seems superior to the one that type 1 individuals inhabit, there is not a significant difference between the estimated values of search. The only way such a result can be rationalized within the current framework is if type 2 individuals have significantly lower utility flow values in the unemployment state.

In terms of the type-probability function, we found that a particularly important "predictor" of type is the schooling level of the individual. The individual's gender is also a statistically significant predictor of type, whereas being black or hispanic is not. What is particularly interesting is the huge increase in the log likelihood function obtained when we allow for two unobserved types, an increase to -4778.698 from -7960.452 when comparing the unobserved heterogeneity specification with no covariates to the perfectly segmented labor market model. In our simple example involving gender, it would be possible to formally "nest" the two specifications in a particular, asymptotic sense. Instead of the setting the binary variable associated with being a female to 1 if the individual is female and 0 if male, set its value equal to -1 in the case of the individual being male. Let the coefficient associated with this redefined binary variable be denote by β_f. Then define

$$\pi_1(X_i) = \lim_{\beta_f \to \infty} \frac{\exp(X_i\beta)}{1 + \exp(X_i\beta)}$$

In this case all women will have a probability of being a type 1 equal to 1, and all men will have a probability of being a type 1 of 0.[17] By allowing β_f to become indefinitely large, we have given infinite weight to gender as the characteristic upon which the market is sorted. Our results indicate that gender itself is not the sole indicator of labor market type.

11.6 Implications of Heterogeneity for Equilibrium and Labor Market-Policies

In this concluding section we consider how the existence of distinguishable sets of agents affects the definition and computation of equilibria. Following that discussion, we look at the important issue of how heterogeneity impacts the determination and implementation of optimal policies.

11.6.1 General Equilibrium and Heterogeneity

As we have done throughout this book, our consideration of general equilibrium in search markets is limited to the use of the matching function framework of Pissarides (1979). The general issues encountered can be considered without loss of generality if we restrict our attention to the case of two types. For the moment we will assume that there exists perfect sample separation information, so that we are able to unambiguously assign an individual with observed characteristics X to one of the two markets.

We have already encountered the two-type heterogeneity case in our discussion of OTJ search in general equilibrium in chapter 10. When there exist separate submarkets, a modeling decision must be made regarding the search technology that exists in the economy. At the two polar extremes are (1) random search and (2) "perfectly" directed search. In the pure random search case, firms encounter individuals from each submarket in proportion to the effective search intensity from that market. In the perfect directed search case, firms can target their search to a specific submarket, and hence will only encounter individuals from that submarket as potential employees.

In discussing these two cases, we will ignore OTJ search so as to simplify matters. Let the steady state proportion of submarket j individuals in the unemployment state be given by U_j, and let the proportion of individuals in subpopulation 1 be given by π. Assuming both types search with the same intensity while in the unemployed state, the total measure of searchers is given by

$$U = U_1 + U_2.$$

If firms create a total measure of vacancies given by V, then the number of potential matches produced is

$$M = m(U, V).$$

The contact rate per searcher is M/U, so that the rate of contacts between type j searchers and potential employers is given by

$$\lambda_u^1 = \lambda_u^2 = \frac{M}{U}.$$

In this case, contact rates are identical.

The number of matches created per unit time does depend on the composition of the population, however, since the reservation match values in the two markets differ. Thus the total number of matches created is given by

$$M = \left(\frac{\tilde{G}_1(\theta_1^*)U_1 + \tilde{G}_2(\theta_2^*)U_2}{U} \right) m(U, V).$$

The situation is different when there exists directed search. Then firms can target their search activities into a localized market consisting of type j individuals. The search technologies may differ in the two markets, and we denote the search technology in market j by $m_j, j = 1, 2$. The measure of firm vacancies posted in market j is given by V_j, so that the contact rate per unemployed individual in market j is given by

$$\lambda_U^j = \frac{m_j(U_j, V_j)}{U_j}, \qquad j = 1, 2.$$

Even if the search technologies were the same, that is, $m_1 = m_2$, the contact rates will in general differ because $U_1 \neq U_2$ and/or $V_1 \neq V_2$. In this case the total rate of matches formed is given by

$$M = \tilde{G}_1(\theta_1^*)\lambda_U^1 + \tilde{G}_2(\theta_2^*)\lambda_U^2.$$

The firm vacancy creation decisions differ in the two cases. Under random search, there is one search technology with an associated cost of forming a vacancy, ψ. In the directed search case, particularly when search technologies are allowed to differ across markets, there is no reason to expect the cost of holding a vacancy to be the same in the two markets; thus it seems natural to allow $\psi_1 \neq \psi_2$. In each case, to close the model, we typically impose a free entry condition. In the usual one search market case, this implies that the value of holding a vacancy is competed down to zero through firm entry. In the distinct markets case, free entry applies to both markets, so that the expected value of holding a vacancy in either market is competed down to zero. In equilibrium, the marginal firm is indifferent between holding a vacancy in market 1 or market 2.

11.6.2 Policy Implications

When there exist submarkets in the economy, an important policy decision is whether policy should be developed for each market individually or whether one institutional environment should be created for all environments. As we discussed in chapter 1, there was a serious debate when the federal minimum wage was first enacted regarding whether or not region-specific minimum wage levels should be set. The question was settled in the favor of those who wanted a uniform level applied throughout the country, though states were free to set a higher minimum wage than the federally mandated value. In a partial equilibrium framework, or a general equilibrium framework with directed search, if minimum wages were set at the submarket level, than the optimal minimum wage analysis could be conducted for each submarket in isolation of the others. Because such market-level policy raises many questions regarding implementation, and because it can be analyzed using the tools we have already developed, we will assume that the minimum wage set at the federal level applies to all submarkets.

In chapter 4 we examined several welfare criteria that could be used to evaluate the welfare effects of minimum wage changes, and that in some cases could be used to determine optimal minimum wage levels. Most of our attention was focused on a Benthamite social welfare function, in which the welfare of all agents in the economy, those on both sides of the market, were given equal weight. This social welfare function approach continues to be well-defined even in the presence of submarkets in the economy. Instead of distinguishing individuals on the supply side solely in terms of whether they were OLF, unemployed, or employed, we would expand the state space to include the submarket to which each individual belonged. This extension is straightforward, since the social welfare function is an additive function of the expected welfare of each "type" of agent in the economy, where type can be define in terms of labor market state and any other characteristic that distinguishes agents.

Say that we consider the case where there exists directed search, as we defined it above, so that firms can be assigned to separate submarkets. Then we can define the social welfare function associated with each of the two submarkets as $W(m, \Xi_j)$, where $\Xi_j, j = 1, 2$, indicates the labor market environment of type j agents (individuals and firms in this case). The overall welfare function is then simply

$$\tilde{W}(m) = \pi W(m; \Xi_1) + (1 - \pi)W(m; \Xi_2).$$

The determination of optimal minimum wages is, in principle, straightforward using the "aggregate" social welfare function $\tilde{W}(m)$.

While no new conceptual issues arise in determining optimal policy in the presence of heterogeneity when the social welfare approach is used, the presence of heterogeneity may lead us to fundamentally question the usefulness of this framework as a guide to actual policy implementation. The rather mysterious "social planner" makes optimal policy determination a bit too easy in the end. Even if we are to believe that the social welfare approach is applicable to a particular "type" of agent, is it plausible that it can be extended to encompass a number of different types, for which "optimal" minimum wages may vary markedly? In our example, imagine that there existed two social planners, one for each environment. Let the optimal minimum wage for environment Ξ be given by $m^*(\Xi)$. Then the two optimal minimum wages are given by $m_j^* = m^*(\Xi_j)$, $j = 1, 2$. It seems reasonable to imagine that in a heterogeneous society, the possibility of agreeing on one minimum wage would depend on the difference in the welfare outcomes associated with it. One measure type $j's$ welfare gain associated with imposing its own environment-specific optimal minimum wage is

$$\frac{W(m_j^*; \Xi_j) - W(m^*; \Xi_j)}{W(m^*; \Xi_j)},$$

where $m^* = \arg\max_m \tilde{W}(m)$. If this value is sufficiently large for either of the two subpopulations, then the cost of implementing the "optimal" minimum wage policy may be too large. In this case some participation constraint should be added to the planner's problem, one that would ensure the agreement of both types to an economy wide minimum wage.[18]

Instead of "convexifying" the policy problem in this way, an alternative is to allow voting to determine the outcome. If we continue to assume that each group agrees to set their optimal minimum wage by optimizing their group-specific welfare function, then the minimum wage set for the economy may be set through active competition between the groups. A median voter rule would then select m_1^* as the economy wide minimum wage if $\pi > 0.5$, while m_2^* would be selected if $\pi < 0.5$.

While we have not come to any definitive conclusion regarding the best way to think about policy implementation issues in this section, we hope to have at least pointed out the manner in which heterogeneity in the population may impact the determination of a (common) minimum wage. In particular, the fact that few groups in the population benefited from high minimum wages may be the most important factor in explaining their low historic level in the United States. Sorting out efficiency versus political power explanations for low minimum wages can only be addressed using a model that incorporates a more elaborated political economy component, and should be an important goal of future policy-relevant research on this topic.

12 Conclusion

This chapter summarizes some of the key features and findings of the analysis we have performed and, at least as importantly, point to some of the most important limitations of our approach. Besides serving as a brief recap, we hope to point to possible extensions and elaborations of the model that could be of particular academic and policy interest.

12.1 Theory

Not surprisingly, minimum wage policies, if imposed on "perfect" markets, cannot have beneficial impacts in terms of the efficient operation of the labor market. This finding, of course, applies to any potential policy intervention, not only minimum wages. For those advocating minimum wage increases, arguments are typically made on normative and redistributive grounds, and the assumption, at least implicitly, is that the labor market is characterized by important "imperfections." While few would dispute this claim, it is important to understand the manner in which the labor market is imperfect when analyzing the impact of minimum wage policy on labor market equilibrium and the distribution of welfare. The best case for minimum wage proponents, as pointed out by Stigler (1946), is a labor market with a "monopsonistic" imperfection. In this case a minimum wage, "correctly chosen," in Stigler's words, can increase wages, employment, and output.

The increasing focus on dynamic labor market processes that has occurred over the past several decades has made the search framework the model of choice in both theoretical and empirical analyses (at least those based on behavioral models). Search frictions are a prominent form of imperfection, and their existence tends to give some bargaining power to both firms and workers. While it may seem difficult to speak about "constrained" efficient equilibria in models with search frictions and bargaining over match-specific surpluses, Hosios (1990) made clear the conditions that would produce an efficient equilibrium in this class of models. He showed that giving the worker a share of the match-specific surplus that was equal to their marginal contribution in producing an acceptable match resulted in an efficient equilibrium. If this condition held, then a minimum wage could not increase output. Our estimates of matching function and bargaining power parameters showed that this condition did not necessarily hold. A minimum (or maximum!) wage policy was viewed as a method to increase the effective bargaining power of the side of the market being undercompensated for their contribution to match formation. Thus minimum wages, besides clearly being a reallocative device, could also produce superior constrained efficient outcomes under certain conditions on the underlying primitive parameters characterizing the labor market.

The theoretical model was especially crafted so as to produce equilibrium outcomes consistent with patterns actually observed in individual-level wage data. In particular, we were interested in developing a model that could provide a rationale for the mass point at the minimum wage commonly observed in US data. We were also interested in formulating a model that is parsimonious but at the same time capable of providing a basis for performing some suggestive types of welfare analyses. We were able to use the model estimates and explicit welfare criteria to obtain precise assessments of what the optimal minimum wage should have been in 1996. This, in principle, meets one of Stigler's (1946) main objections to minimum wage policy, which was that it was difficult, if not impossible, to actually determine the value of a "good" minimum wage.

12.2 Limitations of the Modeling Framework

All models are tautologically incorrect. They are abstractions, meant to help us understand key features of the world around us, or even more fundamentally, to guide us along a path to better understand the mechanisms generating relationships among measured variables. One can only legitimately ask if a model is useful in helping us to understand some particular set of phenomena, not whether it is the "right" model.

Our model of the labor market environment is highly stylized, needless to say. Readers not used to seeing formal behavioral models guide empirical analysis may be uncomfortable with some of the basic modeling assumptions that have been made, so I will explain and defend those that do not seem to be particularly problematic, while pointing to those assumptions that may be troublesome and in need of attention.

To conduct policy experiments involving the minimum wage, we have maintained that it is necessary to employ a search-based equilibrium model of the labor market, where by "equilibrium" we mean a model in which, at the least, the wage offer and steady state accepted wage distributions are endogenously determined. Within the class of equilibrium search models, there are essentially those models that assume wage-posting and those models that allow for bargaining. Of the two model types, we could only see a natural way to produce an equilibrium with a mass of wage offers at the minimum, m, under the bargaining assumption. Now, does each individual actually bargain with each potential employer over their wage rate? No, but the question is whether we can reasonably approximate the observed wage and employment distributions with such an assumption. We think that the histograms presented in chapter 8 indicate that we can.

The actual bargaining process posited to take place in the modeling development may occur "silently" if the match surplus is immediately apparent to both sides, the outside options of each are well known, and if there is agreement as to each side's degree of bargaining power. In the case of most jobs found by the young or low-skilled workers, who are disproportionally affected by minimum wage legislation and, as a consequence, occupy most of our attention in this book, match productivity may be limited in its variability and the bargaining power of the worker may be low. Both such factors tend to reduce dispersion in observed wages. Thus the relatively homogeneous wages paid to workers at MacDonald's, for example, are also consistent with our bargaining story given certain, plausible, values of primitive labor market parameters.

The generalized Nash bargaining framework that we rely on here is often criticized for the presence of the bargaining power parameter, α. The welfare analysis of minimum wage changes depends critically on the value of this parameter, and we have devoted a substantial amount of time to discussing how it could be credibly estimated with the data available to us. While the parameter is arbitrary, at least in the way we have used it here, this has at least one advantage and one disadvantage. We view the bargaining power parameter as a type of summary statistic of all the factors ignored in the model (of which there are many) that play a role in determining the final wage outcome. The disadvantage of this interpretation is reasonably obvious; if at least some of these other factors respond to the level of the minimum wage, then the value of α will change with m, and all of the policy analysis we have performed at a fixed value of α will not be valid. Without an explicit mechanism to determine α, there seems little to be done regarding this point.

The dynamics of the model are limited, to say the least. Most of the analysis is done using steady state distributions, and little attention is paid to transitional dynamics when moving from one minimum wage equilibrium to another. The highly restrictive dynamic setting is used to enable us to derive stationary decision rules and equilibrium outcomes, and is common to virtually all search-theoretic models used in micro- and macroeconomic applications. Moreover, with the exception of chapter 10, the empirical work relies essentially on (repeated) cross-sectional data. This type of information can only be used to estimate dynamic labor market models under the most restrictive of conditions—such as those we have imposed here.

The real problem with the stationarity assumption as it impacts our minimal wage analysis is the implicit assumption of a constant price level. While it is usually straightforward to impose stationarity assumptions on the analysis of wage observations at various points in time simply by dividing each by some measure of the price level in the period, doing so with respect to a fixed (in nominal terms) minimum wage makes the entire model highly nonstationary. This makes the analysis of the model extremely challenging.

12.3   Empirical Findings and Lessons

The model we developed was applied in performing a welfare analysis of fairly recent federal minimum wage changes, those occurring in 1996 and 1997. In terms of the model without on-the-job search, which occupied the bulk of our attention, we used two different methodologies in performing this analysis. Reassuringly, the results were quite consistent across approaches.

The argument we have made consistently throughout the book is that every empirical analysis is based on a modeling framework, though in most cases the model is not made explicit. This is true whether the empirical analysis involves a comparison of wage distributions before and after a minimum wage change, or the estimation of primitive parameters associated with a very specific version of an equilibrium search model. This point was illustrated in chapter 6, where our behavioral model was used to derive implications on the ordering of pre- and post-minimum wage change distributions of wages that were consistent with a particular type of welfare improvement. In our model we found that changes in unemployment or employment rates convey relatively little information as to whether a minimum wage change was "good" or "bad." What information was contained in these state occupancy rates, which are typically the only focus of the minimum wage empirical literature, can only be interpreted when used in conjunction with pre- and post-change wage data.

The chapter 6 analysis did not require any specific assumptions on the form of the matching distribution, or estimates of primitive model parameters, and may be a good illustration of an event study approach. The point of that exercise is that a model is required to determine the features of the data that indicate the manner in which the labor market equilibrium has changed. Because limited prior information is brought to the empirical analysis in this case, the amount that can be learned regarding welfare changes is limited. Nonetheless, we found strong indications that the federal minimum wage changes of 1996 and 1997 had very little, if any, impact on the welfare of members of the 16 to 24-year-old population.

The econometric and empirical analysis carried out in chapters 7 and 8 was of another type altogether, though it was based on the same equilibrium bargaining model. In carrying out that empirical analysis, we first carefully examined the conditions for identification of primitive parameters given the CPS-ORG data available to us. Then under a set of assumptions required for identification, relating to the match productivity distribution and the matching function that determines the contact rate, we obtained point estimates and estimated standard errors for the primitive parameters that characterize the model. In obtaining estimates of the primitive parameters, we went through the intermediate step of actually estimating the value of search. By pooling CPS-ORG observations from months before and after the minimum wage change, we were able to consistently estimate the values of search before and after the change, and perform a "direct" welfare analysis of the impact of the minimum wage changes. Using this methodology, we found little indication that those two minimum wage changes had significant welfare impacts on the population of 16- to 24-year-olds.

First, and most obvious, the two very different approaches to looking at welfare effects yielded similar implications. This consistency was primarily due to the fact that both analyses were based on the same modeling framework. The second reassuring thing we learned is that both results accord with common sense. At minimum wage rates set at such low levels only a small minority of 16 to 24-year-olds are paid the minimum wage or less. So the minimum wage simply should not be expected to have large welfare impacts when changed by what are essentially small amounts.

Can a minimum wage have major impacts on labor market outcomes and welfare? It certainly can, in principle, when set at a high enough level. The main problem we face in performing counterfactual analyses is extrapolating outside the range of the data. Event study approaches, such as the one performed in chapter 6, allow no possibility of extrapolation because they are based on the evaluation of changes that actually occurred. Only when armed with estimates of primitive parameters that characterize the model—namely those parameters that do not change in the face of a particular type of policy change—can the analyst perform counterfactual experiments. However, whether the model is cast in partial or general equilibrium terms, we should always question the results of counterfactual experiments performed well outside the range of the data. This doesn't mean that we cannot hope to draw policy conclusions and recommendations from the limited range of historical policies that have been implemented. It means that we should subject our theoretical and econometric models to rigorous scrutiny and sensitivity testing in this common circumstance.

In drawing conclusions about the optimal minimum wage, we were confronted with something of a dilemma. On the one hand, the empirical results from chapter 8 rather clearly indicated that the minimum wage changes that occurred in 1996 and 1997 had no impact on the rate of arrival of job offers, which in turn implies that those rates can be considered constant with respect to the actual wage changes that occurred. On the other hand, based on our estimates of the partial equilibrium model, in chapter 9 we found an optimal wage rate of $8.66 for September 1996. Is it reasonable to assume that the contact rates between workers and firms would remain the same in the face of a doubling of the federal minimum wage rate? Most probably, that is not a reasonable assumption.[1]

The alternative is to conduct the counterfactual policy analysis in the context of the general equilibrium model. This approach entails problems as well. The implication drawn from the general equilibrium analysis was that the optimal minimum wage was $3.33 in September 1996, which was significantly less than the prevailing minimum wage of $4.25. Once again, data limitations lead us to view this figure with some suspicion. A key component of the general equilibrium model is the matching function, which relates unemployment and vacancies to contact rates between searchers and firms. With no direct measures of vacancy levels, and with limited variation in the equilibrium labor market outcomes due to the small size of the minimum wage change, it is very difficult to obtain credible estimates of this function. From the little knowledge we have of this function it is difficult to trust the policy changes it implies. It may be useful to attempt to merge macroeconomic time-series evidence on the properties of the matching function with individual labor market data to improve on the current state of affairs.

In chapter 10 we added the possibility of on-the-job search to the basic model. In a sense, this was an exercise in studying the robustness of policy inferences to changes, albeit a simple one, to the assumptions on the underlying market structure. Adding OTJ search in a bargaining framework required us take a position on the nature of bargaining and renegotiation among workers, employers, and potential employers when determining optimal behavior and equilibrium outcomes. We saw that under different bargaining assumptions, the minimum wage was binding for different parts of the matching distribution, and as a result produced different welfare outcomes. Our limited testing indicated a preference for a model in which the outside option value of the worker in the bargaining problem is always associated with unemployed search. In this case, the optimal minimum wage in the partial equilibrium case turns out to be extremely high, while the optimal minimum wage in the general equilibrium case is below the federal minimum wage of $5.15 for the period covered by the data. In a qualitative sense, this result mimics that found in the policy analysis performed assuming no OTJ search, which also utilized a different data set.

While we should take the results of policy analysis with a large grain of salt, we do believe that the exercises that have been conducted here are useful ones. Their usefulness stems from bringing to light mechanisms that may be involved in producing observed labor market outcomes, the types of information required to estimate the parameters that characterize the underlying labor market environment, and ultimately the value of counterfactual policy analysis. As Marschak (1953) recognized many years ago, there is no substitute for actual policy variation in attaining credible estimates of economic models. When faced with a paucity of data on problems of immense social and political issue, it is necessary to wisely and immaginatively use the limited information available to us.

Appendix: Proofs of Selected Propositions from Chapter 7

Proof of Proposition 16

If there exist no restrictions relating (c, d, α), then consistent estimators of c' and d' are insufficient to determine all three parameters. Suppose that there exists one exact restriction on the parameter vector (c, d, α) of the form $0 = r(c, d, \alpha)$, and without loss of generality, let us use this restriction to determine a value of α given (c, d), or $\alpha = \alpha(c, d)$. Then with consistent estimators for c' and d', we can solve for

$$\widehat{c'} = (1 - \alpha(c, d))\hat{\theta}^* + \alpha(c, d)c,$$

$$\widehat{d'} = \alpha(c, d)d,$$

which is a system of two equations in two unknowns. Depending on the form of the function $\alpha(c, d)$ and the values of $\widehat{c'}$ and $\widehat{d'}$, there may exist no solution, a unique solution, or multiple solutions. We will say that the model is just identified if the system

$$c' = (1 - \alpha(c, d))\theta^* + \alpha(c, d)c,$$

$$d' = \alpha(c, d)d,$$

has exactly one solution for all values of (c, d) in the parameter space. Note that in this case we have replaced all estimated quantities with their limiting values, so that this should be interpreted as an "asymptotic" identification condition.

The most common restriction will be a direct one on one of the parameters c or d. For example, if $c = 0$ we have

$$\widehat{c'} = (1 - \alpha)\hat{\theta}^*,$$

$$\widehat{d'} = \alpha d.$$

This is a two-equation system in two unknowns, and it yields estimators for α and d of

$$\hat{\alpha} = 1 - \frac{\widehat{c'}}{\hat{\theta}^*},$$

$$\hat{d} = \frac{\widehat{d'}}{\hat{\alpha}}.$$

While in small samples it is possible for these estimators to yield values outside of the parameter space, the likelihood of such an event will be a decreasing function of sample size.

We now establish why a restriction relating (c, d, α) is not sufficient to ensure identification. Assume that G is negative exponential with support R_+. In this case the location parameter is 0, and the scale parameter $d > 0$ completely characterizes the distribution. The likelihood of wage observation w_i is given by

$$\frac{g_0\{[w_i - (1-\alpha)\theta^*]/\alpha d\}/\alpha d}{\tilde{G}_0\{[w^* - (1-\alpha)\theta^*]/\alpha d\}} = \frac{\exp\{-[w_i - (1-\alpha)\theta^*]/\alpha d\}/\alpha d}{\exp\{-[w^* - (1-\alpha)\theta^*/\alpha d\}}$$

$$= \frac{1}{\alpha d} \exp\left(-\frac{w_i - w^*}{\alpha d}\right).$$

Thus the wage distribution can only identify αd, not the two components individually. This is the only continuous distribution with support R_+ that we have found that is not identified under a restriction on c or d so that it may be a pathological case.   ∎

Proof of Proposition 17

The unconcentrated likelihood function $L(\tilde{\gamma}, \alpha)$ satisfies standard regularity conditions for $\tilde{\gamma}^0 \in \text{int}(\tilde{\Gamma}(m))$ and $\alpha^0 \in (0, 1)$. In particular, the support of the distribution of the data is not a function of $\tilde{\gamma}^0$ and α^0, though it is a function of the known constant m. The likelihood function is continuously differentiable in both $\tilde{\gamma}$ and α. The implicit function $\alpha^*(\tilde{\pi}, \tilde{\gamma}, m)$ is continuously differentiable in $\tilde{\gamma}$, so the function $\ln L(\tilde{\gamma}, \alpha^*(\tilde{\pi}, \tilde{\gamma}, m)) \equiv \ln \tilde{L}(\tilde{\gamma}; \tilde{\pi}, m)$ is continuously differentiable in γ on the space $\Gamma'(m, \tilde{\pi})$. Continuous differentiability of α^* is sufficient for $\text{plim}_{\tilde{\gamma} \to \tilde{\gamma}^0} \alpha^*(\tilde{\pi}, \tilde{\gamma}, m) = \alpha^0$, and differentiability of $L(\tilde{\gamma}, \alpha)$ in both arguments is sufficient for $\text{plim}_{\alpha \to \alpha^0}\text{plim}_{N \to \infty} \arg\max_{\hat{\gamma} \in \tilde{\Gamma}(m)} \ln L(\tilde{\gamma}, \alpha) = \gamma^0$. Then $\text{plim}_{N \to \infty} \alpha^*(\tilde{\pi}, \hat{\gamma}, m) = \alpha^0$.

Since the concentrated log likelihood function $\ln \tilde{L}(\gamma;\tilde{\pi},m)$ satisfies all regularity conditions for asymptotic normality, the asymptotic distribution of $\sqrt{N}(\hat{\gamma}-\tilde{\gamma}^0)$ is $N(0,\Sigma_{\hat{\gamma}})$, where

$$\Sigma_{\hat{\gamma}} = \left(\frac{\partial^2 \ln \tilde{L}(\tilde{\gamma};\tilde{\pi},m)}{\partial\tilde{\gamma}\partial\tilde{\gamma}'}\bigg|_{\tilde{\gamma}=\hat{\gamma}}\right)^{-1}.$$

The asymptotic covariance matrix of $\hat{\alpha}$ is derived using the delta method. The variance of $\hat{\alpha}$ is

$$\text{Var}(\hat{\alpha}) = \frac{\partial\alpha^*(\tilde{\pi},\tilde{\gamma},m)}{\partial\tilde{\gamma}}\bigg|'_{\tilde{\gamma}=\hat{\gamma}} \Sigma_{\hat{\gamma}} \frac{\partial\alpha^*(\tilde{\pi},\tilde{\gamma},m)}{\partial\tilde{\gamma}}\bigg|_{\tilde{\gamma}=\hat{\gamma}}. \qquad \blacksquare$$

Proof of Proposition 20

From the augmented CPS data we have consistent estimates of λ_t within each equilibrium, as well as having consistent estimates of $(UI)_t$. Under the Cobb–Douglas assumption we can write

$$\lambda_s = \left(\frac{(UI)_s}{v_s}\right)^{\omega-1},$$

$$\Rightarrow v_s = \lambda_s^{1/(1-\omega)}(UI)_s, \qquad s=t,t'.$$

Substituting this expression into the free entry condition of period s, we have

$$\psi = \lambda_s^{-\omega/(1-\omega)}\tilde{G}(m_s)J_s, \qquad (A.1)$$

where J_s is the equilibrium value of a filled vacancy under m_s. Then we have

$$\lambda_t^{-\omega/(1-\omega)}\tilde{G}(m_t)J_t = \lambda_{t'}^{-\omega/(1-\omega)}\tilde{G}(m_{t'})J_{t'}$$

at the two sets of equilibrium values. From this we have

$$\omega = \frac{A_{t,t'}}{1+A_{t,t'}},$$

where

$$A_{t,t'} \equiv \frac{\ln \tilde{G}(m_{t'})-\ln \tilde{G}(m_t)+\ln J_{t'}-\ln J_t}{\ln\lambda_{t'}-\ln\lambda_t}. \qquad (A.2)$$

The estimator of $A_{t,t'}$ is defined as $\hat{A}_{t,t'}$, which is obtained by replacing all of the quantities on the right-hand side of (A.2) with consistent estimators of them. Under Condition C, the estimator $\hat{A}_{t,t'} > 0 \Rightarrow \hat{\omega} \equiv \hat{A}_{t,t'}/(1 + \hat{A}_{t,t'}) \in (0,1)$ as required. Given this permissible and consistent estimator of ω, we use the consistent estimators of the relevant equilibrium values as well as the consistent estimate of ω, $\hat{\omega}$, to form the consistent estimator

$$\hat{\psi} = \hat{\lambda}_s^{-\omega/(1-\omega)} \widehat{G(m_s)} \hat{J}_s, \qquad s = t \text{ or } t',$$

since $\hat{\psi}$ is identical whether t or t' values are used.   ∎

Notes

Chapter 1

1. The models considered are by no means exhaustive. All but one, that involving equilibrium selection in a multiple equilibria framework, explicitly include search frictions. Since one of the focal points of empirical minimum wage research involves unemployment, and since unemployment is most reasonably generated in a framework with search frictions, virtually all empirically relevant models of minimum wage effects on the market and welfare include search frictions of some type.

2. There are a number of contributions to in the literature that consider the possibility of welfare-enhancing minimum wage rates (e.g., Drazen 1986; Lang 1987; Rebitzer and Taylor 1995; Swinnerton 1996), though the frameworks in which the models are set tend to be relatively abstract and the models are typically not estimable. While these are important contributions, in this book our focus is more on models that have been or are capable of being taken to data.

3. Some examples of labor market models that can easily produce multiple equilibria involve statistical discrimination (e.g., see Moro 2003) and the general equilibrium search model with contact rates determined through a nonconstant returns to scale matching function (e.g., see Diamond 1982).

4. Of course, if the low wage equilibrium turned out to be Pareto optimal, a maximum wage policy would be used as the equilibrium selection device. This type of possibility is why we use the term "wage policy" instead of "minimum wage" when discussing equilibrium selection possibilities.

5. Jovanovic (1979) emphasizes the role of learning about match quality in explaining separation decisions and wage progression at a firm. He expands his framework to include unemployment in Jovanovic (1984). The bargaining process is not emphasized in his approach.

6. In chapter 3 we will explicitly define all of the terms appearing in (1.1).

7. We could invoke an evolutionary argument to claim that firms that are not good bargainers are eventually selected out of the industry, leaving only the good bargainers behind. We don't wish to push this argument too far, however, since we will be considering the case where all firms have the same bargaining power. The case where bargaining power is heterogeneous among firms and searchers is interesting but is an extremely difficult case to analyze conceptually and empirically.

8. In this view, the government plays a somewhat similar role to a union-contract negotiator. Major differences are that the minimum wage does not only impact a narrow class of employees, defined in terms of industry or occupation of employment. More important, the objectives of the government in setting a minimum wage are generally quite different than the objectives of union leaders.

9. Technically, within the context of our model anyone in the minimum wage pool will be paid the minimum wage at some point in their labor market career with probabability one. An individual not in this pool will never be observed at the minimum wage, no matter how long is the sample observation period.

10. It may be the case that historians have made too much of this particular division. In a statistical analysis of voting patterns on this law, Seltzer (1995, p. 1335) concludes that "although southern legislators disproportionately opposed the bill, there was not a unified effort by the South to defeat it. The South was less unionized, had a higher proportion of employment in agriculture, had lower wages, and had more blacks—all of which led to southern opposition to the FLSA. However, if one controls for these characteristics, southern legistlators were no more likely to oppose the act."

11. On a related point, in performing the empirical minimum wage analysis using Current Population Survey data from the mid- to late-1990s, we found few workers paid the state minimum wages in those states for which $m_S > m_F$. One explanation for this finding may be that wealthier states tend to enact higher minimum wage rates, while having wage distributions that stochastically dominate those of poorer states. In these states case, the high minimum wage rate may be less "binding" than in poorer states, resulting in few individuals paid at the high state minimum wage level.

12. If each state has its own labor market, then it follows that our analysis, which assumes homogeneity in model parameters at the national level, is beset by spatial aggregation problems as well. This is a valid argument, and in interpreting the results that appear below, the reader should bear in mind that they apply to some idealized national market that ignores spatial differentiation.

13. This is not to suggest that variability in state minimum wage laws cannot be used to learn about the impacts of minimum wages on labor market outcomes and welfare. I am merely suggesting that a number of preliminary analyses should be performed to assess the likely degree of heterogeneity in state labor market environments in characteristics other than the minimum wage before using state minimum wages as instrumental variables.

Chapter 2

1. The household respondent must be at least 15 years of age and have knowledge of the labor market activities and demographic characteristics of all household members.

2. In the classical measurement error model, it is also typically assumed that ε is continuously distributed, often according to a normal distribution. However, these assumptions are not necessary for the measurement error to be considered "classical."

3. The noncompliance issue in accounting for wage observations less than the minimum wage is emphasized in Eckstein et al. (2006).

4. A distribution F (first-order) stochastically dominates a distribution G if, for every value x, $F(x) \leq G(x)$, with the inequality being strict for some measurable set of values of x.

5. Construction of the short panel is complicated by the fact that unique individual identifiers are not available in the CPS. Household identifiers are available, however. We utilize statistical matching to create the short panels, where an individual in the same household in sample months 4 and 8 is considered to be the same if they have (1) the same gender in both months, (2) they are of the same race in both months, and (3) their age in sample month 8 is no less than in sample month 4 and is less than 3 years greater in sample month 8 than in sample month 4. While some errors in matching may exist, we don't expect them to constitute more than a very small proportion of the total number of observations in the panel.

6. An exception is recent work by Eckstein et al. (2006) who account for such observations in a model of firms' decisions regarding compliance with minimum wage laws.

7. We will revisit the impact of minimum wage changes on the wage distribution of group D members within a much more formal context when we discuss the empirical assessment of the welfare impacts of minimum wages in chapter 7.

8. This discussion assumes that the individual receives no better job offers while employed at the time-1 firm. This is consistent with the assumption of no on-the-job search made in the model developed in the following chapter. If individuals can receive alternative offers, then the fact that an employee is not at his time-1 job at time 2 does not necessarily indicate that his productivity was low at the job. It is consistent with getting a better offer from an alternative employer before or after the minimum wage change.

9. This claim must be tempered by the fact that this information is reported by a household member at both points in time. The household respondent may be different in months 4 and 8, and may not be the subject individual in one or both months.

10. We also repeated this analysis for individuals who *may* have been working at the same job at both observation times—or at least remain in the same major industry and occupational grouping. Since we condition on being employed at both points in time, the conditional probability of being observed in state U at the second observation point was zero in this subsample. We don't know what happens between the two sample points, however, so it is highly probable that some in our subsample have experienced an unemployment spell between the first and second interview times, and/or have had a number of other jobs between these two points in time. While we would like to be able to consider only on those at the same job, this is not possible given the information available to us. In any event, we found transition matrices that were extremely similar to those reported in table 2.3, and for this reason do not include them here.

Chapter 3

1. This will be the case as long as the minimum wage is relatively low in comparison with the median compensation level, for instance. As the minimum wage is raised, we can expect that the proportion of workers directly impacted by it, and the average age of workers paid the minimum wage, would steadily increase.

2. It is possible to rationalize the Nash-bargaining axiomatic solution as the outcome of a strategic bargaining game, as was notably done by Rubenstein (1982). We won't explicitly attempt to model the interactions between negotiating firms and workers. For one attempt to do so in a bargaining model similar to ours, see Cahuc et al. (2006).

3. In the search literature, this is referred to as the case of nondirected search. Directed search occurs when firms not yet contacted are not viewed as equivalent by the searcher.

In this case the individual may rank potential employers or geographic labor markets in a preferred order prior to beginning a search episode. While some form(s) of directed search no doubtedly occur in actual labor markets, the theoretical and empirical analyses of such models are currently at a very rudimentary stage.

4. Under the informational assumptions of this model, jobs, or more properly potential jobs, are pure *search goods*. Once a potential employer is contacted, both the individual and the firm will learn the total value of the match as well as the share of that value accruing to each.

5. See Flinn and Mabli (2008) for a model in which schooling choices are endogenously determined given their impact on the productivity distribution when individuals are differentiated in terms of their ability to convert schooling into productive human capital.

6. In chapter 11 we examine issues in the incorporation of both observed and unobserved heterogeneity into the type of labor market models we consider.

7. As one example, their matching structure implies that any worker that is more productive than another worker at a given firm b will be more productive at any other firm b'.

8. For a consideration of decision-making in a search-theoretic model in which the environment is nonstationary, see van den Berg (1990).

9. Due to this feature of the decision rule, we do not have to take a position on whether searchers have access to previously rejected offers. In a nonstationary model, instead, there typically will arise situations in which previously rejected offers would be accepted if the searcher still had access to them. If so, we say that search is with *recall*, if not we say it is *without recall*. The recall option is not operative under stationary decision rules.

10. For an excellent exposition of this approach, see Burdett and Mortensen (1978).

11. We have already used this invariance property implicitly when we argued that given it was optimal to search at one point in time it will never be optimal to exit the labor market in the future. Obviously, if employment conditions, such as the wage offer distribution, were allowed to vary over time this would not be true in general.

12. Assuming that the distribution function G is everywhere diffentiable, the support of the distribution is defined as the subset of the real line $S \subseteq R$ such that $g(s) > 0$ for all $s \in S$. In this discussion we assume that wage offers are always strictly positive, so that $S = R_+$, the positive real line. This is reasonable since under our assumption that the wage offer is equal to the worker-firm match productivity, which we might posit must be nonnegative.

13. If w is a discrete random variable instead, the decision rule will still possess a critical value property, but the critical value solving the problem will not be unique. Say that wages were drawn from a discrete distribution with three mass points, at $w = 1, 5$, and 10. Then say that the optimal decision was to reject wage draws equal to 1 and 5, and to accept only a wage draw of 10. In this case the reservation wage is not unique, since any value in the interval $w^* \in (5, 10]$ will divide the sample space into the appropriate acceptance and rejection regions.

14. The log normal density is given by

$$g(w; \mu, \sigma) = \frac{1}{w\sqrt{2\pi}\sigma} \exp\left\{ -\frac{1}{2}\left(\frac{\ln(w) - \mu}{\sigma}\right)^2 \right\}.$$

15. This is only a substantive restriction on the form of the offer distribution G in this case.

16. One could argue that certain modifications of the objective function of the searcher could make the reservation wage choice "suboptimal" and lead to the possibility of welfare-improving minimum wages even within a fixed labor market environment. In models of hyperbolic discounting, for example, where the individual makes seemingly time inconsistent decisions, by limiting the agent's behavior the government could increase the long-run welfare of the agent at the expense of her "short-run self." For the exposition of such a model, see Della Vigna and Paserman (2005).

17. This statement is not true if the model is extended to allow for on-the-job search. In this case future bargains struck with either one's current employer or a future employer (met during the ongoing employment spell) may be a function of one's current match value.

18. In a celebrated paper, Rubinstein (1982) shows how the bargaining power parameter is related to the discount rates of two players trying to divide a "pie" in a setting in which they alternate making proposals regarding the division of the surplus until one is accepted.

19. The same argument could be made for many of the other "primitive" parameters, it must be admitted. When discussing estimates of the equilibrium model we will provide some evidence that the rate of contacts between searchers and firms, λ, is not invariant with respect to changes in the minimum wage.

20. As we saw in chapter 2, the principal exceptions occur in the food preparation and serving sectors, where substantially lower minimum wages apply.

21. By well-defined, I mean that the distribution of match values has finite expectation, the discount rate is strictly greater than 0, etc.

Chapter 4

1. There are no mass points, or "spikes," in the accepted wage distribution when match productivity is continuously distributed, as was assumed in chapter 3. If there were match values θ that were acceptable from the standpoint of initiating an employment contract and that had positive probability, then there would be mass points in the accepted wage distribution, with or without a binding minimum wage.

2. We only formally considered the impact of finite minimum wage changes in the previous section, but the positive impact of minimum wage increases on the propotion of labor market participants who are unemployed holds for both finite and infinitesimal changes. In this subsection and the next two, it is less daunting notationally to consider the case of infinitesimal changes.

3. Of course, with a fixed participation rate the unemployment rate in the population is a fixed proportion of the unemployment rate within the set of participants.

4. For the claims we are making in this section to hold *immediately* following a minimum wage change, we require a fixed contact rate. If contact rates are endogenous, following a minimum wage change some jobs will be terminated (those with $m \leq \theta < m'$) and this mass of individuals will temporariliy inflate the unemployment rate. This will have effects on vacancy creation, and ultimately on the contact rate. With a time-varying contact rate, the value of search will be changing continuously over this transition period, until eventually converging to its steady state value. If contact rates are fixed, the temporary increase in the unemployed stock does not impact the value of search, and all contracts are renegotiated using the new steady state value $V_n(m')$.

All the results we report are applicable, even for the endogenous contact rate case, when the new steady state equilibrium has been reached. How long it takes to (effectively) reach

Notes to Pages 81 to 108

the new equilibrium depends on the size of the minimum wage change and the values of model parameters.

5. Hosios considers a slightly more general decision problem, since he allows both firms and searchers to choose a search intensity. Given the severe econometric identification problems we face, the estimation of a model allowing for the choice of intensity is not possible, even though it would clearly be desireable.

6. Our axiomatic Nash bargaining framework provides no explicit mechanism through which α is determined. One possibility for rectifying this situation is to employ a strategic approach to the bargaining problem as in Rubinstein (1982). In the case of an alternating offers game to determine the share of a pie allotted to the two parties, α was found to be a function of the discount rates of the two parties. If this discount rate is considered to be a part of the preference map of the individual parties, then it is not reasonable to consider it a policy variable. It is not straightforward to extend the Rubinstein framework in the presence of a binding constraint on the division of the surplus.

7. This statement requires a bit of qualification. For the case where we are able to estimate a Cobb–Douglas matching parameter, ζ, the standard error is sufficiently large that one could not rule out $\alpha = \zeta$ using standard hypothesis testing methods. However, when using data from only one cross section, in which case we cannot estimate a Cobb–Douglas matching function, the matching function elasticity is significantly different from α. We tend to give more credence to the results obtained using the single CPS samples.

Chapter 5

1. The studies selected are all solid examples of empirical minimum wage research, and have at least one of the characteristics mentioned. The selection criteria used were extremely idiosyncratic, meaning that there are many high quality empirical studes of minimum wage effects on labor market outcomes that could have been included but were not. As mentioned below, the recent extensive survey of Neumark and Wascher (2008) should be consulted for those readers desiring a detailed review of the minimum wage literature.

2. An informative review of this monograph and the authors' research program can be found in Kennan (1995).

3. Policy makers may be directly interested in the employment and/or unemployment rate in the economy, rather than the distribution of welfare in the population or labor market. For purposes of determining whether a minimum wage has improved either of these rates, it is obviously not necessary to use a full-blown behavioral modeling framework. Our focus is on the welfare and distributional effects of minimum wages in the population, and hence our claim of the necessity of a comprehensive equilibrium model underlying the empirical analysis.

4. For example, the job may pay a wage greater than $\hat{w}$, and hence will survive the minimum wage change, but could then be terminated for exogenous reasons prior to the second measurement. If the individual is unable to find a new acceptable job prior to the second measurement, it may appear that the minimum wage change caused the change in employment state. This is only to say that time aggregation leads to a particular type of measurement error that makes causal inference more challenging.

5. See the discussion of van den Berg and Ridder (1998) below.

6. We are more explicit as to what we mean by the "shape" of the wage distribution in the following chapter.

7. See, for example, Card and Krueger (1995, pp. 232–236) and Dickens et al. (1998).

8. A comprehensive and excellent survey of this literature can be found in Petrongolo and Pissarides (2001). Most studies use time series information on unemployment and some measure of search activity by firms, most often an index of help-wanted advertising, as the regressors, and the change in employment level as the dependent variable, in estimating a linear regression model. In this framework, the CRS property implies a linear restriction on the regression coefficients.

9. They assumed "classical" measurement error, that is, to the logarithm of each true wage, which was one of a small set determined in equilibrium, an independent and identically distributed disturbance is added.

10. See Postel-Vinay and Robin (2004) for an interesting analysis of firms' decision to match or not match job offers to their employees from other firms.

11. Given that (instantaneous) revenue is equal to θ, no firm can offer a wage greater than that. The equilibrium wage distribution has finite support, $[\underline{w}^*, \overline{w}^*]$, and over this interval the wage density is increasing.

12. There are a few different minimum wage rates in existence at any point in time. The major indexing occurs with respect to the age of the employed.

Chapter 6

1. The matching values θ are never directly observed by us, but when there exists a binding minimum wage, we know that all draws of $\theta \geq m$ lead to employment contracts. Under our model, given values of α and $\rho V_n(m)$, for all wages greater than m, we know that

$$\theta = \frac{w - (1 - \alpha)\rho V_n(m)}{\alpha},$$

so from any wage observation w we obtain a unique θ value. Thus there is a linear relationship between θ and w that allows us to use the observed wage distribution above m to test competing assumptions regarding the functional form of G. But such tests can only indicate which functional form is more consistent with the data on a subset of its total support, since $[m, \infty) \subseteq R_+$. The point of the Flinn and Heckman (1982) analysis was that we can never test the fit of the assumed distribution of G for values of $\theta < m$ unless we happen to have access to rejected offers. Typically we only observe accepted wages, making parametric assumptions necessary to "extrapolate" probability mass from the observed portion of the match distribution ($\geq m$) down to the unobserved portion ($< m$).

Some analysts, notably Postel-Vinay and Robin (2002), have been able to estimate certain distributions in these kinds of models nonparametrically, but only after imposing conditions that insure that sample information is available over the entire support of the distribution. This type of assumption is problematic within our modeling framework in which we want to allow for the possibility that minimum wage laws prevent the formation of otherwise acceptable matches.

2. In making this statement we are assuming, first, the absence of measurement error here in wages and, second, perfect coverage and enforcement. These conditions will be assumed throughout the analytic discussion and the empirical work we conduct.

3. In a general equilibrium model, firms should alter their vacancy creation decisions to adapt to the time path of unemployment that occurs over the transition path from one steady state to another. This makes it quite difficult to characterize the transition dynamics in the economy.

4. The p-values of the test statistics for equality and FOSD are computed by the bootstrap procedure defined above.

5. Some care is required in interpreting this test result. There is a substantial amount of "heaping" in wage reports, and this measurement problem is to a large extent responsible for the extremely large values of the Kolmogorov–Smirnov statistic that are calculated. To modify the test to allow for measurement error would require that we take a position on its exact form.

Chapter 7

1. Manski (1995) contains an illuminating discussion of identification problems and results across a wide variety of social science applications.

2. A linear regression analogy is the rank condition on the matrix of regressors. In the regression model

$$y = X\beta + \varepsilon,$$

the ordinary least squares estimator of β is $\hat{\beta} = (X'X)^{-1}X'y$, which is unique if X is of full column rank. In any finite sample N, the matrix X (with K columns) may not have full rank, particularly if some or most covariates are discrete. However, as long as

$$Q = \plim_{N \to \infty} \left(\frac{X_N'X_N}{N} \right)$$

is of rank K, the estimator $\hat{\beta}$ is consistent, even if there are some X_N for which the rank condition fails and $\hat{\beta}$ is not unique.

3. Flinn and Heckman actually assumed that match rents were evenly divided between workers and firms, though they did not explicitly utilize a Nash-bargaining framework in their analysis. Within a Nash-bargaining framework the assumption of an exogenously determined wage offer distribution is only consistent with the assumption that $\alpha = 1$.

4. A distribution is defined as *recoverable* if knowledge of the truncated distribution is sufficient to determine the population distribution. In the context of a search model with a reservation wage w^* and population wage offer distribution F assumed to be uniquely characterized by the vector of parameters δ, recoverability requires that

$$F_\delta(w|w \geq w^*)$$

be a function of all of the elements of δ, not only a subset of them. Flinn and Heckman gave several examples of distributions that are not recoverable, such as the Pareto.

5. For a further discussion of forward and backward recurrence time, the reader is referred to standard texts on stochastic processes such as Cox and Miller (1965) or Karlin and Taylor (1975).

6. This statement is only true when using a likelihood-based estimator in which wages at successive jobs (with no intervening unemployment spell) appear in likelihood function. The estimator used in the estimation of the on-the-job search model in chapter 10 is consistent and well-defined even when the wage at a new job is less than the wage at the job that the individual left. More details are provided in chapter 10.

7. Treating θ^* as a parameter in the estimation does not imply that all of the behavioral restrictions are not being imposed. The model is inherently underidentified in the sense that θ^* is determined by ρ and b in addition to the other parameters that appear "directly" in (7.8). Once we estimate θ^*, we can assume a value for ρ or b and then (uniquely) solve for the other. Conversely, we can directly estimate ρ or b after fixing the value of the other, and our estimate of the parameter along with the others in the likelihood function will uniquely determine θ^*. This last procedure is less attractive from a computational standpoint due to the necessity of imposing a complicated, implicit restriction on the parameter space so as to ensure that the (implied) value of θ^* is strictly less than m.

8. We could consider slightly more general classes of distributions, such as those that also possess a shape parameter, though the negative results of this section regarding the identifiability of α would only be reinforced.

9. Given that the location parameter is set to 0, the lognormal distribution is characterized in terms of its scale parameter μ and shape parameter σ. Thus there are two unknown parameters of the distribution, as in the location-scale case. The difference is that sample moments above the second order convey information on these parameters, which is not the case for location-scale distributions. The content of this sample information is not sufficiently great to enable identification in practical situations, for the reasons described in the subsequent footnote.

10. Whether in Monte Carlo experiments or using CPS data, the log likelihood function invariably is monotone in α, resulting in maximum likelihood estimates of this parameter that converge to 0 or 1.

11. See Johnson and Kotz (1970, p. 129).

12. Another alternative would be to collect aggregate wage share information by firm, and to estimate the subpopulation-specific share using variability in subpopulation employment rates across firms. The use of such a procedure raises questions regarding the source of the variability in subpopulation employment rates across firms or industrial sectors and also encounters the problem that few firms report wages as a separate item in their CSI.

13. Under an assumption regarding the value of the discount rate ρ we are able to infer the value of b - hence its inclusion in the list of estimable parameters in the previous paragraph.

Chapter 8

1. We also estimated the model after deleting all cases with wage observations less than the minimum wage in the period. There was little substantive difference in the point estimates.

2. In all continuous time models in which the rate of leaving a state is not a function of the time spent in the state, the duration of time between events has a negative exponential distribution. In terms of the time between the arrival of job offers, the duration distribution is given by

$$f(t) = \lambda \exp(-\lambda t),$$

and the expected value of t is simply λ^{-1}. Thus the maximum likelihood estimate of $E(t)$ is simply $\hat{\lambda}^{-1}$, where $\hat{\lambda}$ denotes the maximum likelihood estimate of the parameter. In the same manner, we can compute the expected duration of a job, which is $\hat{\eta}^{-1}$.

3. Cahuc et al. (2006) are able to estimate group-specific values of α given their access to employer–employee matched data and their assumption that match values are the product of the idiosyncratic productivity values of an employer and an employee.

4. This point is borne out in chapter 10, where we formulate and estimate a model of minimum wages that allows for on-the-job search. We estimate that model using a different (panel) data set, a different estimator, and an elaborated bargaining mechanism. Because of the complexity of that model, explicit identification conditions are much harder to obtain, even with the richer data potentially available.

5. If one rounds all hourly wage rates below the minimum up to the minimum wage, then the proportion of the sample paid the minimum in the simulations would be over 10 percent in each of the two months. In this case, the overprediction of the minimum is not substantial.

6. For both the sample and simulated duration distributions, we have rounded all durations above 12 months to 12 months for the purpose of graphical presentation.

7. The respondent reports search duration in weeks, which we have converted to months here since the econometric model parameters are denominated in that frequency. Heaping in the weekly data is especially pronounced at 4, 8, 12, 36, and 52 weeks.

Chapter 10

1. If there was a fixed cost, say, of changing jobs given by $C > 0$, this would create a "wedge" between the reservation wage $w^*(w)$ and w, with the size of the wedge increasing in C. If the wage offer distribution is assumed to be continuous, then

$$\frac{\partial w^*(w, C)}{\partial C} > 0.$$

The standard case assumes $C = 0$, and so $w^*(w, C = 0) = w$.

2. The reader should recall that "partial–partial" equilibrium, in fact, really signifies no equilibrium. In such a model the wage offer distribution is taken as exogenous, as are the rate parameters describing contact and termination frequencies. Partial equilibrium models of search typically take all rate parameters as fixed, but endogenize the wage offer distribution. General equilibrium search models also endogenize some subset of the rate parameters.

3. This analysis used data on men in their mid- to late-twenties from the National Longitudinal Survey of Youth, the 1979 survey. These data are among the most commonly used for conducting studies of labor market dynamics in the youth labor market.

4. Classical measurement error models typically assume that the measured characteristic x^* is related to the "true" value x by

$$x^* = x + u,$$

where u is a continuous random variable that is independently and identically distributed in the population. This implies, most important, that the true value x and the measurement error u are independent.

5. This is due to the fact that the value of a job offer is an increasing function of w and a decreasing function of η. If η is a deterministic, nonincreasing function of w, then jobs can be ranked in terms of w alone.

6. This is especially true in our case, even when one-time transfers could potentially be large. This is due to the assumption of linear utility invoked in virtually all search models. In this case there can be no income effects of large income transfers on the mobility and wage process.

7. Since the value of being employed is strictly increasing in the match value for any value of the outside option, if a match value $\theta^A(m)$ is acceptable, then all higher match values are also acceptable.

8. Since the searcher has the option to not report any alternative match value, she will only do so when her employment value at the current firm will increase, which only occurs when her wage at the current job increases.

9. This event has positive probability given our assumption that θ is a discrete random variable.

10. We drop the explicit dependence of the unemployment and employment values on the (binding) minimum wage m in this section to economize on notation.

11. The mapping $\tilde{V}_U = T\tilde{V}_U$, while typically not a contraction, is monotone increasing. Subject to existence conditions, there exists a unique fixed point solution.

12. Given the simplicity of the bargaining process in this case, it is trivial to allow for shocks to match productivity to occur that would change this implication. In particular, say that a current (acceptable) match value of θ_j increased to θ_{j+1} at rate γ^+ for $j < L$, while it decreases to θ_{j-1} at rate γ^- for $j > 1$. This type of process would generate wage increases and decreases during a job spell, and would could obviate the need for an exogenous dismissal rate η if there were a measurable set of unacceptable match values coming out of the unemployment state.

13. Of course, this result is in large part attributable to the distribution of θ being discrete. If θ were continuously distributed, then the minimal acceptable match value would change with m in general, as long as some observed wages were equal to the minimum wage.

14. To see that these contact rates are the appropriate ones, note that the total rate of contacts can be written as

$$\lambda_U U + \lambda_E E = \frac{m(S, V)}{S} U + \frac{m(S, V)}{S} \tau E$$

$$= m(S, V).$$

15. Once again, how long it takes for the cross-sectional wage distribution of a cohort of labor market entrants to converge to the steady state cross-sectional distribution depends on the rate parameters characterizing the market and the properties of G, in particular, the degree of dispersion of the distribution.

16. By this we mean that in contrast to the likelihood based estimator described in chapter 7, the estimator is well-defined even if the data include outcomes that have zero probability under the behavioral model. In the likelihood-based estimator, if it is assumed that there is no measurement error in wage observations, a wage observation less than m has 0 probability under the model, and hence the likelihood function is not well defined. Using a moment-based estimator, we see that this is not the case. For example, if we use the mean wage of employed workers at a point in time as a sample characteristic to fit, there is no restriction on the individual wages in the sample that are averaged to form the sample characteristic, even though all simulated wage draws from the model would be constrained to be at least as large as m. Furthermore we could include a characteristic in

the vector of sample characteristics used to define the estimator that was zero probability under the model, and the estimator would still be well defined in a particular sense. An example would be the proportion of sample wage observations less than the minimum wage. No matter what the value of the primitive parameter vector, this proportion would always be 0 under the model, even if it happened to be 0.12 in the sample, say. While this characteristic would have no value in selecting the "best" value of the primitive parameters, an estimator that included this characteristics would remain well defined, namely computable.

17. Unlike estimation in the case of $\lambda_E = 0$ that was discussed in chapter 7, we found that reasonable estimates of the bargaining power parameter α could be obtained under all model specifications without using firm revenue and cost information. This is most likely due to the additional information obtained from the wage change distributions associated with job-to-job movements within employment spells.

18. We were limited to fifty replications because of the time it takes to estimate the model with renegotiation, which on our quad-core Sun workstation was about 35 hours per replication.

19. The model is estimated using a thirty-point discrete match distribution. Given our parameter estimates, the first eight match values are not accepted in equilibrium.

Chapter 11

1. It is not strictly necessary to assume that the searcher is infinitely-lived for the stationary reservation wage policy to be optimal. If she were to die at the constant rate ω, then the form of the reservation wage function remains the same. The actual value of w^* is determined using ρ' in the place of ρ, where $\rho' = \rho + \omega$.

2. If a mixture of a particular family of distributions has the same functional form as its component parts, we say that the distributional family is closed under mixing. For instance, the untruncated normal distribution is closed under mixing. Clearly, the truncated lognormal family is not closed under mixing. Mixing also has a marked impact on the population distribution of unemployment spell durations.

3. Since the only duration distribution with a constant hazard is the negative exponential, and since the support of the negative exponential distribution is the entire nonnegative real line, the mixture of two constant hazard duration distributions has the entire nonnegative real line as its support, and hence negative duration dependence will be observed everywhere on R_+.

4. If the distribution G is log concave, Flinn and Heckman (1983) and Burdett and Ondrich (1985) show that $h_1 < h_2$. Van den Berg (1994) derives this result using a weaker set of conditions on the distribution G that nest log concavity as a special case.

5. The wage rate of an employed individual only matters in jobs with OTJ search, that is, when $\lambda_E > 0$.

6. The gamma distribution also nests the negative exponential as a special case. Either one can be used to conduct a parametric testing procedure like the one described here.

7. In the presence of OTJ search, the rate of exit from a job spell is a function of both η and the current wage. However, it remains true that the hazard of exiting an employment spell, which consists of one or more job spells, is η.

8. If we were able to conditon on the value of θ associated with a particular job spell, then the conditional hazard should be independent of the duration of the job spell. Even if job-specific wage information was available, we would face the problem of recovering the value of θ from the observed wage, a feat that would be especially difficult under the OTJ search model that allows wage renegotiation (since in this case w is a function not only of θ but also of the second best match value revealed during the current employment spell). These issues imply that probably only unconditional (on wages) job spell information could be used in conducting this relatively informal specification test of the general OTJ search model.

9. We say at least two subpopulations since the mixture of two single-peaked distributions can produce a marginal distribution with one peak.

10. When some information over which the estimator is defined is not available at the subpopulation level, then this partitioning strategy has to be adjusted. In chapter 7 we formulated a maximum likelihood estimator that incorporated data from the firm side of the market to aid in identification of the Nash-bargaining weight α. Since revenue and labor cost data are not available separately for population subgroups, one has to impute (using the model and the representation of each group in the population) their representation in the workforce of the firm(s), as well as restricting all subgroups to share the same bargaining parameter. These problems are largely particular to this particular application, however.

11. This is not to suggest that theoretical considerations do not come into play that would place restrictions on parameters across subgroups, particularly in general equilibrium versions of the model. For example, under random search in the market (so that firms randomly encounter males and females rather than being able to direct their search to one of the genders), the likelihood of encountering a potential match for each gender would be related through the aggregate matching technology. These types of restrictions, however, would not typically suggest equality of contact rate parameters.

12. The proportions paid the minimum wage are computed before any adjustment is made for wage reports that are below the nominal minimum wage. When estimating the model, we assumed that all individuals who reported a wage below the nominal minimum wage were actually paid the minimum wage, which increases the mass point at m significantly.

13. The number used is 0.576, which was taken from the Consolidated Income Statement of MacDonald's Corporation in those years. The corporation no longer breaks out wage information in the same way, so that it was not possible to update the information to the 2009 environment.

14. By not restricting the contact rates to be equal when in fact they are, one is only losing (asymptotic) efficiency when estimating the partial equilibrium model. If one mistakenly restricts the contact rates to be equal when they are not, then all model estimates are, in general, inconsistent. Researchers usually opt for forgoing potential efficiency gains when facing such a choice.

15. A likelihood ratio test yields a test statistic of 33.008, which follows a χ^2 distribution with six degrees of freedom under the null hypothesis of equality. The probability of such a value under the null is less than 0.0001.

16. If we observe that at least three sample members have wages equal to the minimum wage, we can conclude that at least one type must face a binding minimum wage constraint. This is the case in our sample.

17. This will be true no matter what values the rest of the variables in X_i or the other coefficients in β take, as long as they are finite.

18. These constraints might involve the welfare gain function given in the equation above. For example, we might allow the social planner to choose an m for the economy subject to the condition that neither side would gain more than ρ percent from establishing their own optimal minimum wage m_j^*.

Chapter 12

1. Another important issue regarding the plausability of such a high minimum wage being "optimal" involves the subpopulation being analyzed. As the minimum wage is increased, it begins to become binding for a large number of other subpopulations in the labor market, such as older and more skilled individuals. To evaluate the welfare effects on the general population, these groups should be brought into the analysis as the minimum wage is increased.

Bibliography

Abadie, Alberto. 2002. Bootstrap tests for distributional treatment effects in instrumental variable models. *Journal of the American Statistical Association* 97, (457):284–92.

Abowd, John, and Martha Stinson. 2005. Estimating measurement error in SIPP annual job earnings: A comparison of census survey and SSA administrative data. Working paper. Cornell University.

Albrecht, James, and Bo Axell. 1984. An equilibrium model of search employment. *Journal of Political Economy* 92 (5): 824–40.

Barlow, Richard, and Frank Proschan. 1981. *Statistical Theory of Life Testing: Probability Models*, 2nd ed. Silver Springs, MD: To Begin With.

Bell, Linda. 1997. The impact of minimum wages in Mexico and Colombia. *Journal of Labor Economics* 15 (S3): S102–35.

Bound, John, Charles Brown, Greg J. Duncan, and Willard Rodgers. 1994. Evidence on the validity of cross-sectional and longitudinal labor market data. *Journal of Labor Economics* 12 (3): 345–68.

Brown, Charles. Minimum wages, employment, and the distribution of income. In Orley Ashenfelter and David Card, eds., *Handbook of Labor Economics*, vol. 3B. Amsterdam: North-Holland, 2101–63.

Brown, Charles, Curtis Gilroy, and Andrew Kohen. 1982. The effect of the minimum wage on employment and unemployment. *Journal of Economic Literature* 20 (2): 487–528.

Brown, Meta, Christopher Flinn, and Andrew Schotter. 2009. Real time search in the laboratory and the market. Working paper, New York University. Forthcoming, *American Economic Review*.

Burdett, Kenneth, and Dale Mortensen. 1978. Labor supply under uncertainty. In Ronald G. Ehrenberg, ed., *Research in Labor Economics*, vol. 2. Greenwich: JAI Press, 109–58.

Burdett, Kenneth, and Dale Mortensen. 1998. Wage differentials, employer size, and unemployment. *International Economic Review* 39 (2): 257–73.

Burdett, Kenneth, and Jan Ondrich. How changes in labor demand affect unemployed workers. *Journal of Labor Economics* 3 (1): 1–10.

US Bureau of Labor Statistics, US Department of Labor. 2006. *Characteristics of Minimum Wage Workers*. Washington, DC: GPO.

Cahuc, Pierre, Fabien Postel-Vinay, and Jean-Marc. Robin. 2006. Wage bargaining with on-the-job search: Theory and evidence. *Econometrica* 74 (2): 323–64.

Campolieti, Michele, Tony Fang, and Morley Gunderson. 2005. Minimum wage impacts on youth employment transitions, 1993–1999. *Canadian Journal of Economics* 38 (1): 81–104.

Card, David. 1992. Do minimum wages reduce employment? A case study of California, 1987–89. *Industrial and Labor Relations Review* 46 (1): 38–54.

Card, David, and Alan Krueger. 1994. Minimum wages and employment: A case study of the fast-food industry in New Jersey and Pennsylvania. *American Economic Review* 84 (4): 772–93.

Card, David, and Alan Krueger. 1995. *Myth and Measurement: The New Economics of the Minimum Wage*. Princeton: Princeton University Press.

Coles, Melvyn, and Eric Smith. 1996. Cross-section estimation of the matching function: Evidence from England and Wales. *Economica* 63 (252): 589–97.

Cox, David R., and H. David Miller. 1965. *The Theory of Stochastic Processes*. London: Methuen.

Della Vigna, Stefano, and M. Daniele Passerman. 2005. Job search and impatience. *Journal of Labor Economics* 23 (3): 527–88.

Dey, Matthew, and Christopher Flinn. 2005. An equilibrium model of health insurance provision and wage determination. *Econometrica* 73 (2): 571–627.

Dey, Matthew, and Christopher Flinn. 2008. Household search and health insurance coverage. *Journal of Econometrics* 145 (1–2): 43–63.

Diamond, Peter. 1982. Aggregate demand management in search equilibrium. *Journal of Political Economy* 90 (5): 881–994.

Dickens, Richard, Stephen Machin, and Alan Manning. 1998. Estimating the effect of minimum wages on employment from the distribution of wages: A critical view. *Labour Economics* 5 (2): 109–34.

Dinardo, John, Nicole Fortin, and Thomas Lemieux. 1996. Labor market institutions and the distribution of wages, 1973–1992: A semiparametric approach. *Econometrica* 64 (5): 1001–44.

Douglas, Paul, and Joseph Hackman. 1938. The Fair Labor Standards Act of 1938 I." *Political Science Quarterly* 53 (4): 491–515.

Douglas, Paul, and Joseph Hackman. 1939. The fair labor standards act of 1938 II. *Political Science Quarterly* 54 (1): 29–55.

Drazen, Allan. 1986. Optimum minimum wage legislation. *Economic Journal* 96 (383): 774–84.

Eckstein, Zvi, Suqin Ge, and Barbara Petrongolo. 2006. Job and wage mobility in a search model with non-compliance (exemptions) with the minimum wage. IZA discussion paper. Institute for the Study of Labor, Bonn, Germany.

Eckstein, Zvi, and Kenneth Wolpin. 1990. Estimating a market equilibrium search model from panel data on individuals. *Econometrica* 58 (4): 783–808.

Eckstein, Zvi, and Kenneth Wolpin. 1995. Duration to first job and the return to schooling: Estimates from a search-matching model. *Review of Economic Studies* 62 (2): 263–86.

Eckstein, Zvi, and Kenneth Wolpin. 1999. Estimating the effect of racial discrimination on first job wage offers. *Review of Economics and Statistics* 81 (3): 384–92.

Flinn, Christopher. 2002a. Labour market structure and inequality: A comparison of Italy and the U.S. *Review of Economic Studies* 69 (3): 611–45.

Flinn, Christopher. 2002b. Interpreting minimum wage effects on wage distributions: A cautionary tale. *Annales d'Économie et de Statistique* 67–68 (July–December): 309–55.

Flinn, Christopher. 2006. Minimum wage effects on labor market outcomes under search, bargaining, and endogenous contact rates. *Econometrica* 74: 1013–62.

Flinn, Christopher, and James Heckman. 1982. New methods for analyzing structural models of labor force dynamics. *Journal of Econometrics* 18 (1): 115–68.

Flinn, Christopher, and James Heckman. 1983. Are unemployment and out of the labor force behaviorally distinct labor market states? *Journal of Labor Economics* 1 (1): 28–42.

Flinn, Christopher, and James Mabli. 2008. An estimable equilibrium model of search, bargaining, and schooling choice. Working paper, New York University.

Flinn, Christopher, and James Mabli. 2009. On-the-job search, minimum wages, and labor market outcomes in an equilibrium bargaining framework. Working paper. New York University.

Hashimoto, Masanori. 1982. Minimum wage effects on training on the job. *American Economic Review* 70 (5): 1070–87.

Hosios, Arthur. 1990. On the efficiency of matching and related models of search and unemployment. *Review of Economic Studies* 57 (2): 279–98.

Johnson, Norman, and Samuel Kotz. 1970. *Continuous Univariate Distributions*, vol. 1. New York: John Wiley and Sons, 1970.

Jovanovic, Boyan. 1979. Job matching and the theory of turnover. *Journal of Political Economy* 87 (5): 972–90.

Jovanovic, Boyan. 1984. Matching, turnover, and unemployment. *Journal of Political Economy* 92 (1): 108–22.

Karlin, Samuel, and Howard Taylor. 1975. *A First Course in Stochastic Processes*, 2nd ed. New York: Academic Press.

Kennan, John. 1995. The elusive effects of minimum wages. *Journal of Economic Literature* 33 (4): 1950–65.

Koopmans, Tjalling. 1949. Identification problems in economic model construction. *Econometrica* 17 (2): 125–44.

Kooreman, Peter, and Arie Kapteyn. 1990. On the empirical implementation of some game theoretic models of household labor supply. *Journal of Human Resources* 25 (4): 584–98.

Lang, Kevin. 1987. Pareto improving minimum wage laws. *Economic Inquiry* 25 (1): 145–58.

Lawless, Jerry. 2003. *Statistical Models and Methods for Lifetime Data*, 2nd ed. Hoboken, NJ: Wiley.

Machin, Stephen, Alan Manning, and Lupin Rahman. 2003. Where the minimum wage bites hard: Introduction of minimum wages to a low wage sector. *Journal of the European Economic Association* 1 (1): 154–80.

Manski, Charles. 1995. *Identification Problems in the Social Sciences*. Cambridge.: Harvard University Press.

McFadden, Daniel. 1989. Testing for stochastic dominance. In Thomas Fomby and Tae Kun Seo, eds., *Studies in the Economics of Uncertainty in Honor of Josef Hadar*. New York: Springer, 113–34.

Marschak, Jacob. 1953. Economic measurements for policy and prediction. In William C. Hood and Tjalling C. Koopmans, eds., *Studies in Econometric Method*. New York: Wiley, 1–26.

Meyer, Robert, and David Wise. 1983a. Discontinuous distributions and missing persons: The minimum wage and unemployed youth. *Econometrica* 51 (6): 1677–98.

Meyer, Robert, and David Wise. 1983b. The effects of the minimum wage on employment and earnings of youth. *Journal of Labor Economics* 1 (1): 66–100.

Moro, Andrea. 2003. The effect of statistical discrimination on black–white wage inequality: Estimating a model with multiple equilibria. *International Economic Review* 44 (2): 467–500.

Nash, John. 1953. Two-person cooperative games. *Econometrica* 21 (1): 128–40.

Neumark, David, and William Wascher. 2008. *Minimum Wages*. Cambridge: MIT Press.

Oaxaca, Ronald. 1973. Male–female wage differentials in urban labor markets. *International Economic Review* 14 (3): 693–709.

Pereira, Sonia. 2003. The impact of minimum wages on youth employment in Portugal. *European Economic Review* 47 (2): 229–44.

Petrongolo, Barbara, and Christopher Pissarides. 2001. Looking into the black box: A survey of the matching function. *Journal of Economic Literature* 39 (2): 390–431.

Pissarides, Christopher. 2000. *Equilibrium Unemployment Theory,* 2nd ed. Cambridge: MIT Press, 2000.

Postel-Vinay, Fabien, and Jean-Marc Robin. 2002. Equilibrium wage dispersion with heterogeneous workers and firms. *Econometrica* 70 (6): 2295–2350.

Postel-Vinay, Fabien, and Jean-Marc Robin. To match or not to match? Optimal wage policy with endogenous search intensity. *Review of Economic Dynamics* 7 (2): 297–330.

Rebitzer, James, and Lowell Taylor. The consequences of minimum wage laws: Some new theoretical ideas. *Journal of Public Economics* 56 (2): 245–56.

Romano, Joseph. 1988. A bootstrap revival of some nonparametric distance tests. *Journal of the American Statistical Association* 83 (403): 698–708.

Romano, Joseph. 1989. Bootstrap and randomization tests of some nonparametric hypotheses. *Annals of Statistics* 17 (1): 141–59.

Rubinstein, Ariel. 1982. Perfect equilibrium in a bargaining model. *Econometrica* 50 (1): 97–109.

Seltzer, Andrew. 1995. The political economy of the Fair Labor Standards Act of 1938. *Journal of Political Economy* 103 (6): 1302–42.

Stewart, Mark. The employment effects of the national minimum wage. *Economic Journal* 114 (494): C110–16.

Stigler, George. 1946. The economics of minimum wage legislation. *American Economic Review* 36 (3): 358–65.

Swinnerton, Kenneth. 1996. Minimum wages in an equilibrium search model with diminishing returns to labor in production. *Journal of Labor Economics* 14 (2): 340–55.

Van den Berg, Gerard. 1990. Nonstationarity in job search theory. *Review of Economic Studies* 57 (2): 255–77.

Van den Berg, Gerard. 1994. The effects of changes of the job offer arrival rate on the duration of unemployment. *Journal of Labor Economics* 12 (3): 478–98.

Van den Berg, Gerard. 2003. Multiple equilibria and minimum wages in labor markets with informational frictions and heterogeneous production technologies. *International Economic Review* 44 (4): 1337–57.

Van den Berg, Gerard, and Geert Ridder. 1998. An empirical equilibrium search model of the labor market. *Econometrica* 66 (5): 1183–1222.

Wolpin, Kenneth. 1987. Estimating a structural search model: The transition from school to work. *Econometrica* 55: 801–17.

Yashiv, Eran. 2000. The determinants of equilibrium unemployment. *American Economic Review* 90 (5): 486–522.

Index

Vacancies, 9, 267, 271
  econometric issues and, 147–48, 162–66
  endogeneity of rate of contacts and,
    67–71
  heterogeneity and, 256–57
  labor market careers model and, 36–37,
    43, 54–55, 67–71
  labor market outcomes survey and, 110
  model testing and, 175–79, 280n3
  Nash bargaining and, 53–56
  on-the-job search and, 201–202, 213–14,
    220, 223–25
  optimal minimum wages and, 185–88,
    191
  welfare impacts and, 78–79, 82–84, 87–88,
    130, 277n4
Van den Berg, Gerard, 4, 108, 110–15, 149,
  276n8, 278n5, 284n4

Wage density, 58, 106, 114, 121–22, 126,
  232, 279n11
Wage distribution, 1, 5, 274n11
  conditional, 121–23
  cross-sectional analysis and, 126–27,
    131–36
  cumulative distribution function (c.d.f.)
    and, 64, 66, 119–21, 126, 162, 215, 234
  descriptive evidence on minimum wage
    effects and, 17, 21–24, 30, 275n7
  econometric issues and, 147–50, 155
  heterogeneity and, 231–32, 236–37, 241,
    247, 250, 252
  labor market careers model and, 43,
    59–60, 63–66
  labor market outcomes survey and, 95,
    104, 107–11, 279n11
  model limitations and, 263
  model testing and, 180–81
  on-the-job search and, 206, 209, 211, 216,
    219, 283n15
  optimal minimum wages and, 186
  panel data testing and, 127–29
  policy lessons and, 264, 270
  spillover and, 30, 121–23, 126, 131, 134–36
  statutory minimum wage increases of
    1996/1997 and, 125–29
  stochastic dominance and, 2, 44, 119–21,
    126–27, 131, 134–35, 231, 236, 280n4
  truncation effect and, 80, 88, 120–22, 154,
    188–90, 232
  unconditional, 119–21

welfare impact studies and, 73, 80–82, 88,
  94, 121–38, 277n1, 279n1
Wascher, William, 97, 278n1
Wealth maximization
  econometric issues and, 149
  heterogeneity and, 230
  labor market careers model and, 36,
    43–44
  on-the-job search and, 225–26
  optimal minimum wages and, 187–88,
    191
  welfare impacts and, 85–87
Weibull distribution, 183, 238–40
Welfare, 1–8, 273n1, 274n3, 275n7, 286n1
  average value of individual, 185–86
  behavioral models and, 118
  Benthamite social welfare function and,
    73, 83, 258
  Canada and, 101–103
  Colombia and, 100–101
  conditional wage distributions and,
    121–24
  contact rates and, 73–81, 84, 88, 277n4
  cross-sectional wage distribution results
    and, 131–36
  Current Population Survey (CPS) and,
    117–18, 125, 128–30, 136–39
  demand side parameters and, 177
  employment impacts and, 73–84, 89–93,
    277n1
  endogeneity and, 73, 76–79, 88
  equilibrium and, 73–77, 80–85, 88–94,
    117–20, 125, 128–30, 277n4, 279nn9,11
  ex post (short-run), 88–89
  general criteria for, 82–84
  heterogeneity and, 258–59, 286n18
  impacts of changes in minimum wage,
    34, 73, 80–94, 117–39, 258
  labor market careers model and, 34–38,
    58, 70–73, 80–94, 97–100, 109, 277n16,
    278n3
  labor market status and, 73–82
  matching and, 73–82, 87, 91–94, 117–39,
    177, 277n1, 278n7, 279n1
  Mexico and, 100–101
  Nash and, 80–81
  on-the-job search and, 207, 217, 225–27
  optimal minimum wages and, 185–93
  Outgoing Rotation Group (ORG) data
    and, 129
  panel data testing and, 127–29